Breaking Trail

by

EDGAR HETTEEN

with

JAY LEMKE

Breaking Trail
Edgar Hetteen with Jay Lemke

Grateful acknowledgment is made to Pantheon Books and
Random House Books for permission to reprint previously
published material from a book called THE EXPERTS SPEAK,
BY CHRISTOPHER CERF AND VICTOR NAVASKY.

Cover design by Richard Schaefer.

ISBN 1-885904-99-1

Printed in the United States of America
by
Focus Publishing, Inc.
Bemidji, Minnesota

This book is dedicated...

… To the original employees we had at Polaris who worked such long periods of time without compensation.

… To the farmers who paid a cash deposit to a greasy young guy for a non-existent company, a company they had no guarantee would ever exist.

… To people like Norman Flagstad, who took a flyer and put up money in those early embryonic days.

… To the guy in Crookston, George Bang, who sold us the building when we didn't have any money.

… To Jay Lemke, for the writing of this book, for his patience in extracting the information, cataloging it, and making it readable and interesting.

… And to those who didn't believe, who told us we were wrong. They provided a very special kind of motivation.

– Edgar Hetteen

… To Paige, my wife and best friend, for insightful advice that made this book better, and for understanding the late, late nights.

… To my parents, who made it all possible.

… To Edgar Hetteen, for putting up with a thousand questions, and for putting his faith in someone who'd never written a book.

– Jay Lemke

ACKNOWLEDGMENTS

In writing this book we are left with many people to thank. First, to all those who read the book in its infancy, found the mistakes, and offered suggestions. Remaining errors are ours, not theirs. In no particular order, thanks to Paige Wallin-Lemke, Henry Fiola, Lee Lynch, Maurice Hurley, Allen Eide, Gary and JoAnn Lemke, Brad and Jamie Lemke, Donna Hansen, Carol and Jerry Wallin, Jeff Drake, Kelly and Lisa Tarbell, John Ehlert, C.J. Ramstad, Jerry Bassett and Rudy Billberg. Thanks to Jeanne Pauletti and David Churchill for their expertise in editing the manuscript. Thanks to Joe Gillaspie for his early work on the cover. And thanks to Stan Haley, Rich Schaefer, Rob Yuretich and LouAnn Muhm at Focus Publishing for guiding us through the difficult process of publishing a book.

Edgar Hetteen and Jay Lemke

FOREWORD

by Bob Bergland

Bob Bergland, born and raised in Edgar Hetteen's hometown of Roseau, Minnesota, represented Minnesota's 7th Congressional District in the U.S. Congress from 1971 to 1977 and served as President Jimmy Carter's secretary of agriculture. He was CEO of the National Rural Electric Cooperative Association until retiring in 1994. He now serves on the University of Minnesota Board of Regents.

I was about twelve riding my old bike past Hetteen Hoist and Derrick machine shop at the intersection of Highways 11 and 89 in Roseau, Minnesota. Out front was the most awesome looking motorcycle I had ever been near. It was exciting to just touch such a machine. A man in greasy clothes came out and in his soft voice asked if I would like to take a ride. Never in my wildest dreams could I have imagined such a wonderful invitation. That night I told my Dad about my thrilling day, and Dad said the man was Edgar Hetteen.

Fifteen years later, I was married with three small children and starting to farm. But with too much rain, too much debt, and poor prices, we lived in poverty. I found some part-time odd jobs to keep body and soul together, but hundreds of my friends and neighbors were not so lucky. They had to leave their families and hunt for work.

It was a time of upheaval and hurt for rural people, but fortunately for Roseau, Edgar Hetteen was busy at his company, Polaris Industries. They built many things, but their snowmobile would bring a better life to our small town.

Polaris now employs 2,000 at its Roseau plant, pumping $50 million a year into the local economy and we now have a prosperous and fun place in which to live and raise our families. Edgar Hetteen, his brother Allan and brother-in-law David Johnson started this economic miracle.

This book is about true grit. It is a fascinating story. Even though I knew much of the history, I found it difficult to put down.

– Bob Bergland

Breaking Trail

❧ ❧ ❧

❧ ❧ ❧

PREFACE

Note: This book was written over the course of four years. Learning not only about, but from Edgar Hetteen has been a valuable experience that will stick with me. If you have dreams of greater things, if you want to start a business, or if you simply love snowmobiles, this book was written for you. I hope Edgar's thoughts will stay with you as well.

— Jay Lemke, Winter, 1998

❧ ❧ ❧

The policeman with the yellow raincoat fought a losing battle in the winter of no snow, 1994. His face was flushed red under windy, gray skies, his arms a whirlwind as he waved traffic through with a left hand and held it up with a right.

The lack of snow did not stop the people from coming, and coming. Their destination: The Northland Hotel in Blaine, Minnesota, where the new snowmobiles were to be unveiled. On a Saturday morning in the middle of March, a jam of vehicles branched off I-694, the thoroughfare that cuts across the northern Minneapolis-St. Paul metro area. One by one, with headlights on, drivers searched for somewhere to park. Most had to go far down the road and hike back; but they didn't seem to mind.

Polaris Industries had booked the hotel for two days. It was displaying its latest machines to the public, and the resulting smiles were larger than life – the visitors loved Polaris. Like all snowmobilers, they were fiercely loyal to their brand.

Approximately 3 million men, women and children proclaim themselves snowmobilers; and a large percentage ride machines built by two companies – Polaris Industries and Arctic Enterprises. Polaris builds its sleds in Roseau, Minnesota, a few miles south of the Canadian border, and Arctic resides 100 miles south in Thief River Falls.

The companies combine for annual sales of approximately $1.5 billion and control more than 60 percent of the market. Both have made men rich and towns strong. As the millennium nears, it appears their dominance will continue.

Through the din at the hotel stepped Edgar Hetteen, wearing khaki slacks, brown shoes and a flannel shirt. With his left hand tucked inside a pants pocket, he strolled easily. He was 74 years old, sporting a white goatee. Polaris had given him a room on the fifth floor, anything for its founder, anything for the man who made this all possible. Ironically, Edgar Hetteen also started Arctic Cat, its great rival.

He was asked if this is what he expected 50 years ago. He laughed a throaty laugh and resorted to his usual sarcasm.

"Yep, this is exactly what I had in mind," he said.

No, not really. It's not what he pictured when he opened his first business in the dark corners of a car garage in 1944. It is not what he pictured when he set up the world's first snowmobile dealer on the windswept snows of northern Alaska. It is not what he pictured when he rode across 1,200 miles of Alaskan frontier to prove the snowmobile was viable.

He simply wanted to build machines that worked and could be sold. He had no premonition of the great heights or the great lows he would see through his life.

As he mingled with the crowd, stopping now and then to sign an autograph, it was clear the snowmobile industry had not forgotten him.

That was good. Chances are, things would have been different without Edgar Hetteen. Much, much different ...

Chapter 1

<u>ALASKA – THE</u>
<u>PROVING GROUNDS</u>

Polaris stood on the brink of greatness. Edgar Hetteen knew it, as did his brother Allan, and brother-in-law David Johnson. They may have been the only ones to believe in the 15-year-old company. Snowmobile sales were stagnant, and the firm was making due building and selling straw cutting attachments for combines.

In the spring of 1960, something had to be done about the snow machines, the enterprise of six years. Though they were setting up dealers here and there, now and then, the idea wasn't catching fire. Board members were restless and, indeed, hated the little machines.

Still Edgar, Allan and David believed. Farm implements were the past, snowmobiles the future. So gambling the fate of Polaris – and his own life – Edgar set out on an adventure that continues to live in snowmobile folk lore. On March 4, 1960, on the western shores of Alaska, Edgar Hetteen, Polaris employee Earling Falk, and friends Rudy and Bessie Billberg, set out on three Sno-Travelers.

They would brave 1,200 miles of rocks, sand, ice and deep snow. They would ride through blizzards, torrential winds and terrifying sand storms. They would struggle to Fairbanks, seemingly on the other side of the world.

❧ ❧ ❧

Dead; it was dead.

It had slowed, it had sputtered, and then with a warble and a choking pop, died. A hard wind off the frozen Yukon River now whipped down across the ice, like a voracious monster, and came on me and my little snowmobile. I sat for a moment, my heart falling to my stomach, and I looked around. As far as I could see, the ice, topped with whirling, hard snow extended on and on. I was miles from the nearest outpost, and the way the snowmobile had quit left me wondering if it would ever start again.

As I stepped to the snow, I became truly aware of how hard the wind was, and how really cold, likely 30 below. I shivered, and I moved to the back of the snowmobile, where the engine sat on those early models.

My companions, Rudy and Bessie Billberg, and Earling Falk, pulled their machines even with mine. Their faces said it all: "Is it OK, Edgar?" Nerves ran high, for they knew if we lost one of the machines and the other two had to take all of the loads and all the people, it'd be tough to complete the 1,200 miles to Fairbanks. We were in our 10th day out, not even halfway to the goal.

It began to snow. I crouched to check the engine. A hard gust hit my face and my eyes watered, but not long, because the tears froze instantly to my cheeks. It was miserable. The group pulled out a big tarp, one on which Earling and I slept, for our tent had no floor. They held that tarp high to block me from the wind. Still, it whipped furiously, threatening to jerk out of their strong hands at any moment.

I quickly determined the engine had no spark; it probably needed a new coil. The coil, which introduces electricity to the engine, was located under the flywheel. I ripped off the shrouding that covered the flywheel, and struggled to get the flywheel off. My hands grew stiffer and stiffer, and the tips lost feeling. Attacked by a pliers and a hammer, the flywheel finally, reluctantly, snapped off. I pitched it to the snow.

I fitted a new coil and put the flywheel back on. As I spun it by hand, the engine seemed to have spark. Perfect. But, just to be sure, I decided that before refitting the covering and the cooling ducts, I would run the engine. I cranked it and the rumble was music to my ears – until the hammer somehow tumbled from my hand into the flywheel's spinning fins.

No! Without the protective shrouding, the hammer stripped every one of those cooling fins, just as slick and clean as could be. They blew around me like shrapnel.

Fear set in. Without those fins, there would be no air on the engine and it wouldn't cool. I shook my head and replaced the covering. I had only one choice. I'd go as far as I could, and hope the machine could make it. I didn't share my thoughts with the rest of the crew. No sense scaring them quite yet. I crossed my fingers and prayed.

On our way, I tried to keep calm. This was not the first, nor would it be the last time I had to fight off panic. I took a deep breath, the cold air flying deep into my lungs. I had to think of anything but that engine. It was running fine, but who knew for how long? I forced my mind to wander. For some reason, my thoughts turned back.

The trip had been incredible, taxing us in so many ways. It would change my life, and the lives of millions. And yet, despite its ultimate impact on the sport of snowmobiling, we might never have tried it had things not been desperate back home at Polaris Industries.

ɕ ɕ ɕ

By the fall of 1959, things were not going well. Our farm implements were selling fine, but the snowmobile, our Sno-Traveler, the machine that could make our future, was slowly dying. The catcalls came hard and fast: "Edgar, what are you doing?" "Edgar, you're crazy." "Edgar's been flying too high in that plane of his." "Edgar, who would want to ride on that crazy contraption you and the boys are building?"

Unfortunately, it wasn't just the kibitzers at the local café laughing. The sniggers were coming straight from our board room. It had been building for years, but only in the last few months had things reached a head. We knew our machines were good. We knew they would sell. We had discovered the joys of winter. Proving that to our board, however, was proving impossible.

They hated that we ran around in the nearby field, testing the Sno-Traveler. They hated the ridicule the company received. "Let's quit this foolishness, let's be respectable," they told me. "Let's sit at a desk like a president is supposed to. Let's act like one."

In the face of our success with farm implements, it was foolish to build snowmobiles, they said. Why quit a good thing for a risky thing? Who would buy them? Who in their right mind would go out and play in the snow?

"Nobody," they said. "That's who."

Nor did the public view the snowmobile as the answer to winter recreation. Most saw us as simpletons who believed we could play in the snow. They saw the machine as a silly invention they'd never use.

Yes, there was a long row to hoe between our own convictions and being able to establish a market. It became obvious that we needed to stir the imagination. We needed to draw out the adventurers. We needed people to understand the joys of winter. Bouncing around hour after hour in that beautiful expansive wilderness, your mind goes blank. It's an escape. You can forget for a few moments that the note is coming due at the bank. We needed people to know that. We needed to prove our snow machines worked.

If we could do all of that, perhaps we could make some sales and, more importantly, perhaps we could convince our board to back the idea. We needed Alaska, though I didn't know that until November of 1959.

It was then that Rudy Billberg and his wife Bessie came to my home in Roseau. I grew up with Rudy in Roseau County, but he eventually moved to Alaska and became quite a famous bush pilot. He and Bessie were real-life adventurers, living in Nome, Fairbanks and many points between. It was always nice to visit with the Billbergs because, to me, they represented Alaska, a place I loved.

Rudy sat on my sofa. He ran his fingers through his thick hair.

"Edgar, I've been thinking about something."

"Yeah?"

"You like Alaska."

"You know I do."

"You've been wanting to test those snow machines?"

"That's right."

"What if we took a trip on those machines from around the Bering Sea Coast up into the interior of Alaska and then finished in Fairbanks?"

I paused. My eyes bugged and I smirked. He was crazy. He might just as well have said, "Edgar, I think we should launch a rocket ship to the moon." Only my friend was not smiling. He was serious.

"It's an interesting idea, Rudy, but I frankly don't know if the Sno-Travelers could make it," I said. "You've seen them. Sometimes they work, sometimes they don't."

But we continued to talk. And as the day wore on, the weather frigid in the far north of Minnesota, the idea began to hold a certain fascination for me. The more I thought about it, the more my blood raced. What an adventure – to a place I loved, to try something that might help the sputtering snowmobile industry. If we really could make the trip, it would prove to the world that we were not some rag-tag company building a goofy machine. It could move us ahead by years. Eventually, Rudy and I put together a plan.

It went like this: Our caravan would consist of three Sno-Travelers, two of which would pull 900 pounds of supplies on a pair of freight toboggans. Two of the sleds would be sky-blue Ranger model Sno-Travelers, powered by 10-horsepower Kohler K-241 gasoline engines. The third would be a red Trailblazer model, powered by a 7-horsepower Kohler K-161. In addition to Rudy, Bessie and me, I would ask Earling Falk to join us. Quiet, reserved, and always dependable, he was one of the top production men at the factory.

We would leave from Bethel on the edge of Alaska's western coast, then move east along the Kuskokwim River. We eventually would find the Yukon River and follow its valley through the unpopulated, unbroken wilderness, move through passes north of Mount McKinley, and finally finish in Fairbanks, 1,200 miles away.

I arranged to leave the company in the good hands of Allan Hetteen, my brother, and David Johnson, my brother-in-law. They were among the few who believed the snow machine had a future. They would keep in line those who thought otherwise.

As we planned, the days stretched into months. We worked on our bodies; I did push-ups and sit-ups as I prepared for the rigors to come. My muscles tightened and grew strong. I was ready. I hoped the Sno-Travelers would be as well.

A few weeks before setting foot in Alaska, I went over the route on a map hanging on the wall of my office back in Roseau.

March arrived, and it was time for Earling and me to catch a plane to Alaska. Two days later, I found myself staring out a window of the Westward Hotel in Anchorage. It snowed gently outside and I was deep in thought, looking ahead to the following day, when an airliner would take us to the coast, where Rudy and Bessie waited. Though I was anxious to be off, questions swirled in my head.

Could we really make it? I had no doubt the weather and terrain would be brutal.

That brought me to the main question. Would the sleds hold up? Sure, we'd put them through their paces in Roseau, and we actually had a dealer in Fairbanks, but nobody had tried anything like this. The machines would be pounded hard, and something easily could go wrong. We hadn't asked for any publicity, because we didn't know if we could make it. A bad report in a newspaper might very well ruin us.

I also wondered about the state of the company. How much longer could I put up with a board that was losing faith in me? How much longer could I put up with financial problems, bank loans that didn't come through, sitting behind a desk and doing the day-to-day business of running a company – all the stuff that drove me crazy? How much longer? I honestly didn't know. I had trouble relaxing that night, but finally got some sleep.

On March 4, 1960, we flew into Bethel on the Bering Sea Coast. Rudy and Bessie met us at the airport and took us to their home, where we spent the night. We rose early the next morning and transported the snowmobiles to the frozen Kuskokwim River, which we would follow until we cut cross country to the great Yukon.

It was a fine day. The sky was blue and the air a crisp and healthy 25 degrees. Most of Bethel turned out to see us. Their breath, and ours, froze in a smoky haze. Cameras pointed our way clicked furiously. For a short time, we were celebrities.

I checked and rechecked the machines. The grinding bumps and unseen holes would take their toll; best to start in as good a condition as possible. While I made my preparations, the others made theirs.

Bessie looked over her supplies. She'd already baked several loaves of bread, and with those went a healthy supply of meat – bacon, hamburger and hot-dogs – plus dehydrated vegetables and packets of soups, cereals and navy beans. She wore several layers of clothing under a white-knitted sweater covered with red roses and a large army-green parka. The sun sparkled off her cat-eye glasses, and a white bonnet protected her brown hair. At 5 feet, she was not a large woman, but she was every bit as sturdy as the men, and indeed, without her two meals a day and her great attitude, the trip might have been impossible.

Rudy said goodbye to several friends. He and Bessie lived in Bethel, having moved there a few years earlier from Fairbanks. Rudy stood on the Kuskokwim, seemingly growing out of the ice. He had recently left his job as station manager for Northern Consolidated Airlines, so he and Bessie could prospect for gold in the Yukon. He was a solid man, with a square face turned rough by years in the wilderness. He wore a furry brown hat and dark sunglasses that covered steely eyes.

Earling Falk was quiet, usually waiting until asked before speaking, and he helped me prepare the sleds. He was dressed much like me, with a mid-length heavy green coat over layers of clothing and floppy black mukluks, the kind worn by Eskimos. They were warmer than any boot made.

We didn't start until noon, but finally, to the pleasant hum of the Kohler engines, we were on our way. Rudy took the lead, driving one of the few collapsible snowmobiles ever made. We'd built it mainly for Alaska. I had seen the extreme difficulty of doing work in the bush and the idea was born. You could take it apart in 15 minutes, toss it into a small plane and go anywhere. It was a fantastic little machine.

Rudy broke trail, the snow swirling behind. I followed, and Earling brought up the rear. Bessie, as she would most of the trip, stood on a toboggan behind Earling. The snow on the Kuskokwim was hard from high winds, and the Sno-Travelers purred along.

Bessie Billberg (left), Earling Falk (middle), and Rudy Billberg prepare to depart from Bethel on the frozen Kuskokwim River.

It was nice to be off, and I let the dusting snow and the wide, expansive wilderness wash away my thoughts. All I knew was the gentle rumble of the engines and that this was not a foolish venture, but a great one. Occasionally, I zoomed to the lead or slowed to the rear taking movies and photos.

We'd gone 60 miles when in the late afternoon, we came upon the tiny village of Akiachuk. It was tucked in the middle of that vast wilderness but didn't seem out of place. As our machines, which the natives called Iron Dogs, roared near the village, children poured onto the river. There must have been at least 20 of them, scampering from their small wooden homes and speaking in the native tongue we didn't understand. We pulled the caravan to a halt, but as we peppered them with questions, it was clear they didn't know our language either.

"How many people in your village?"

"What do you think of our machines?"

"Are there places to camp along the river?"

We got little response, but their warm, toothy smiles were enough. And soon, we again were on our way. We drove another half hour before stopping for the night. Though we might have found a place at Akiachuk, we stopped farther along because we were eager to set up camp. We needed the practice. There'd be nights ahead when getting those tents up would be the most important thing in the world.

We dug through three feet of snow and cleared a space for the tents. We erected them, moved in our belongings, and settled in for the night. It was warm and comfortable in my sleeping bag, and I scribbled my thoughts in a brown and green Steno notebook. I'd forgotten to pack my air mattress, and each time I moved, hard snow crunched and crackled beneath.

❦ ❦ ❦

The sun broke in through the white walls of the tent and woke us early on March 5. While the men rolled sleeping bags, folded tents and repacked the toboggan, Bessie hovered over the campstove. We got in trouble with her when we poked at what we thought was oatmeal and gazed suspiciously at some black lumps.

"Never mind that," Bessie ordered. "Eat it before it freezes."

We obeyed, as we always did, and gobbled up our breakfast. It was good, and we climbed back on our rides. The engines fired up as if they were on the factory floor, and by 9 a.m., we were back on the river. Though we'd gone through drifts before, they were nothing like what we now encountered. Ice crusted, and a couple feet high, they hammered and twisted the Sno-Travelers. Dull pain crept up my spine and soon the

Bessie Billberg shivers slightly as she cooks us a fine meal along the trail.

ache was a constant companion. This was not good. Not only was it still a long way to Kalskag, the village we hoped to make that night, but it was many days to Fairbanks.

Several hours later, about 6:30 p.m., we rolled into Kalskag. Once again the children flocked around. They called us gussocks, a colloquialism that means "white man." Their curiosity was obvious, and we happily let them go over the sleds as much as they wanted. Our arrival touched the lives of those people far out in the wilderness.

Twenty years later, I found myself in Kalskag again. I walked into the general store. Sitting on a bench was an old Eskimo and we began talking. I asked if he remembered me, if he remembered the snowmobiles that had come through. "Yeah," he said slowly, nodding with a distant look in his face, "I remember."

We wound up spending the night of March 5, 1960, with a young couple fresh to Alaska from Virginia. A few Eskimos who spoke English pointed us to their door. The Smiths were school teachers at the Bureau of Indian Affairs, and after their eyes narrowed upon finding four weary travelers at their door, they welcomed us heartily.

Over dinner, the Smiths bombarded us with questions. We obliged them, but we also had something to ask. We needed to know about the condition of the portage from the Kuskokwim to the great Yukon River. The Yukon, one of the longest rivers in the world (just a hair shorter than the Mississippi), lay 48 miles north of Kalskag. We soon would leave the relative comforts of the Kuskokwim and venture into the wild. The Sno-Travelers were running well, but how would they perform in country tough to walk through? And, more worrisome, could we find our way?

The Smiths advised us to see a man named Alex, a native Alaskan and the only local who'd made the portage that year. They sent someone to find him and an hour later, he arrived at the Smith residence. We asked him about the trail to the Yukon River. He seemed a pleasant man, but looked at us as if we were children straight from the city. We wouldn't find the trail, or what was left of it, he said. Fire had destroyed all the markers and strewn trees blocked the way. He'd gotten through, but only with great difficulty.

We clearly needed help, and so Rudy began to negotiate with Alex to be our guide.

"I think you can't find the trail," Alex said.

"I can navigate by compass, like I do in my airplane," Rudy countered.

"Yes, but then you would have to cut trail for the last seven miles through thick woods," Alex replied.

"OK," Rudy admitted. "Will you go along and show us the way?"

Alex was pleased. He nodded, a half nod, a maybe nod.

"I'll need another man to go along with dogs to bring me back," he said.

Rudy gazed at him. With a pipe in his mouth and a thick flannel shirt on his back, he blew smoke and asked the question.

"How much?"

"Wait," Alex said, shuffling to the door. "I go see my friend. If he can go, then I come back. Then we talk money."

In an instant, he was gone. The door slammed behind and stopped a sudden blast of frigid air from sneaking into the room. Thirty minutes later, Alex was back. Good news.

"OK, we go," he said.

"I'll give you $35," Rudy replied.

"I dunno," Alex said. "I dunno. That maybe not enough."

Rudy repeated his offer. After a long silence during which his eyes sized us up, Alex spoke.

"We want $50."

Shaking his head and pulling the pipe from his mouth, Rudy said he was sorry, but that we couldn't afford $50. I looked on. Just what was Rudy doing?

With that, Alex left. As the door closed, I believed our trip had just gotten a lot tougher. An hour later, we rolled out our sleeping bags and slept on the Smiths' wooden floors.

The temperature had dipped to zero by the next morning, but the day dawned bright. Though I grew apprehensive about taking the sleds through an inhospitable wilderness, it was exhilarating to be heading into the unknown. We threw down Mrs. Smith's scrambled eggs, bacon, toast and coffee, and prepared to leave.

As we were placing the final packs on the toboggan, we saw Alex hiking over. As he grew closer, we saw he was grinning. Soon, so was I.

"We go," he said. "Dog team already gone ahead."

His friend, Sergei, had left to prepare the cabin where we would stay. Alex pointed across the tundra through the mountains. That was the way, he said. The wind blew hard at the fur from the hood that circled his face. Alex took his time examining the snow machines and then climbed on the back of a toboggan. He seemed eager to go and he held on tight.

In single file, we followed the dog-sled trail that would take us around the end of the Nivit Mountains. The engines rumbled with a pleasing rat-tat-tat sound. For the first two or three miles, we picked our way around large drifts and traveled steadily. We soon slipped into a forest. It was like moving into another world, where it didn't matter whether you wore a tie, didn't matter if you weren't at that meeting on time. All that mattered was that you took care of yourself and took care of your machines. That feeling, the one of having to rely on your own mettle rather than the whims of financial institutions, was a good one indeed.

Snow hung heavily off the trees, and they drooped majestically. The trail – if you could call it that – snaked in and around the trees and wild brush. Though it was slow going, perhaps it wasn't as bad as Alex had made it sound.

All at once, however, we broke into the tundra, and the pleasant day came to a grinding halt. It was clear why the snow had gathered in the forest. Heavy winds – ones that tore into us and our machines – blew hard off the land and scraped it bare. It was the toughest of going, with glare ice and rough tundra stretching, it seemed, to the end of the earth. A profusion of bare moss hummocks rose up before us. As we pushed on, our sleds and toboggans tilted crazily. I looked ahead and saw Bessie clinging to the toboggan behind Earling. Suddenly, he hit a ridge of ice, and the toboggan flipped. Bessie held on with one hand, her body dangling over the ground for a second that seemed an eternity. Finally, the toboggan swung level and Bessie was saved.

The old trail was useless. Only remnants remained of the markers that once showed the way. Many had burned. Others had fallen on their sides, wildly wobbling in the wind. Some had simply rotted away, stuck like glue in the ground. It was a stark image compared to the serene quiet of the woods – this chaotic tundra where nature ruled with an iron fist, and where we were mere visitors who hoped to make it through.

An hour later, we lost all trace of snow and ran into bare ground. Huge patches of frozen moss dotted the tundra. The sleds had no snow, but they ran quite well, albeit much slower.

We went on like that for hours. The bumping and grinding wore at me and my arms jittered. Finally, just when it seemed it would never end, as if the whole world were tundra, we hit the timber line, a band of forest that bordered the Yukon. Once through that, we could find our way without a guide. We then would follow the river.

We stopped briefly and asked Alex what lay ahead.

"Seven miles through it," he said with a shrug.

In the forest was snow – lots of it. And yet, there would be no ease to this leg of the journey. The snow was three feet deep and the place was thick with trees. They lay strewn about, as if someone had tossed in a bomb.

It wasn't long before we came across a large tree – probably a foot in diameter – blocking the trail. Because of the density of the forest, we were stuck. Rudy, Earling and I hopped off our sleds. We grabbed a saw from our equipment and took turns at the log. Sweat gathered uncomfortably deep inside our clothes. It was a good feeling when we'd sliced through, and the three of us grunted to pitch the tree aside. In the middle of Alaska, we were forcing our way through.

Unfortunately, not all the trees sat atop the snow. Not all could we cut through. Some were buried deep and we hit those hard. Each time I struck a hidden tree, I worried for the sleds. Would that be the collision that did it? Would it be the next? Or the next? Or would these machines bear up under the stress? If they did, what a testimony it would be.

We picked our way along. The trees seemed to close in on us. It was plodding, and we grew frustrated. But finally, some miles later, we intercepted a slough, a meandering arm of the Yukon, which we would follow to the main river. As the trail alongside the slough straightened for a time, the snow seemed to grow even deeper, and we punched the gas. Bessie hung onto the toboggan behind me, while I followed Earling, who had taken over the small, collapsible sled. Rudy and Alex brought up the rear.

We zipped toward the main river. The wind swirled heavily and threw up huge clouds of white. Suddenly, just ahead, Earling vanished. One moment he was there and the next, he and his Sno-Traveler had dropped off the face of the earth. But since it was not at all unusual to briefly lose sight of someone, I pushed on, figuring Earling would turn up ahead.

I found him, about 10 seconds later. It was the strangest of feelings as I went off the cliff, an 80 degree ridge, dropping 25 feet down. Alex had failed to mention that the river bank we were following dropped vertically to the ice below. As we fell, I wondered if we just might crush Earling. I wondered what would become of my passenger, Bessie.

It was a miracle we didn't hit my employee, or his machine, and ruin the trip. Instead, we landed with a thud next to Earling's sled, about three feet to the right. I was thrown hard at my windshield.

*The snowmobiles of today, much less those of the 1950s,
would have trouble negotiating this rough and difficult trail.*

Bessie, meanwhile, tumbled off the toboggan about 15 feet up the cliff. She rolled and bounced into the snow. Earling watched it all, having already scrambled out of harm's way. The snowmobiles were upright, but the three of us stood waist deep, thinking we might never get out of such a mess.

Maybe a minute passed. We heard a rumble and then quiet. Rudy and Alex poked their heads over the bank high above us.

"What happened?" Rudy said with a good humored smile. He could tell we weren't seriously hurt, though definitely bruised.

"We seemed to have had a little trouble," I said.

The cliff would cost us a couple hours. We had to push and pull the two machines and the toboggan back to the top. Finished, but doggedly tired, we turned to Alex, who didn't seem bothered by our struggles. We asked him how to get to Paimut, the village on the Yukon where he and Sergei had their cabin.

Alex shrugged and said it was only three miles by direct route, but that we'd have to climb another cliff just as high and as steep as the one we'd just encountered.

"Otherwise," he continued, sinking in deep snow like the rest of us, "we must follow the slough, and it is much farther that way."

We had no choice. It was impractical and dangerous to shove three sleds and two toboggans up another steep bank. Meanwhile, the sun was going down.

"How much farther the long way?" Rudy asked.

"I dunno, quite a ways, I think," Alex said.

"Well, about how far?" Rudy asked. He was getting frustrated with poor Alex, who never gave us much information.

"Not too far," he said.

"A couple miles or so?"

"No," Alex said. "Lots farther than that."

"Well, about how far?"

"I dunno."

Rudy sighed, gave up, and I pulled out a map. We brushed snow off my snowmobile and laid the map on its seat. We bent over it, and Rudy traced our way with a large finger. As near as we could tell, Paimut was at least seven more miles.

Of all the hardships that day, those miles may have been the worst. We had to follow a small river that had two horrible features – thin ice in the center and soft, deep snow along its steep banks. As we stopped to look at our chosen path, Rudy, with ax in hand, climbed off his machine. We possibly could ride along the river's edge, but first we had to test it. Rudy lifted the ax over those large, sturdy shoulders, and brought it down on the ice. It sank in so fast and so easily that our hearts sank. Where could we ride? Perhaps on the banks, but would it be possible? They were so steep, it hardly seemed likely.

We tried. At such an angle, I wondered if we wouldn't tumble down, crash through the ice and drown. Quite often, the sleds tipped so dangerously, we were forced to cross to the other side, where the going might be better.

Each time we did that, however, we had to find a way to cross the ice. We took turns walking ahead with an ax. If the ax went through in one blow, it wasn't safe. If it took two chops we considered it good enough. We would hop on the sleds and race across at top speed, hearts beating wildly. In that fashion, bank to bank, we criss-crossed the slough. It seemed our progress would not be fast enough to beat the sun, which barely hung in the sky. I was getting worried, and for good reason.

Eventually, we ran out of banks, which were now impassable on both sides of the small river. Our choice was clear: We had to go on the ice. We stopped the caravan. Rudy and Alex stepped lightly to the river. Their axes fell and split the ice. The two men flinched as freezing water splashed at them. They did this over and over, and finally, they learned the ice running down the center was the safest.

There remained one burning question. Just how would we get to the center? The ice on either side was too thin, so riding to the middle would be risky. Up and down the river we chopped. It took us nearly an hour to find thicker ice, and when we did, we still weren't sure it was thick enough.

We decided Rudy would test the passage with his smaller Sno-Traveler. We watched nervously as he gunned the engine. Bessie winced and chewed on her lower lip, and the machine took off, spewing out the slushy snow. He appeared to have no trouble as he came to rest in the middle of the river, and he waved us to follow. He must have been more than a little nervous waiting, especially with his wife on a toboggan. But we made it, and with relief in our hearts, we headed down the middle of the river. We were careful not to stray too far left or right.

About a mile up, the slough widened as we approached the main river. The sun dipped below the horizon, leaving every color in the world shimmering off the land. We hit the great Yukon.

The river was a mile wide and spectacular. We zipped across it on hard, windblown snow. A lightness bounced in my heart; we'd made it. Just reaching the Yukon brought a surge of confidence. Perhaps the snowmobiles would make it after all.

A couple of miles later, we neared the abandoned village of Paimut, where Alex and Sergei had their cabin. We eagerly drove to it. My muscles cried for a rest. I needed to stop, and I kept my eyes peeled for any sign of the cabin. Only, it never came. It was supposed to be along the river. Where the heck was it? The hazy sunshine turned to dark twilight, and I began to doubt Alex.

Much, much later, we came to a steep hill, and Alex motioned us to stop. He leaped off a toboggan and pointed to a small cabin sitting way up on top. When asked exactly how we would get up there, he shrugged once again.

"Walk," he said.

We tried one run at the hill but buried the machines, so we did as Alex suggested. We climbed. It was slow, and then it was slower.

Rudy turned a flashlight up the hill and lit up Bessie, who was crawling through the snow. We followed, carrying the sleeping bags, food and duffels. Near the top, we crawled, too. Finally, we were there, and we stared gratefully at the cabin. Puffs of smoke rose from the chimney and its dirty windows glowed.

We stepped through the door and let our bundles drop. It was wonderful. Alex's friend Sergei had arrived earlier with the sled dogs, and now a roaring fire was going. We collapsed in various chairs, but somehow, Bessie, after bouncing around all day on the back of the toboggan, with no windshield to guard her from the high winds, cooked us a wonderful meal. Before long, we fell asleep on the floor.

Many years later, in 1982, I went down the Yukon River in a boat. I had three friends with me – Lee Lynch, Bob Johnson and Denny Dunham – and as we passed a curve, I noticed that same cabin sitting high on the hill. Near the river, an Eskimo woman was cleaning fish.

"Hey, I spent the night in that old place," I told my pals.

"Sure, Edgar, sure," they grumbled.

They didn't believe me, because the cabin was falling down and it just was too preposterous. Lynch, who handled all of Arctic Cat's advertising, walked up to the woman and asked if he could buy some fish. She shook her head harshly. It was against the law for Eskimos to sell fish.

Then I stepped up.

"You know, I spent a night in that cabin 22 years ago," I said. "I was with two guys called Alex and Sergei."

"Sergei is my brother," she said, a huge grin tearing into her face.

Well, from her we then got fish, we got coffee, we got fresh bread, we got everything. Plus, my friends, those yahoos who didn't believe, finally knew the truth.

൙ ൙ ൙

The sun rose over the bleak surroundings, and we woke to cold and crisp weather. We threw down Bessie's breakfast of coffee, bacon and oatmeal, said goodbye to Alex and Sergei, and were on our way.

High rolling hills, backed by mountains, ran along the river. I took the lead and we clipped along at a fine pace until Rudy's machine decided to go for a little drive. By itself.

Chunks of large ice dotted the Yukon, and though we took care to avoid them, Rudy hit one. His machine pitched hard to the right and Rudy couldn't hang on. The Sno-Traveler didn't have the throttle mechanism of today's machines that automatically closes when released, so off it went down the river.

"It pitched me like a bronco," Rudy said as we watched the sled zoom away.

"It should come back," I said. "They usually do."

On those old machines, a riderless sled often made a large circle, and returned like a faithful dog. Rudy's snowmobile did just that, and it flew into our midst. Quickly, I unhooked my toboggan and in a few seconds, Rudy and I raced down the Yukon after the machine. We gained and gained, about to catch it, when suddenly it hit a piece of ice and tipped over, skidding to a stop.

Chuckling and shaking our heads, we flipped the machine upright. It was no worse for wear, and we were off again. We came to much softer snow, and battling higher winds, we slowed to eight miles an hour. We huddled behind our windshields while Bessie faced backwards on a toboggan. At about 2 p.m., we came abreast of Holy Cross.

Since it was early afternoon, we decided to make nearby Anvik. For that leg, Bessie took control of the smaller Sno-Traveler, but soon we noticed her slowing down, then stopping. We pulled up next to her, and discovered that the engine had died. I wasn't happy. It was too early in the trip for breakdowns.

I knelt over the engine and saw the trouble. The bolts were loose around the case and oil was flying onto the pulleys. My hands were cold, and it would be difficult to work outside. Fearing a blown gasket, we turned back to the Holy Cross Catholic Mission.

Occasionally on the Yukon, we would meet a dog team, the only way to travel until we came along.

The native children again gathered at the river to see who the heck we were. Later, Father John Fox, head of the mission, said that as we drove into sight, the kids announced our approach with shouts of "Airplanes without wings are coming."

Earling and I worked until 10:30 that night. We fixed the small Sno-Traveler's gasket and tuned the others. Then we lit a couple of cigars and relaxed, stretched out against a wall as the sweet-smelling smoke warmed our faces.

೪೬ ೪೬ ೪೬

We left the Catholic mission at 10:30 a.m., March 8. We broke trail for 40 miles and made Anvik at 4 p.m. We stayed with Rudy's friend, Jack Wharton, who was a trader and sold us gas for our long trip to Kaltag, the next stop up. He opened his store and Bessie replenished her supplies. It had been an easy day, a necessary easy day.

It was eight degrees below when we left Anvik the next morning. We rode on rough snow and choppy ice, and my clothes grew wet from blowing snow. As the wind grew fierce throughout the day, I shivered like a child with a fever.

We covered 54 miles, but finally could take it no longer. We considered pitching our tents on the banks of the Yukon, but gratefully spotted a cabin high on a hill. We slid off our machines, strapped on snowshoes and trudged on up. But as we arrived at the cabin and opened the door, we were overcome by a strange odor. Our joy turned to dismay. In the middle of the floor was a huge pile of salmon – very old salmon. Martens had also made camp, and droppings sat on the chairs, on the stove and on the beds.

Rudy and I stood in the doorway, nearly gagging. As Bessie walked in, her eyes grew three sizes. Her nose shriveled.

"Good grief!" she said. "We can't stay in here."

"I don't know," I said. "That snow is four feet deep if it's a foot, and making camp out there doesn't thrill me."

Earling nodded.

This cabin had marten droppings and rotten salmon inside before we cleaned it up. The pile to the left of the cabin is all the dead fish. Once clean, the place provided shelter for at least one night of sleep without cold. Earling, Bessie and Rudy huddle in the doorway.

"I suppose we could clean it up," she said, rubbing her hands together and, as she did many times, took charge. "All right, then, let's get to work."

Earling and I grabbed shovels, Rudy and Bessie brooms, and we swept the stuff outside. It wasn't fun after a day of bouncing up and down on a hard seat, but before long, we had the cabin cleaned out, and it made us feel good.

After another of Bessie's fine dinners, we retired to the sleeping bags which for months would smell of dead fish and marten droppings. With a candle glowing nearby, I scribbled down my thoughts. As I began to drift off, I blew out the candle. I slept well, which was good, because our minor troubles soon would become major ones.

๛ ๛ ๛

March 10 started on the Yukon in three-below weather. We fought headwinds of 20 to 30 miles per hour, and even behind the large windshields, needles of cold sneaked around and nailed us. Bessie huddled on the toboggan, arms covering her face. The smelly cabin had been much better.

The wind not only battered us, but it built incredible snow drifts on which the machines bounced crazily. Visibility was down to less than a mile, and soon snow clogged the machines' carburetors and running parts. It slowed us badly, but it would not be the wind, snow or the engines that made our day miserable. That would be left to the great Yukon itself.

The river brought us overflow ice, caused by heavy snow that forced water to seep up through tiny cracks. The water pooled on top and was hidden by new-fallen snow. We learned that the hard way when Rudy hit a patch.

Trailing Bessie and me, he began to sink. A seasoned outdoorsman, Rudy immediately knew what it was. He punched the accelerator and sped across the slush to solid ice about 30 feet ahead. As he stopped, he turned to warn Earling, who brought up the rear. Too late. Earling's machine plunged into the water, and his tracks began freezing. Earling leaped from his sled, sloshed through the snow and hoisted the track out of the water. The engine howled above the ice, spewing water from the track. Rudy turned his machine around and headed back to help.

"Great job getting that track out of the water," Rudy yelled. "I thought I was going down myself, but I managed to punch the gas and barely made it through."

"I didn't notice until it was too late," Earling shouted above the roar. "I gunned it, but it just sank."

When the slush and ice was removed from the track, it was time to get the machine out. Rudy and Earling tied a rope between the two snowmobiles. Rudy then revved his engine and began pulling. He had barely begun to tug, however, when bad went to worse. His machine crashed through more overflow ice.

Earling came running. They moved fast, very fast, and hoisted Rudy's machine up. They looked hunchbacked as they battled Mother Nature and a machine that weighed 500 pounds. But it was too late – water had already iced up the track.

Rudy marched out to me and Bessie, 20 yards from the action.

"It's all overflow, and I got my machine frozen," he said, shaking his head with disgust.

"Well," I said, trying to be in good spirits, though I knew chipping the snowmobile out of the ice would take hours. "We'd better start."

With hammers and chisels, we chipped. And chipped. Three terribly long hours later, the drive chains moved once more, and we had the little thing running. We tied a 100-foot rope onto Earling's machine and, with the two other sleds, pulled it out of danger.

Wanting to get the heck out of there, we took off up the river.

∞ ∞ ∞

When bad luck hits, it can hit hard. It was later that same day that my machine died, and I dropped the hammer into that exposed flywheel.

The future hung in the balance, but it was too late to fret.

My plan was simple. I would run the engine as long as I could, until inevitably, it overheated and the engine stopped. Much to my surprise, the engine ran better than the other two. Apparently, in that climate, we'd been running our engines too cold. Stripping the cooling fins proved to be a solution, not a problem. Another hurdle, another dangerous situation, was avoided. Luck was on our side, though it always chose its time and place to help.

Deciding to call it a day before anything else went wrong, we set up camp in deep snow close to the bank of the river to gain shelter from the wind. Due to our problems that day, we made a tough decision: We had to leave supplies behind. They were too heavy, and if we had to go through more deep snow and overflow ice, we had to be as light as possible. We spent much of that night deciding what to keep and what to leave, and hoped we were making the right decisions.

We built a big fire. More than ever before, we felt the need for heat that night in the frigid far north.

ॐ ॐ ॐ

It could hardly get worse, we thought. But as usual, the Alaskan frontier had it own ideas. Considerably lighter on March 10, our seventh day out, we drove in sub-zero weather and in low spirits. The wind was light in the morning, but by midday picked up and exceeded its strength of the previous day. We moved slowly, a noisy caterpillar plowing through the expanse of Alaska.

We got stuck twice that day, partly because of the winds and partly because of our inability to avoid snow traps. Our drive belts slipped, and the machines ran slower and slower. Though we'd gone only 15 miles, we had to bed down for the night.

As we sought shelter, Rudy spotted a cabin high on the left bank. Pleased that we might have a place, we threw on our snowshoes and again trudged up another steep hill. Tired – emotionally and physically — I thought how nice it would be to get inside a cabin, where we could light a fire and have a good meal. But to our dismay, we discovered the front of the cabin was the only wall standing. It was like a movie prop. Down the hill we went, our spirits sinking with each step.

We found another cabin about a half hour later, also up on a hill. As we opened the door, we saw that it belonged to trappers. They weren't home, but we feared if we bedded down, they would return and have no place to sleep. We trudged back down the hill and set up camp near the river bank. To keep the wind from blowing down our shelters, we tied the tents to the motor sleds.

A hearty supper warmed our stomachs and our hearts, and we settled in for the night. It was chilly in those tents. I laid in my sleeping bag and again tried to write, this time by flashlight. My fingernails ached from the cold. So penetrating was the wind, we slept with fur caps on our heads.

Day eight began nicely. As we ate breakfast, Rudy spoke with one of the trappers who'd just returned home. He said there was a trail all the way to Kaltag, about 60 miles away.

"I think we should be able to make Kaltag today," Rudy said hopefully.

"It'll be nice to have a path," I said. "I'm tired of breaking trail."

It was great – oh, was it great. The machines flew across the Yukon on a real, honest-to-goodness trail, and we were making good time. The path was smooth, almost groomed by the wind and dog teams. I could see us in Kaltag by nightfall and, for the first time in days, laughing about the trip instead of complaining.

Then we hit the rough snow. I didn't notice it at first, but subtly, more and more, my body began to shake and my wrists and arms began to shiver as if I were in a small earthquake. We crossed into another world.

Our beloved trail vanished, destroyed by the wind. Instead, sharp drifts rose before us. We bashed into them and our machines crawled. As we plodded, three men ran down from their cabin, a small wooden structure with a neat red chimney on top.

We stopped and they eyed the snowmobiles as if they couldn't believe we were riding across a terrain that usually chewed up machinery.

"What the heck you got here?" said the tallest man, one with a heavy beard.

I explained how the Sno-Travelers worked and where we were going. When I said we'd like to reach Kaltag by nightfall, the three shook their heads. The fellow with the beard put a large, strong hand on my shoulder and chuckled lightly.

"It's still 40 miles to Kaltag, but in about 22, you and your snow machines are going to hit a patch of ice that's some of the worst I've seen," he said. "That ice is glare, and it goes on for several miles."

We said thanks, but were on our way, still hoping to reach Kaltag by nightfall. About 10 miles later, we met a dog team. The driver, a Kaltag Indian and the fourth member of the trapping party, agreed with his comrades.

"You'll never make it past the ice today," he said, wind tugging hard at his jacket. It whipped a flap into his face and he flipped it off with a quick hand.

"The wind is so strong that my dogs and I blew helplessly downstream on the ice," he said. "The dogs laid on their bellies and slid and slid. I thought they'd slide forever. We were lucky to get out of there."

He told us of a cabin near the ice where we might spend the night. We thanked him heartily, and were on our way, still planning to give it a try.

Not long after the encounter, the winds reached 60 mph and whipped up an almost continuous cloud of snow, sand and silt. It covered us and cut visibility to 600 feet or less.   It was a blizzard; it was a sandstorm. The snow cut coldly into our faces, and sand peppered our eyes. Worse yet, the elements tore into the engines. Our faces could take it; the engines, perhaps, could not. I worried that the silt and sand might affect the motors, and yet they plowed on, like little tanks.

We drove like that for an hour before stumbling upon the ice. Through a cloud of dust, we saw it lying 100 yards ahead. We saw that the snow, drifting three feet high in places, no longer was white but an ugly brown.

Whirling dust reduced visibility to an eighth of a mile and forced us to stop on a sand bar. Hopping off, I motioned Rudy to follow. The howl of the wind was loud, so through hand gestures, we decided Earling and Bessie would wait while we checked out the ice ahead.

We rode off. A few minutes later, we came to a turn in the river and got a good look. As far as we could see, a sheet of ice shimmered dangerously. Suddenly, the wind knocked me to my knees, and I grabbed the machine. I then watched Rudy drive onto the ice. Against a wall of wind, his machine stood still. In a snap, he and the sled were carried down the river. I watched him go, helpless to do anything but wish him well.

Somehow, through sheer determination, he zigzagged back to me. He plopped down in the snow and caught his breath; and then we tried our luck again. Except, whenever Rudy and I ventured out, the wind grabbed our machines and swung them like a weather vane. The trappers were right. We would not be able to beat the ice. I pulled close to Rudy.

"I think we better call it a night!"

My words were carried away by the wind.

"Let's turn back and look for that cabin," Rudy shouted.

We first had to find Earling and Bessie, but the weather made it nearly impossible to do so; we just couldn't see.

"Which way?" I yelled.

"I think there!" Rudy said, pointing into the whiteout. He flinched as a small pebble struck his cheek.

It probably was only a few minutes, but it seemed forever before we spotted their outline in the snow. Rudy's instincts were the best.

"We're going to look for that cabin the trappers talked about," he told Earling and Bessie, and with Rudy in the lead, we began our search in dark dusk. We returned through the sandy, snowy terrain. We again crossed the hummocks three feet high, and as I accidentally ran into one, a sharp, gritty pain rifled from my lower back to the base of my neck.

One of our typical campsites on the Yukon River.

As night descended, we were in trouble. We couldn't find the cabin. Then, with another terrific blast of wind and snow, I saw nothing. I looked ahead and looked behind, trying to see an outline, a small movement, anything. Not only was visibility down to zero, but my sled had no headlights.

Suddenly, I remembered a big hill along the river. Perhaps I could go there and rest in the lee side, out of the wind. At least there I'd have time to go over my options. I moved back slowly, bumping and bouncing over hard snow until finally, like entering a bright home at Christmas, I found the hill. Even better, I found Rudy and Bessie sitting on their still-warm sleds, with Earling just driving up. After being together for 10 days, I guess we were starting to think alike.

Instead of using two tents, we set up only one, my seven-foot pup tent. As I fell asleep, it seemed as though I had done nothing but drive Sno-Travelers on the Yukon.

❧ ❧ ❧

The bright sun – and as always, a healthy breakfast from Bessie – raised our spirits the next morning – but the river and the Alaskan wind still were not content to let us pass. The day was hazy, and we gazed down the river, to that glare ice and to those sand bars where dust swirled heavily. It seemed as inhospitable a place as any on earth.

We plowed through to the sand bar, and gravel tore at our runners. We came upon the ice, and once again, the wind grabbed the machines and manhandled them. We could go no farther. Frustrated, we sat. We brooded. We thought. Finally, by walking alongside our machines and giving a little push now and then, we moved ahead. Slowly.

We slipped and slid against the wind for hours. My heart thumped and I thought my lungs would explode. My legs were rubber.

But wishing for relief was pointless. When the glare ice came to an end, it was replaced by a stretch of jagged, broken ice. We maneuvered around the dangerous needles and then came upon hard drifts.

The final 18 miles to Kaltag were rough, but about mid-afternoon we rolled into town. We received a warm reception, and our machines were the center of attention. We stayed the night in the home of teachers from the Kaltag School. Mr. and Mrs. Clifford Fossman fed us and allowed us valuable down-time. Our stopover gave us a chance to wash – we were smelly – dry our clothes and repair some gear.

Compared to what we had been through, the next few days were easy. On March 14, we spent a short day on the trail to Nulato – about 35 miles in all – and stayed the night in the company of Father Baud and four sisters at a Catholic mission. On March 15, we traveled 40 miles to Galena, where Rudy and Bessie lived when he worked for Northern Consolidated Airlines. We spent two nights there, where in the FAA shop, Earling and I went over the engines, piece by piece, until they purred like kittens. Rudy and Bessie stayed at the home of airfield manager Russ Hart, while Earling and I slept in the FAA visitors quarters.

We made good time on March 17, and reached the village of Ruby 50 miles away. It had been cold, as low as 30 below, but the trails were good and the wind low. Rudy and Bessie stayed with friends, and Earling and I slept in what used to be an old theater. A local woman cooked us dinner.

We were moving deeper into Alaska and closer to Fairbanks. It was a good feeling. We saw more people, more civilization. For too long, mile after mile, I had gazed ahead, gazed behind, gazed to the left and right, and seen nothing but windswept snow moving on forever.

On March 18, we left Ruby and made 60 miles to a small cabin on the Yukon at a point called Birches. That day, we passed through the village of Kokrines, a sad place. Wind whistled down the town's only road, past rotting, abandoned shacks. Had it been the Old West, a tumbleweed surely would have rolled on by. The people were pleasant, asking us questions about the machines, but didn't seem nearly as happy as those in other towns. A local legend, Rudy said, explained the difference.

It was many years ago, Rudy said, that a missionary came to Kokrines and established a mission. The man worked hard building a church. One day, while he was away, someone destroyed the new building. They tore up fixtures, smashed windows and wrecked the floor. On his return, the angry missionary decided to leave the village. But before he left, he issued a curse.

"The village of Kokrines will decay," he said. "Its people will die in violence, and grass will grow in the streets."

He never returned, and the village was ruined. Rudy said violence, wholesale murders, drownings and disease had decimated the population. Looking around, it was hard not to believe the story.

March 19 came, and with temperatures 25 below (snow froze to my eyebrows), we pulled into the village of Tanana. Trails had been good and the snowmobiles were running well. We stayed the night with the Rev. Melvin Jensen of the Arctic Mission. I was encouraged by the last few days, so I wrote a letter home, informing my wife that we would be in Fairbanks by March 22. Done writing, I stepped to the window and stared out over a thick, snowy forest. I asked to use the reverend's phone, and I called Anchorage to have our luggage sent ahead to Fairbanks. As it turned out, I was too optimistic.

About to leave Tanana, fierce wind and cold came at us. It would hound us all day.

"Looks like a cold one, Edgar," Rudy said.

From the toboggan attached to Earling's machine, Bessie yelled, "We only have a few more days, so let's get going, boys."

Whether she was feeding us or encouraging, Bessie was an invaluable member of the group. Had she not been along, I doubt we could have made it, even with those powerful old sleds.

Not long after, I felt silly for sending that letter. It would be a struggle to get there by my predicted date. The snow was rough, and it didn't look better up ahead. We made our way from the Yukon to the Tanana

Here we all are, well into our Alaska journey. From left: Bessie Billberg, Rudy Billberg, myself, and Earling Falk.

River, a distance of 15 miles. We now were leaving the great Yukon, our friend and enemy for nearly 1,000 miles. It was the start of our final leg to Fairbanks.

It should have made us feel wonderful, but I don't know that it did. The terrain changed, and once again there was sand and impassable ice. We were on a frozen stretch of river called Squaw Crossing, a confluence of streams between the Yukon and the Tanana. Snow, swirled with sand, blew hundreds of feet into the air. All we could do was bow our heads and push on, but still the elements cracked us and our engines. The wind blew our caravan this way and that, and the machines spun helplessly. For mile after mile, we barely moved; finally, we had to stop.

I got off my machine. The wind knocked me to my knees.

"Better get out and walk," I yelled.

And so we walked. We pushed, we crawled, we tugged. Visibility grew poor, and when Rudy went ahead to scout for a better trail, he came back shaken. He had lost sight of us momentarily and was virtually blind. He had, however, found a trail.

It had taken us five hours to go 12 miles, but on the path we made good time until it grew dark. The night was much lighter than it was back home, but still, with no headlights on the snowmobiles, we needed to stop. We pulled out the map and the flashlights. Our position, we saw, was the mouth of the Manley Hot Springs. We looked for the shortest route into the springs and to the Hot Springs Roadhouse, where we thought we could find a warm bed and a hot shower. Fairbanks was 400 miles east.

We needed rest, and my snowmobile needed work. It had begun to lose power and was now wheezing like an asthmatic. The crew didn't know, but I thought they'd better, in case I started to fall back.

"My machine sounds terrible," I said. "We better get to this place as soon as possible."

"Let's take that small creek," Rudy said, pointing at the map.

We drove down into the stream, but soon noticed that it carried the waters of the hot springs, and because of that, we worried about thin ice. Instead, we hopped onto a dog-sled trail, which we figured was safe. It certainly was, and we took it a few hundred yards, until it disappeared. We stopped and huddled. Rudy stood before me, with Bessie on my right and Earling on my left. As night chilled our bones, we decided Rudy should walk ahead with a flashlight and point the way. He was the best man for the job, with years of Alaskan experience. He nodded his agreement, and though it was dark, I could tell it was a nod of concern.

Slowly, Rudy forged ahead until all we could see was his bobbing light about 40 feet away.

At times Rudy lost the trail and the light stopped, flashing this way and that. It sometimes flashed straight back at us and glittered in our eyes. It reflected on open water, and then ran, jiggling low and fast for several yards across the snow. As the hours passed, Rudy kept walking, his beam swinging in wide patterns one moment and then down to earth the next. As he walked, I found myself in awe of his stamina, especially after the harrowing hours on the glare ice. If his legs were as tired as mine, they must have been ready to give way.

The light and Rudy came to a stop. We drove and circled him. He was a mess. From sweat that had frozen and melted a hundred times, his bangs were matted against his forehead. When he let out a breath, his cheeks ballooned. His hands went to his knees as he tried to rest, and then he sat himself on a toboggan.

It was more than a tired body that had my friend slumping. It was frustration. The trail had disappeared, and the river now shot off in two directions; each heading into the night.

"I know we're near the springs," Rudy said, shaking his head. "I can tell by the hills, and it should be right here. Only, it isn't."

He pointed to those hills he'd seen so many times from the air and shrugged.

Suddenly, Bessie's face brightened. "I think I see a light," she said.

We snapped our heads and looked to where Bessie was pointing. I looked everywhere, but saw nothing. Neither did Rudy. But she continued to nod. "Yup, it's right over there," she said.

"Yeah," Earling agreed. "I saw it, too, for a second."

We took the right branch of the creek and soon it was clear to all. A light flickered through the trees. We continued to ride, my machine sputtering badly, and then we saw the dim outline of a cabin. As we got close, the pleasant smell of smoke came from the chimney and warmed our spirits.

I stepped to a door built with sturdy strips of oak, and knocked.

"Who is it?" a male voice called warily from inside.

"Travelers going through," I said. "We're looking for the roadhouse."

We heard scurrying, and a man opened the door. A flashlight was in my eyes.

"The roadhouse is a quarter mile up the trail, but it's closed for the winter," the voice said.

We stood in the snow as this man looked us up and down, then shined the light on the Sno-Travelers. He quickly made up his mind.

"My name is Chuck Clements," he said. "My wife and I are alone, and we have an extra room. You're welcome to it."

As we unloaded our gear, Mary Clements got up and cooked us a big supper. It was 10 p.m. Such was the hospitality of Alaska.

The next morning, I worked on my failing machine. I pulled the head from the engine. I held it close and my breath quickened as I saw the damage. One of the intake valves had a deep groove burned into it, perhaps from the swirling sands of a day earlier. It was very unusual for this to happen, so I hadn't bothered to bring along any replacements. I sat down on the sled and, for a moment, pondered what to do. In its condition, the machine would not make it to Fairbanks.

Somehow though, I wondered, couldn't we erase the groove? It'd be difficult, but maybe, just maybe, we could. So, scrounging around the debris at Manley Hot Springs, I found a V-Block, a clamp, and some odds and ends. From the stuff, we spent much of the day fashioning a makeshift tool. We built a crank and then set the damaged valve in our little machine. Rudy was the first to crank it, and as we took turns, slowly, the groove began to disappear.

By late afternoon, it was fixed. I was proud of our little team. We illustrated man's ingenuity in the face of disaster.

We thought about putting a few hours in that day, but the Clements asked us to stay, saying we could swim in the hot springs. It turned out to be a great break as we indulged in their hospitality and Mary's fine cooking, not to mention the wonderful pools of warm water.

ॐ ॐ ॐ

Before leaving the morning of March 22, we sat at an oak table that overlooked the springs. Chuck Clements' large hands waved as he talked.

"Now listen closely," he said. "This is how you should go. There is an old telegraph trail from Manley to Tolovna, the second to last stop before you make Fairbanks. It was used by some old gold miners."

A little while later, we shook hands with our wonderful hosts and got back on our rides, refreshed. For the first time in many days, we left the river and went cross country. It was tough finding the old trail, and we worried until we came across a native who showed us the way. It was hilly and the bush was thick, but it proved smoother than the river. Later that day we arrived in Tolovna, and stayed the night at an abandoned roadhouse.

By March 23, we were growing excited, for the end of our journey was in sight. We followed a trail to Minto, where we bought gas, and where we met a representative of the Kohler company, who'd flown in from Fairbanks. He wondered how his engines were doing. We said they were good, but also discussed a few of the problems we'd had.

The meeting didn't last long, and we continued to Nenana, about 30 miles away. We followed an old dog trail part of the way, and Fairbanks neared. But Alaska was to leave us with one more challenge. A bull-dozer had destroyed much of the trail. Fallen trees, dirt and snow blocked the way.

We gingerly made our way around the obstacles. How horrible it would be to hit something now, to get dirt or wood inside the tracks, or for something to break I couldn't repair on the open trail. But we were careful, and the machines plugged along.

It was on that rough, uneven snow, in sight of our goal, that my brain cleared and I saw the future. I knew the machines were here to stay, that they would be a success. What I didn't know was how big a success. There were unknown factors, but the fact that the Sno-Travelers would succeed was not unknown. Not now. Not with Fairbanks almost in sight.

It was dark as we neared Nenana. We traveled along the road, and an occasional car lit our way as we found a nearby inn. The next day, March 24, would be our last on the trail. Fairbanks was only 65 miles away.

Starting at 6:30 a.m., we followed the Tanana River (there was no trail to Fairbanks). For the first 10 miles, we clipped along at a pace that had me thinking we'd arrive by early afternoon. But from that point on, the snow on the river grew deeper and wetter, and we slowed to a walk. Once, we slogged down a river channel for an hour before realizing it went in the wrong direction. Twice during that detour, we ran into overflow ice and its menacing water, and with hearts beating fast, zipped across as fast as we could. Though Fairbanks was still on our minds, it was easy to grow disheartened.

Back on course, we spotted open water. Rudy, in the lead, motioned for us to stop on a sandbar. We looked the situation over.

"It's not good," Rudy said.

Quite true. The water extended far and wide. Deciding to scout ahead, Rudy zoomed off. We stared at the mocking waters and waited. Our friend returned with bad news.

"There's another big area of open water ahead," he said. "It easily could swallow up one of our machines, probably never see it again."

"Any ideas?" I asked. "Is there a way to go around it?"

***Once, a banana Air Force helicopter descended out of the sky
and landed near us. The pilot took me up, and I surveyed the
land.***

"Probably; I saw an island in the river that we should be able to get close to," he said. "There might be solid ice nearby."

As usual, Rudy was right. Still, the snow was deep and as the day warmed to nearly 30 degrees, it became sticky.

Once more in the late afternoon, my snowmobile plunged through the top of the ice and hit water —overflow – and I spun out of it before freezing down. Because of that, and other close calls, we left the river. Approximately 15 miles from Fairbanks, we climbed up off the Tanana and began following an old logging road.

Later, losing the road, we returned to the Tanana and finally met the Chena Slough, which should have taken us to Fairbanks. We followed the Chena for three miles, but as the day grew dark, we had to pull off for fear of thin ice.

Just 12 miles from our goal, we now thought of camping. We had no trail and we couldn't follow the river in the dark. We stopped, even though we were anxious to finish the trip.

"I hate to say this, but I think we should call it a night," Rudy said. "Without a trail, we could wind up just about anywhere."

"I suppose you're right, Rudy," I said.

Disheartened, but knowing good sense meant putting off the celebration for one more night, we'd unloaded a few packs when Rudy pointed into the darkness.

"I see a pair of wolves," he said.

"That's just great," I said. "Do they look hungry?"

"I don't know, I only saw their eyes."

Fortunately, he had not seen wolves, but a pair of Sno-Travelers with headlights coming at us. They twisted and turned through the woods, and finally pulled to a stop with a loud growl. The Persinger boys, Sno-Traveler dealers in Fairbanks, stepped off and gave us all hearty handshakes. They wore smiles larger than their faces; and soon, so did we.

"The ice is bad up ahead," one said. "But we've got a way into Fairbanks.

A host of Alaskan children stare at this curious stranger on a strange machine.

My goodness, I thought. We would make it that evening!

We took a trail most of the way. The final mile saw us riding up the Chena River abreast of the city, which glittered over the snow. The last few hundred yards ended at the airport. We pulled up side by side and turned off the engines. They warbled and popped. We'd made it.

Several people were waiting for us, and they shook our hands over and over. How wonderful. Mayor Jack Wilbur drove us to the Chamber of Commerce, where there was a great reception. The Kohler men, Ed Anderson and George Gallati, were there, as were many civic leaders, even Miss Alaska.

Our overland journey had covered 1,200 miles in 21 days, 19 of which were spent on the trail. The sleds had performed wonderfully – better, perhaps, than our own bodies, which were sore beyond belief.

In the following days, our machines would sit on display in front of the Chamber of Commerce. Men, women and children, especially the kids, gawked at those machines, those battle-weary machines. They got down on hands and knees and eyeballed the slide rails which drove the tracks of those early models. They knocked fists on the huge squarish windshields that rose from the equally squarish front frame. They wandered around the sleds like cavemen around a wheel.

As I looked over my machines with a touch of pride, up strolled a little old man. He wore a black coat that hung on a tiny body. He frowned to himself. He looked at the sleds and he looked at me and he looked back at the machines. His hands were shoved deep inside his pockets and his shoulders were hunched. He shook his head four times and rocked back on his heels.

"They'll never work," he said. "They'll never work."

With a slight grin, I nodded. It was a comment we'd heard frequently, but coming off 21 days that proved snowmobiles definitely did work, I could only chuckle.

❦ ❦ ❦

Twenty years later, riding in a boat down the Yukon, it became apparent that snowmobiles had become the main form of transportation for Alaskans. I saw few dog teams. No longer did the Eskimos have to fish most of the summer for dog food, so the animals could work hard for them in winter. Our 21-day cross-country trip had brought us credibility and those people a more productive life. Back home, similar things had happened. Resorts stayed open in the winter, something they had not done before. Our economic impact was felt throughout the snowbelt of the North American continent, to say nothing of the recreational joy brought to families who discovered a way to conquer winter. We touched the lives of millions.

"They'll never work," that old man had said. "They'll never work."

Incredibly, even after our historic trip across Alaska, that's just what a couple members of our board thought.

Chapter 2

GROWING UP

In his late-70s now, Edgar Hetteen has a habit of referring to himself as an eighth-grade graduate from a country school. It seems odd to hear this, coming from an intelligent, witty fellow who is largely responsible for billions of dollars that now flow into the United States economy. Thousands owe their livelihood to him. He is not a typical eighth-grade graduate. And yet, it was that simple beginning that likely turned Hetteen into what he became, a resourceful entrepreneur who never gave up.

It's time to step back a moment from those heady days of Alaska and the quickly changing world of Polaris to a time when I still played; when I learned you can always improve, when I learned to believe in myself in the wilds of rural Roseau.

This goes back 70 years to the early school days, though school was not one of the things that appealed to me. Each year, I had one real happy day in school – the day when school was to be let out for the summer. I could look forward to a time of chasing gophers and squirrels and roaming around the farm, then down by the river, all of those things.

Helping my parents on the farm was far better than school – though as I look back, I wished I'd paid a whole lot more attention to school and what it could do for me.

That one-room school house was about three miles from our farm. Mom or Dad usually shook me out of bed at five. We'd eat early, and then I'd wipe my eyes a billion times before chores. I'd start out for school about 7 a.m. I often was late on a warm day, because a seven-year-old boy found a lot to explore along the way. Blades of long, wide, green grass were picked and shoved into my mouth. I'd get a loud, screeching whistle by blowing hard. I chased insects and ran around trees. I'd kick a rock until it went askew and tumbled into the high weeds. In winter, I trudged through snow, holding the scarf up above my mouth and crossing my arms tight to keep in the warmth. By the time I arrived at school, my nose and cheeks burned.

When my parents moved me to the Brandt School, where I spent most of my schooling, it was a two-mile hike in a different direction. It, too, was a one-room country school. It had no indoor plumbing and was heated by a large wood stove in the back of the room. The fire was usually nice and comfortable, sometimes a little too warm, sometimes a little too cold.

We drank water that came from a well a quarter mile away at the Brandt Farm. It was great to be asked to go for water, and we boys looked forward to our turn. It was a chance to get out of school, and we certainly didn't hurry back, nor did we bring back much water. With two of us carrying the pail, most of it had spilled out over the ground and onto our pants. But after all, that wasn't bad because maybe we'd get another trip the same day.

As I began school, I spoke little English. Though my mother and father knew English, Swedish was the dominant language in our farm home. Many years earlier, Grandpa and Grandma had immigrated, and settled in the far north of Minnesota because it was so much like Sweden. Even at school, few students knew the American language. There were Swedes, Norwegians and Germans, all speaking their native tongues, all having to learn English because that's what the teacher was speaking, that's what our country was speaking. We spent extra time on it, so we could get on and learn other things.

My one-room schoolhouse.

Compared to present-day schooling, my experience was unique. With 30 to 40 of us, all different ages, in one room, I was able to draw on their knowledge. I believe I had an advantage over children who never got to associate with those younger and older.

Each day as school began, the first-graders would march up and take the first row of wooden desks. The second-graders, third-graders and the rest followed suit; and the teacher taught us each in turn. While she taught another grade, we did our assigned work. If we messed around, punishment came quickly in the form of a rap on the fingers. The teacher probably was in her late 20s, but we thought she was older than heck.

School was a big part of growing up, but life revolved around my family and our farm. I was an only child until age nine, when my brother Allan was born. Three years later, a sister, Doreen, came along. She, however, perished in a fire when our house burned down. My father and I learned of her death upon arriving home by train after attending the World's Fair in Chicago. I'm sure the fair had been wonderful, but the news of Doreen's death wiped clean those memories.

Dad had 80 acres, 20 of which were in river woods and pasture land. He had a four-horse team, cattle, sheep, chickens, pigs and turkeys. Much of my childhood was spent feeding those animals. Though our farm was relatively small, we never did lack for food. By today's standards, you probably would have called us poor, but we certainly had clothes and shelter. Dad worked hard. In summer, the animals grazed nearby, but in winter, my father traveled many miles to get hay for the animals. It was in those early years, watching Dad work hard from dawn till dusk, and often longer, that I learned what it takes to succeed. Though my father may not have been a success by worldly standards, he took care of our family.

Sometimes I tagged along, and learned what it was to be drained at the end of a sub-zero, wintry day. After milking the cows, we'd leave early in the morning on a bobsled pulled by a team of horses, and it seemed like we drove all day to a barren swamp area where we'd piled the hay. It was frozen in the snow and we had to hack it out. Blisters rose on my hands as easily as weeds in a garden. We'd stack the hay high onto the bobsled. Before leaving, we ate frozen sandwiches.

We'd finally take off for home. The horses snorted as their breath shot out of flaring nostrils and froze in the air. They thumped through powdery snow, while strands of hay fell from the mound and left a trail. We'd arrive late, only to trudge out to feed the cows. It might sound like hardship, but it wasn't. It was all we knew.

When I was nine, Dad got a Fordson tractor. It was so much better than our old Plowman. How my mouth dropped when I saw it, a large gray machine, standing proud in the barn. Wow! And though Dad would let me ride with him, I yearned to drive it myself. I waited and waited, and then one day, Mom and Dad went to town. There I was alone. What to do?

I checked to make sure they were really gone, and I twirled the steel crank in front. The Fordson rumbled to life, and I climbed aboard. The sound of the engine was music to my ears, a music deep inside me. I smiled and bounced up and down on the seat. I had to drive it. It was cold that day, and the oil was stiff, but I put the tractor into gear.

In the chilled air of fall, I drove toward the river near our house. I pushed the throttle, and the beast grunted. It jolted ahead. But then, that fence, the brown fence that separated our land from the water, drew closer and closer, and then closer. I jostled with the clutch but it had frozen; I couldn't get it out of gear. With me in a panic, the Fordson plowed through the fence. We were heading straight to the river. Fun had turned to fear.

Down the hill I went, the machine ripping up huge chunks of grass. Fortunately, now rising in front of me was a big oak. I struck it hard. Tossed forward, I rapped my chest against the steering wheel. I somehow stayed in the seat, and watched smoke rise from the engine.

Had I gone into the river, it certainly would have ruined my day. As it was, worrying about what my Dad would say when he got home also ruined my day. Fortunately, Dad was quite understanding. He knew how the mind of a nine-year-old farm boy worked, and he didn't say much about his brand new tractor.

By then I knew I liked engines. I could see in my mind how they worked. I could see the gears and the pistons and how they meshed together. To my benefit, Dad wasn't mechanical, and I was given free rein of the farm machinery. In me was a desire to build and to fix, to make things better than they were.

I looked forward to days when my parents might hitch that two-horse team to the caboose, a seven-foot long box heated with wood where they sat. It meant they would drive the 10 miles into Roseau, and they'd be gone most of the day. It was exciting because I could stay home and experiment, both on the machinery and even in the kitchen.

I tried many times to bake bread. A big bowl on the counter served as my caldron, and into it I poured flour, water and yeast. I had no idea what I was doing, but I tried. I never could seem to get the mixture right and the bread usually failed to rise. As the day ended, with powder all over the kitchen and globs of dough on the floor, I scurried to hide the evidence. My parents would have taken a dim view of a farm boy trying to bake bread. It just wasn't done. I'd take the evidence and put it in the trough, where our pigs got rid of it fast. Occasionally, they got a little round and bloated and looked a little funny, but luckily, none ever died. I also tried to make cake and sometimes cookies, most of it winding up as pig food. But all of it was a whole lot more fun than riding in that bouncing caboose all the way to Roseau and back.

I looked forward to every day. I mixed and I tinkered and I built things that didn't do anything, but which I thought were neat. With a few empty spools of thread, some round pieces of timber and a couple of boards, I could make the darnedest machines. Spools became belt pulleys, and grocery string became belts. I could fashion a crank and, by gosh, to my young mind, fascinating devices.

As I grew older, the machines became more elaborate. A cousin, Bob, from Virginia, Minnesota, came to visit each summer, and one July I'll never forget.

Earlier that year, Lavern Larson, a neighborhood boy, and I discovered a coffee grinder in the woods. We took to dumping big old oak leaves in it and made up stories that we had a little tobacco grinding business. When the leaves came out of the grinder, they sure did look like you could roll them and smoke them.

While Bob was visiting, he and I discovered a small gasoline engine, and we hit upon an idea. We carried that engine to the grinder, we belted the two together and, wow, it really worked. We scooped up handfuls of oak leaves and stuffed them in, then sat back and watched. The little engine smoked, and the leaves were chewed up and spit out. Bob had scrounged some cigarette paper, and on an old stump we rolled cigarettes.

It was exciting and quite an adventure. Until one day, as we dashed through the woods, avoiding branches, we discovered that our factory was gone. Our parents had discovered our setup and made sure we no longer ground leaves for tobacco.

❧ ❧ ❧

The childhood games of exploring hills, trees, and spotting wild animals would come to an end, but the fascination with machines never did. It followed me my whole life, like a good friend. As I grew older, they became a part of me. As I neared my teenage years, I knew they would be woven in my life, a life I was eager to start.

Time for my motorcycle hill climb with Rueben Larson.

Almost before I knew it, I was in the eighth grade. I'd soon be done with school. Oh, how I looked forward to that time. Then it was there, the last day of school. Forever. I'd had eight great days of school, each of them the final day before summer vacation. But that last one was the best. Not only did I have the summer free, but there was no further schooling. I was ready for the world, I thought.

With school out, Mom took Allan and me to Roseau. By most standards, Roseau was not big, but it seemed so to me. It was a place teeming with crowds and buildings stacked high. It was daunting, because farm boys were scared of the city kids. We just knew they were tougher and better fighters than us. We just knew it would be hard to hold our own. Despite all that, it was thrilling to be there.

I was 14 and my life was about to change. I went to see Uncle Oscar Hetteen. Though not formally educated, he was extremely well-read and could talk about the stars, the moon, anything.

"Edgar, my boy," Oscar said, patting me on the shoulder. "Knute Grohn and I are starting a new business. A machine shop. We'll mostly be working with farmers."

He now looked me over.

"Edgar, how would you like to stay with me in town and help in the new business?"

I was speechless. What a dream! To work in a shop, with tools and metal and engines meant leaving my family and living in a city that still scared me, but I accepted with several fast nods. I got my mother's permission to live with Oscar, and before long, I was working.

I probably learned more in the first six months than I learned in all my years in school. Though I would later work on machinery, early on, I cleaned. I kept the wood stove filled, scrubbed and swept the floors. And eavesdropped. I'd lean on a big barrel, elbows on rusty metal. I listened, taking everything in. To me, that machine shop was the best place on earth.

Unfortunately, it was a seasonal business. Farmers paid their bills once a year, right after the harvest, and places that catered to them slowed with the snows. Ironic, considering my future. However, as a result, there wasn't much to clean.

This picture was taken in 1936 at the OK Welding Company, my first employer. From left: Knute Grohn, Manfred Holm, an Allis Chalmers Sales Manager, Wayne Kenworthy, myself, another man and Oscar Hetteen.

With nothing to do, I was laid off. My pay stopped coming, but still I kept going to the shop, day after day, just to be there. Finding something you love is so important. And by age 15, I had.

Six months passed, and I kept showing up at work for free. Business must have picked up, because Oscar and Knute decided to give me back pay and actually put me on salary at $20 a month. Of that, I gave Oscar $12 each month for room and board. Left to me was the biggest sum of money I'd ever seen.

Around this happy time, however, sadness touched my life. My mother and father separated (they never divorced), and Mom brought my younger brother, Allan, to Roseau, where we all rented a house. Mom found a job as a chamber maid at a hotel, earning 15 cents an hour. Times were tough and my mother, an uneducated farm girl, was happy to find anything. But because of her tremendous drive and determination, which I believe I inherited, she would work her way up to become a reporter at the Roseau newspaper. Much, much later, in the '60s, she became a billing clerk at Polaris Industries.

I worked with Oscar and Knute for five years. I grew much in that time; and I credit the OK Machine Company (O for Oscar and K for Knute) with not only teaching me but instilling my desire to build things and to improve upon existing machinery. They taught me about gas and electric welding, about machining and metal shaping. But perhaps the best schooling of all was listening to them deal with the public. People came in with problems, and Oscar and Knute came up with solutions. Sometimes it was a simple idea, and sometimes it was complex, but their ideas usually worked.

When someone came into the shop, I'd slip near and try to hear as much as possible. One day, as I was slinking off the job, Knute looked in my direction.

"Boy, we sure are blessed with floor weights in this place," he said to no one in particular, but loud enough for me to hear.

I wasn't sure what he meant. Confused, I looked around and didn't see anything that looked like a floor weight. It wasn't until years later, when I hired people of my own and watched them stand around, that I knew Knute was talking about me. Sometimes I learned slowly.

And sometimes, I wasn't too smart. One evening, when I was somewhat older and earning $100 a month, I stayed late to do a job for a farmer. It was a Saturday night, but it didn't matter what day it was. And it didn't matter what time. I loved it there.

The job involved a shaft and a turning lathe. As I went around the end of the lathe and reached up for the lever to change speed, my long shop coat got caught in the shaft. As quick as a shot, it wrapped me up and pinned my arms down. It lifted me off my feet. I was sure within seconds I'd start whipping around the shaft and either be killed or seriously injured.

Fortunately, the customer was still in the shop. I swallowed my pride and let out a high-pitched scream.

"Say! Could you help me!"

He moved quickly. He reached up to the lever that came out of the ceiling and put the machine in neutral. Slowly, he turned the machine and began to unwind me. I wasn't hurt, but my muscles were sore and my ego had taken a severe blow. Thank God somebody had been there. From that day forward, I was a lot more careful about exposed moving parts and wearing shop coats.

❦ ❦ ❦

Time passed. I turned 19. There's something about being a teenager that makes you think you know everything, even though you don't. It was the bullheadedness of youth that would send me packing from the OK Machine Company.

I'd welded a mailbox bracket for a local man, Elmer Evans, and charged him 35 cents. When I told Knute, he suggested it should have been 50 cents. That little exchange so upset me that I determined I had to leave. I walked across the alley to the Chevrolet garage, found the owner, Cap Nelson, and asked him for a job.

He looked me over and quickly made up his mind; he knew me well enough from my work at OK. If I would go to Dunwoody Institute in Minneapolis, he said, and take a course in body work, then I could be his body man. I agreed. I walked across the street and told Oscar and Knute that I was leaving.

I could have left under better circumstances, but they wished me well, and we would always be friends. They have since passed away, but without their guidance and teaching, I believe things would have turned out differently. I don't know if they realized what they were doing, but they prepared me well.

I loaded up my old car and drove down to Minneapolis. I enrolled at Dunwoody and took an advanced course called Reappearance Reconditioning of Automobiles. The course lasted four weeks, and I returned to Roseau, to the Chevrolet garage. I was to fix wrecks and rollovers, plus some fender benders now and then. But when World War II came, suddenly, it wasn't patriotic to fix the appearance of cars, not when there were cars needing mechanical work. So when the body work business died, Cap Nelson simply hired me as a mechanic.

In those days, the only way I earned my living was with my hands. I could overhaul a Chevy in one day – rings, bearings, pistons, valves, clean them up and do it fast. For all of that, my commission was six dollars and some cents. Later, we hired other young people, such as David Johnson, my brother-in-law, and Gordon Hetteen, my cousin. My job was to teach them how to do the things I did. At first that was fine, but I grew to feel it unfair. I wasn't paid to teach, I was paid to fix. My teaching time, in a sense, robbed me.

So I kept my eyes open for another job. When a chance arose at the county highway department, I jumped at it. I was put in charge of all maintenance for the county's fleet of bulldozers, road graders and other vehicles. The highway department was on the edge of Roseau, so there was little walk-in traffic. I could work in peace; no teaching.

As I stepped into the garage for the first time, my future as an entrepreneur may have been forged. Scattered on the floor were the guts of a grader. The transmission had blown and the case was cracked. The fellow I replaced hadn't put it back together, because the department was waiting for a new transmission.

Well, this was 1943. The war was ravaging Europe, and back home, it was nearly impossible to get engine parts, much less a transmission. I'd never laid eyes on one of those graders, but the county wanted it rebuilt. Though a daunting task, I went to work.

I managed to fix the crack, but then I said to myself, "Now that I have this heavy casting patched, how am I going to put all these gears and bearings, bolts and nuts together so they work and relate?" But in my head, I just knew. I'd known since I was a boy. I put them all into the transmission, all where I thought they should go, then hung it on the grader. I hopped in the driver's seat, started the big diesel engine and nervously shifted into gear. The thing moved. I drove it out the door, and I don't believe it ever broke down again.

It was that kind of experience that told me I could do more – that if I could assemble a sorry, torn-apart road grader, perhaps there was more in the world for me.

❦ ❦ ❦

It was 1944, and I watched my friends leave for the war. I wondered if I, too, would soon have to go, though with a wife and two small girls, Patty and Nancy, it was unlikely. In 1939, I'd married Ruby, David Johnson's sister. Sadly, she would die in the late 1960s. As the war continued, however, I worked at the county highway department and felt guilty about staying safe in Roseau.

One day, Cap Nelson, my former boss, sent one of his guys over. It was early morning, and the fellow meandered over to me, where I was working under some piece of machinery. He looked down, bent slightly at his knee and waited for me to look up.

"Hey, Edgar," he said. "If you come back and work for Cap, we might be able to keep you from going into the service." By working in a necessary business such as his, there was a chance I could avoid the draft.

"Tell Cap I'll think about it."

That afternoon, however, when I went home for lunch, perhaps in an act of defiance, I stopped by the draft board. I enlisted and was put on the next shipment out of Roseau. It was a terribly impulsive thing to do, but it was typical of me. My friends were going in and they were doing their part, and here I was staying home, by virtue only of the fact that I was married. I didn't think that fair. Besides, I never liked being told what to do; it made me want to do the opposite.

Shipment day arrived and I left Roseau – not to Europe, but to Idaho as part of the Navy. I adapted to Navy life fairly well, but I had other things on my mind. I was waiting for a package, a package from the United States Patent Office. Each day at boot camp, I anxiously checked my mail. While at the county highway department, I'd invented a hoist and winch for placing poles and moving just about anything. I thought it could be a great business – if, that is, I ever could get enough money to build them. Then one day, it came. I was probably the only sailor in boot camp who got a big envelope with a patent inside. I later learned a patent doesn't mean much, but just then I held it like a newborn babe. I was eager to get back to Roseau, and a few months later, I was discharged. The war had ended, and I never fought anybody.

I could have easily resumed my old life. I could have found work as a mechanic, and probably still be doing the same kind of work today. But I guess in a sense – I'm not sure how to define it – such a lifestyle was not sufficient for me. I'd quit milking cows because I'd felt there was more to life than tugging at udders. That was the first change in my life, to go to town and get away from the farm. So maybe, without knowing it, that was a philosophy I had – there had to be more to this business of living.

And yet, that attitude didn't make me any happier, didn't make me any better than the guy satisfied with his eight-to-five job. There was just something about me: I had to go into business for myself.

Chapter 3

<u>ON MY OWN</u>

They would build their first snowmobile in the mid-'50s, but when that happened, Edgar Hetteen and company already had been in business for 10 years. Ten years had gone by since he and his two partners – brother Allan Hetteen and brother-in-law David Johnson – began work on more machines and gadgets than can be counted or remembered. A decade had passed since Edgar bought a tiny building, and began the long march. Without those years of struggle, perhaps nothing would have happened. If you love snowmobiles, or admire perseverance, be thankful Hetteen managed to stay in business, and that he learned from his mistakes.

That I got started was a miracle. In the days after the war, times were tough in Roseau. Young fellows had little, if any, discretionary money. We treasured every penny.

I borrowed and I saved, and managed to scrape up enough to buy a welder and a drill press. They were the biggest buys in my life. I was almost 25 and knew why I'd been placed on earth. An entrepreneurial spirit was driving me. In the fall of 1944, I opened Hetteen Hoist and Derrick, named after my invention.

If you wanted to hire me, you either had to know where I was or be clairvoyant. I wasn't in the phone book, nor did I have a shop on Main Street. You had to go down to Hjalmer Sunsten's Pontiac Garage, and you had to wind your way around the cars and step over a couple mechanics. You'd work your way to a dark, little corner. I'd probably look up and then flip off the dark shield that covered my eyes from the welding flame. An inauspicious beginning, indeed.

The owner of the garage was my wife's uncle, and though I did a few jobs for him and worked with some customers, I spent most of my time on the electric winch and hoist.

The place was fine for a start, but I simply couldn't stay there. That little corner of the garage was too confining. Plus, I had to deal with the public wandering over and interrupting. To solve the problem, I moved to the Stordahl Truck Line Garage, which was off the main street and where the public didn't come in as often. I became the Stordahl mechanic and drove their trucks, but in exchange I had a place to work on the winch and hoist. As I worked, however, and started to think about other products I'd like to build, I knew I had to be completely on my own.

I needed money. I had a growing family to feed, and if I left Stordahl, where would the money come from? Starting a new business might very well starve us. But still, I had to.

I went to many of the farmers I'd done work for at the OK Machine Company. "I'm going to start a business of my own," I told them. "Could you give me payment on account for this company? I'll work it off as I get things going."

I had the audacity to ask them to pay for work not yet done. But those farmers, God bless them, trusted me. Maybe it was only $25 per farmer, but it was enough to feed my family and get the business started.

I searched for a place, and found what I wanted, a 30' by 60' building on the edge of town. It was incredibly small, and a little rickety, but I thought it was perfect. It could house me and several employees. And yet, how do you buy a building when you hardly have any money? I was naïve enough not to know I shouldn't be able to do it.

George Bang owned the building. As a Coca-Cola distributor in Crookston, Minnesota, he'd been subleasing the building to the REA, though he really hoped to use it as a warehouse. However his plans, I learned, weren't working out, and I thought I could make use of this

***Hetteen Hoist and Derrick in the 1940s. The sign would change
to Polaris Industries in the 1950s.***

knowledge. So at age 24, I hopped in my truck and drove the hour to Crookston. I had no money and no plan. Just a lot of gumption. Before long, I found Mr. Bang.

"I understand you own that building," I said.

"That's right, young man," he said.

"Well, I'd sure like to buy it," I said. "Maybe we can help each other out."

The rest of the conversation has long since vanished from memory, but when I left, I had bought the building. Somehow George Bang and I came to an agreement in which I would make payments to him. It was the only way. The banks wouldn't have touched me with a 10-foot pole.

At the beginning of 1945, I moved into my own building. It wasn't a beautiful structure, but in my eyes, it was the Taj Mahal. Years earlier, it had served as a dance hall out in the country. In its wild and crazy days, in the '30s, a man had been shot and killed there. Not long after, perhaps because of that, the dance hall failed. It was moved into town and stood there until I found it.

Inspecting my building for the first time, I discovered, still up on the back wall in huge letters, the dance hall's former name: Pine Needle Inn. I left the sign up and, for years, got letters addressed to the Pine Needle Inn. Perhaps, just perhaps, I should have called my new company Pine Needle Manufacturing.

I partitioned off a little office and went to work. I didn't quite know where to start; but fortunately, I had a lot of help.

❦ ❦ ❦

I needed steel, and to get it I had to go south to the Twin Cities. I walked over to Stordahl Truck Lines, found my old boss, and said, "Hey, I'd like a ride to Minneapolis." Anything to save money. The answer was yes, as it always was, and I hopped on the seat next to the driver. I ate lunch from a paper bag and was on my way. Yes, I had very humble beginnings.

I was dropped off in Minneapolis at a steel company I knew from my days at the OK Machine Company. I walked into their office, and a receptionist greeted me.

"I would like some steel," I said simply.

"You'll have to go to the city desk," she said.

I furrowed my brow. That was odd, I thought. After all, I was from the country and here I had to go to the city desk? I didn't know that was where they took orders. But soon enough, I met a man there. We discussed my situation and put together a small order of steel, priced at $40.

"Now we have to go to the credit manager," he said.

Uh-oh. It would be a shaky deal as it was, but now I had to go to the credit department? How the heck were they going to approve me? I didn't have $40. All the same, the man and I walked up a flight of stairs and found a messy office in which a hefty fellow was eating a sandwich.

The guy looked me up and down, in a way that suggested he knew I had no money. Perhaps my dirty parka and black boots gave me away, or perhaps it was my tousled hair and five-o'clock shadow.

"Just what are you going to use this steel for?" the credit man asked.

"I've begun a business and I needed a start-up supply."

"How will you pay for it?" he wondered.

"Well, you could just ship it to me COD," I said.

"No, I won't send you anything."

I didn't get any steel, and it sure looked as if this kid from Roseau was in trouble. Who would give me steel? Someone back home might have helped, but in Minneapolis? In St. Paul? After scanning the phonebook, I found another place, a company called Paper, Calmenson on East Seventh Street in St. Paul.

This time, I went straight to the credit department and found Cy Brennan. I didn't know it then, but he was to play an important role in my life.

"I'm Edgar Hetteen," I said, as if it mattered. I wasn't anybody in Roseau, much less St. Paul.

"How much steel do you want?" Cy asked. He'd been joined by a fellow from the city desk. That guy bobbed his head up and down while he looked me over. I don't think he liked what he saw.

"How about $400 worth?" I said. As long as I'd been rejected for $40 earlier that day, why not shoot for the moon?

Cy said only four words to the other man, but they were four wonderful words.

"Ship it to him!" he ordered.

It was the start of an association that lasted a long time, through the early days and both snowmobile companies. Cy became so instrumental that, when he retired, Polaris and Arctic got together and set up an extravaganza in Thief River Falls. Arctic sent their airplane for Cy, and when he landed, we took him by limo to a tremendous party. What an oddity it was for two competing companies to honor one man. Songs were sung and poems were read – all in honor of Cy. We did it because, more than any individual, he was responsible for those two companies. He was with us through the good times as well as the bad; his loyalty never wavered. He gave us credit when nobody else would even touch us.

Why did he do it? For some reason, he took a liking to me, and then later to David Johnson and Allan Hetteen, who would run Polaris after I left. We never said we were going to Paper, Calmenson, but to Cy Brennan.

I'll never know why Cy risked his job to help us, but once he told me it was a struggle. "Edgar, I hope my bosses never discover our arrangement," he said, chuckling. "I hide the books when they come around, because I don't want them to see how much you owe me."

He took up our cause. Cy and I were at a hockey game once in St. Paul, watching the Roseau team play. Sitting directly behind us was my banker. It made me nervous, because I was never good around bankers.

I didn't like them, and they didn't like me. Cy was what he always was; a man apart. We watched the game, and Cy threw back a few beers. He kept getting louder and louder, and I began to cringe.

"Quiet, Cy, it's my banker," I said in a loud whisper.

"Eh! that's your banker," Cy yelled. He turned around to stare at the money man.

"What are you doing for my friend? I'll bet I give him more credit than you do!"

The banker looked back coldly, and I had to laugh. Cy was a special man.

❧ ❧ ❧

Fortunately, we attracted those who believed in us, trusted us and helped us. I needed them badly and was thankful for anyone who'd give me a break.

Whenever I needed special materials, even at night, I went to Norman Flagstad's Coast to Coast hardware store. Quite often, the store was locked. When that happened, I'd stroll over to Norman's home. I would ask him to open the store, and he always did. But one night as he stood in his doorway, seemingly tired, he handed me the keys.

"Go help yourself," he said.

I did, but kept track of what I took and left the bill on the counter. A few weeks later, I was at his store again.

"How's life, Edgar?" he asked.

"Fine," I said. "But to get my business really going, I need more equipment. There is just so little I can do right now."

"How much would that cost?" Norman asked, leaning back on the counter.

"About a thousand," I said.

I still have trouble believing it, but before I left the store that day, I had a check for one thousand dollars. There was no talk of how I would pay it back, or what the schedule would be; no papers to sign, nothing.

I kept after him for a long time to get something in writing. "Norm, we have to have a promissory note." "Norm, what if I fall out of a tree and get killed?" A lot of time went by and a lot of haranguing on my part, and finally he wrote out a promissory note and I signed it. He was paid back, but I was an extremely risky investment for him.

I don't know why Norman Flagstad did what he did, same as I don't know why Cy Brennan did what he did. Norman was another of our unsung heroes. His thousand dollars bought a lot of equipment, and I soon had the foundations of a business.

For the first few months, I was my only employee. I fixed whatever was brought in, whether it was a toaster or a farm implement. I was learning, too. Running my own business meant a lot more than welding and tinkering. It meant that no matter what, I had to be there. If it needed to get done, it was my responsibility. It didn't matter if there was a hockey game I wanted to go to, or whether I just wanted to relax. No, when you have your own business, you put in the hours, or it fails.

Through 1945, I continued to do repair work and continued to build my hoist. Then, as I hired a few employees, we started to make other machines and, wow, what a feeling! That year we built and sold fertilizer spreaders, and because of a grasshopper infestation we made poison spreaders. It was a good feeling, and it made me want to design more and more products.

My first employees made that possible. One was Orlen Johnson, who was only 15 or 16 at the time. He stayed with me a very long time. He had no formal training, but he was a brilliant young man, who could and would do anything. If you said, "Climb a greased pole," he'd figure out a way. I loved surrounding myself with those kinds of people, because if I couldn't do something, they probably could.

Another employee was my cousin, Ruth, and she worked in the office. When we finished a project, we always painted it red. The paint went everywhere. When Ruth arrived in the morning, she was a blonde, and when she went home, she was a redhead.

Another was Leelan Brandt, who worked for me only a short time. He was probably too young to legally work, but he was likable and I knew the rest of his family; my country school was named after them. Leelan would become successful in his own right, and now owns a couple of hotels and a restaurant in Roseau.

Yes, my first employees were good, but they were only the start. I had bigger plans. They included David Johnson, whom I'd known since childhood. He soon would be coming back from his duty in the Navy. I looked forward to this, because David was sharp. I wanted him as a partner, and I wasn't about to take no for an answer.

In China, David was making $21 a month training the Chinese to use U.S. vessels through our lend-lease policy. I wrote to David and told him he was now a partner in Hetteen Hoist and Derrick. He must have liked the arrangement, because he sent me $10 a month for the business. David may not have been recognized as a partner by the public, but he was in my mind. Moreover, I needed his money. Desperately.

I also needed him. I knew if I got David, things would run much smoother. Not only would he take part of the load off my shoulders, he'd do some things better than I. My prayers were answered when, a few months later, he was discharged, and he became an active partner.

Everyone loved David and would go to almost any length to please him. If someone had a problem, they simply had to find David, and he'd know what to do. Aside from a few months at the Chevrolet garage, Hetteen Hoist and Derrick (later Polaris) was his only employer. He meant much to our early efforts, and in the future he would mean much to the snowmobile. Albeit slowly, the company was coming together. And soon, we would find the final piece of the puzzle, my brother.

Allan was nine years younger than I and still in high school. He wasn't an official employee and wasn't paid, but just about every afternoon, he'd be in the shop. I knew he would fit in, and when he finished school, he became a partner in our little operation. He did a lot of shop work and as he grew older, he took on more and more responsibility.

There was much to do, so many hours and so little sleep, but it was a fun place to work. It really was. Allan, David and I were business partners, but also friends. I saw how well we worked together, how we'd develop a product and make it better and better. I saw our roles forming.

David, I determined, would be the operations manager and run manufacturing. Allan would take over the business end, for which he had a real knack. He was young, but wise in the ways of cash flow and keeping things running. I, meanwhile, would drum up business. We were in Roseau, so we had to go out and make things happen; couldn't wait for the world to come to us. They were happy for me to freelance, whether it was designing new products, or zipping around the country to make ourselves grow.

In David and Allan, I saw great things. They, as much as I, were responsible for any success the company would experience. They had honesty, integrity and sincerity. They were dependable and trustworthy. Their character and talent would take us through many hard times; and would serve them well when they took over Polaris in 1960.

Also with us in the small factory was my dad, who'd been farming most of his life. He was approaching 60 and there wasn't much employment for people his age, so I asked him to come on board. He did a lot of our shop work, and spent several years with us, before passing away. Much later, after I left the company, my mother worked for the firm as a bookkeeper.

It was very much a family business. Uncle Oscar, who'd loaned me money to start it, became a part-time employee. I don't remember if he was looking for work, but I conned him into helping me. He and Knute Grohn had peacefully separated when their business fell victim to progress.

It was strange to have authority over my father and even more unsettling with Oscar. I'd gone full circle with him. And yet, nobody told Oscar how to do something. I said what needed to be done and watched him do it. He was an absolute genius.

In our group, we also had a fellow moonlighting as an undertaker. We had a highway patrolman, and we had a minister. We used to say, "We can arrest you, we can marry you, we can bury you."

Allan, left, and David, right, and I stop for a moment in our tiny plant in Roseau.

❧ ❧ ❧

We truly were a family. Working in such close quarters and striving every day together made us close. So it was very hard when I couldn't afford to pay them. Understand, as much fun as we had, times were tough. When the end of the week rolled around, too often there wasn't enough money. I'd stare at what we had and sigh heavily, knowing what was to come. We would gather around the till, a little box. The money would be taken out and placed on a table. I'd scoop it up and pass it around, dividing it evenly among the group. David, Allan and I got the same as everyone else. Sometimes it hardly fed the family.

Had it not been for our wonderful employees, we would not have survived. Their hardships must have been great, especially for their wives and children, but they stuck with us. So for them, for us, we did anything to earn a buck.

When it was time for the new cars to come out, I would go to the dealerships. I'd find the owner and say, "I'll build some hitches for those new cars. Would you buy some?" When they agreed, it maybe would amount to $1.50 a hitch. Not much, really, but it was money for the till.

At Christmas, when there was little cash flow, a friend of mine, who grew trees, and I would load up my truck and haul them to the Twin Cities. The truck had a poor heater, and it was cold on that long trip, but I got cash.

Or maybe a farmer would need his harvest taken to market. We would do it. We did things we never would have otherwise. The public looked at us and said, "What business are you guys in? Trucking? Car parts? Or is it really manufacturing?" Nobody understood that we had to do those other things, just to stay afloat.

❧ ❧ ❧

Our first major task was to sell my hoist. It was big, heavy and crude by today's standards, but it worked. Unfortunately, the public did not rush out to buy it. I quickly became discouraged. The world didn't beat a path to my door, and I threw in the towel, though I shouldn't have. If we'd known a little more about promotion and pushing a product, we might still be building hoists today.

*Part of the early crew at Hetteen Hoist and Derrick. From left:
Olger Foss, Erhard Lisell, Allan Hetteen, Roben Johnson,
Wayne Gabriel, David Johnson, Albin Larson and Edner Lisell,
our office man.*

We did however, try other things. I was never scared to do something new, because I'd had such a good education with Oscar and Knute. They'd left me with a feeling that there is always a better way, and you'll find it if you look. We built pulpwood loading equipment, grain boxes, boats, trailers, cultivator hitches and fertilizer spreaders. Later came a straw cutting attachment for combines and other farm implements.

*I made a few of these tillers. They worked well,
but there were too many other products to finance.*

The main difficulty was that we were too ambitious. We designed things faster than we could possibly put them on the market.

We built a four-wheel-drive ATV, which we hoped not only would go on land, but also float. We'd spent a few months on it, and it was time to see if it actually worked. I have a certain reluctance for testing before an audience, so I waited until late one night, then along with employee Albin Erickson drove it down to the river's swimming hole.

Albin scampered onto the beach. He watched as I rumbled toward the water. We didn't know what would happen, but if the machine floated, we thought the spinning wheels would act as a propeller and send me safely back to shore.

I entered the river and waited nervously as the water rose around the wheels. It bobbed, and then floated, quite well in fact. I had not, however, reckoned with the current, which soon pushed me away from the beach. Spinning my wheels proved no good.

"Follow me," I shouted to Albin as I began drifting down river.

The shoreline changed and the banks grew steep. Even if I could reach land, which against the current was proving difficult, there was little chance the machine would climb out. It also was growing dark, and I had no lights.

Spinning those great big wheels, which had cleats and lugs, I moved a little. I managed to get near land, but the tires just wouldn't take hold and pull me out. I kept trying, and I kept floating downstream.

Albin, who'd been running in and around trees and through mucky ground, yelled encouragement.

"Keep trying, Edgar, we'll get you out of there!"

I grew concerned, because if I kept floating, I would plunge over a small dam in Roseau. I knew very well that going over the dam would ruin my night. So I kept trying, desperately spinning my wheels against the shore, but the current kept pushing me closer and closer to the dam. I sailed into the city, and houses drifted by.

"Edgar! I think there's a place up ahead," Albin yelled. His pants were muddy from where he'd fallen. After several hundred yards, he was panting.

Lo and behold, I came to a spot where the bank was a little more gentle, and by nudging the machine up against it, the wheels found firm ground. I began to climb out.

It was pitch black now, and I crawled into a man's yard with my rolling, wet monster. To my dismay, the yard was fenced in and the gate was locked. There was no way out. I went up to his door and knocked. It took him several minutes to peek his head out. He'd been sleeping.

"Uh, I'm stuck in your yard with my swamp machine," I stammered. "Could you open the gate and let me out?"

He looked beyond me and saw the dark mass of my monster. He took a dim view of the whole operation. I'm sure he thought I was hurting his yard, perhaps tearing it up, but I wasn't. Finally with a sigh, he opened the gate. I picked up Albin, and we drove back to the plant, shaking our heads and laughing.

Suffice it to say, we didn't do much with amphibious ATVs. That night in the river, I'd come to the conclusion that other machines held more promise.

❧ ❧ ❧

Every day was something new. At times, it seemed we were the crossroads for every guy with a problem, for every guy with an idea. Anyone could just wander in, and often did.

"I've designed an elevator for moving grain into bins," said this fellow who'd found us. "Would you be interested in building them?"

He had a sheaf of papers, and he thrust them at me. I looked at what he'd drawn – a device made of wood and old Model T wheels, stuff you might scrounge from a junkyard. And yet, we were eager to have any kind of business, so I agreed to build some.

When our little partnership came to an end, we decided to go into the elevator business ourselves. We redesigned his device and made it out of metal. We turned it into something professional.

I'd grown up in an area dominated by the Farm Labor political party, so I knew farmers got products from their locally owned co-op. The co-op, in turn, bought from a place called the Farmer's Union Central Exchange on South Concord in St. Paul. If we could get our elevator accepted by the Central Exchange, we'd have gone a long way into cornering the farm market, at least in Minnesota.

I drove to St. Paul and met with the Exchange people. They accepted me and were impressed with our elevator. So much so, that they agreed to sell it to their local co-ops. If, that is, the price was much lower. With such an opportunity, I returned home and designed a scaled-down model that was just as good as the other. We dubbed it the One Man Marvel. Satisfied, the Central Exchange people began selling our product in their four-state area.

We shipped them carloads of elevators that year, but I had stars in my eyes: I wanted to sell nationally. I called up the Central Exchange manager of the Farm Implement Division, Verne Robinson.

"I understand you people belong to a national association of co-ops," I said.

"Yup," he said.

"I'd like to sell these elevators around the country."

"Hmmm, it's possible. Edgar, we have our national association meeting in Chicago next week. You're welcome to come along. You'd be able to talk to directors from nearly every state."

The economy model of the grain elevator built at Hetteen Hoist and Derrick.

I went with a simple plan. I hoped to establish contacts, so important in business. I had visions of catching some poor guy in the hallway and selling him an elevator. I didn't expect much more than that.

The meeting was in a large convention room. Curious, I walked in and sat near the back. It was a formal session of their association and was chock-full of gray-haired, distinguished looking people. I tried to blend into the woodwork.

Throughout the rather tedious meeting, I daydreamed. Then, suddenly, from the podium came the announcement that a special visitor, Edgar Hetteen from Roseau, Minnesota, would give a presentation.

What?!

What had the man said? Unsure, I sat firm. A few men already were looking my way. Ten long seconds passed. The man repeated the announcement.

Finally, with more folks staring, I rose and walked what seemed a hundred miles to the front. I will never know just what I said. It was a terrifying ordeal and taught me plenty. Thereafter, I decided to never, ever be caught unprepared again.

However, because of my speech – whatever I said – we got orders from California, Kansas and a few other states. I don't know why, but we did.

We had a fair amount of success with the elevator, but it eventually died out. It used a couple of chains to convey hay bales, corn and grain, and did it well, but that world had changed. The auger conveyer, which sent grain through a tube, was more efficient, and our sales dropped dramatically. I briefly explored following the trend of auger elevators, but we simply didn't have the equipment or the manpower to keep up, though we certainly had the knowledge and enough forewarning of what the trend would be.

I did attempt to beat the curve by building a few pneumatic grain conveyers, where grain was picked up by air rushing through a tube, and conveyed to wherever it was needed. We had the talent to make the project a success, but once again, we didn't have the time. Too many ideas and too many machines were already on the shop floor, and had priority.

Again, we had so much going on in that little 30' by 60' building. It was jammed with people and hardware, and a day wouldn't go by when you didn't trip over someone. So many products, so little time. We had ATVs, we had farm implements, including a combine attachment that chopped up straw. We had corn cribs, trailers and the beginnings of a snow machine. We were too doggone ambitious and probably too good at knowing what the market wanted and having the talent to fill those needs. We probably should not have built so many machines, but we couldn't stop; the ideas flowed like water and we were compelled to build. Unfortunately, our ideas and know-how did not match our financial structure, nor the room we had. We simply could not bring many of them to market, no matter how good they were.

Why did we have so many ideas? Easy. We listened to the public and became intimately involved with their problems. We'd see what they were doing; and then say, "Hey, there is a better way to do that." Finding a better way was always my challenge, and that's why we had so many products.

The biggest problem I have had, all my life, is that I was ahead of the times. It's very difficult to introduce new products. It's much easier to come along, say "Me, too," and build an existing product. The public then knows what your gadget is, and they'll accept it. But to be ahead of your time, as just about every one of our products was, is hard. You have to convince the public that the new device not only works but can improve their lives. We would do that with the snowmobile, but most of those other things never made it for us – though today, all of our ideas are manufactured by someone somewhere, and they're succeeding. If we'd only known about marketing and had some money, we'd have been a conglomerate you couldn't believe.

We were an example of what the world so desperately needs. More than ever, our world must have entrepreneurs. We should help them be successful. We should invest in them. Only the entrepreneurs of this world will make up the payroll of all the companies downsizing.

Many people did help us and had faith in us, but for a time, it didn't seem like anything great would happen. We struggled day after day, occasionally battling those who did not believe. All the while, we hoped at least one of our products would break through. Then finally, came the straw chopper.

Here it is - the little 30'x60' shop where I began business in Roseau. If you look closely, you can see the sign on the back wall: Pine Needle Inn. It was so cramped. Bumping into people was commonplace.

Chapter 4

CHOPPING THE STRAW

A burgeoning Roseau business with a promising new product should have been greeted with open arms at the local bank. Not only would the bank likely get its money back, but it would mean more and more people employed, would mean the growth of Roseau, would mean higher revenues for the bank. You would have thought all of that as Edgar Hetteen geared up to push his straw chopper, a machine that bolted onto combines and pulverized straw. But the hoops Hetteen says he was forced to jump through to gain assistance from the bank, and then from his own customers, are nothing short of amazing.

✤ ✤ ✤

It took all the courage I had to open that bank door. I paused and composed myself. I breathed deeply, knowing that if they said no, it could mean the end of our business, the end of my livelihood. But they just couldn't say no. The local bank could not do that to a farm kid who had just nailed down a $100,000 purchase order from International Harvester, the sale of his life.

Inside, I was greeted with that bank smell, the one of power, where they hold your life in their hands. Wanting to get back to our small company as soon as possible, I stepped up to a secretary and asked to see the loan officer. Smiling faintly, she said it would be a few minutes. I sat in a chair and waited.

I thought back to what had brought me here, to this point in my entrepreneurial career. My mind drifted, back to a few days earlier, when I made the deal with International Harvester, and further back, to the ideas that led me to International.

❧ ❧ ❧

Several months earlier, in the late '40s, we decided our straw choppers worked so well that we should sell them to International Harvester. It was ambitious, but Minneapolis Moline, a combine manufacturer in Hopkins, Minnesota, was recommending us to their dealers. We had distributors selling the chopper nationwide. Local farmers were buying, too.

We hoped International would take us a step farther, really make Hetteen Hoist and Derrick grow. We wanted International to buy the choppers, then sell them as their own, in that trademark red. It certainly would solve a lot of problems.

Our first step would be to get approval from International's engineering department. From there, we would have to convince the sales department and then move to marketing. All of them had to say yes before we even got to purchasing, which would make the final decision on whether to buy. That made four hurdles, none of them small.

We were confident in our product. For years, farmers had put chemical fertilizers into the soil but had trouble putting in organic matter, such as straw from the harvest. That was better for the ground, so they'd try to plow or disc it in, but that didn't always work. They often were forced to rake it or burn it, all of which was a difficult process. The chopper, a combine attachment, cut and spread straw onto the ground. It then could easily be returned to the soil.

Unfortunately, few saw us as the solution. Farmers needed our device, but didn't know it. There was no market. It was a theme throughout my career. Whoever said, "Build a better mousetrap and the world will beat a path to your door" was dead wrong as far as I'm concerned.

However, getting International Harvester would go a long, long way to establishing a market. So on a hot summer day in the late '40s, I left Roseau and set out for East Moline, Illinois, headquarters of mighty In-

The straw chopper. Here it is attached to a combine by Gleaner Works of Independence, Missouri.

ternational Harvester. I drove through Thief River Falls, which one day would become my home, down through the Twin Cities of Minneapolis-St. Paul, then south to the quad cities of Rock Island, East Moline, Davenport and Bettendorf on the border of Iowa and Illinois. I drove it straight through, 16 hours in all, and thought about the tactics I would use.

I checked in at the Le Claire Hotel, and began planning how to tackle International's chief engineer. His name was Harold Sieger, and I was in awe of him; I figured he must sit on the right hand of God. I started studying him like I never studied in that one-room school house. Some of the vendors who supplied us with materials also supplied International Harvester. From those men, I found out all I could about Mr. Sieger. I scribbled down notes, and before falling to sleep each night, I memorized them. I would be prepared. There would be no repeat of the farmer's meeting in Chicago.

By the time I went to see Harold Sieger, I knew how many children he had. I knew whether I should rush in and talk business, or if I should talk family. Or if he liked politics, maybe religion. I had done my homework.

Finally, it was time. I pulled into a huge parking lot littered with cars. I walked across the warm blacktop to the huge factory that rose before me. Unlike our plant in Roseau, where my office, the factory and the warehouse were all contained in one tiny building, International Harvester was massive. I walked in and a receptionist greeted me.

"I would like an appointment to see the chief engineer," I said.

"I'll check his schedule, sir. He's pretty busy."

Before long, however, she said I could see Harold Sieger. A few minutes later, he strode up and shook my hand. He was a short, muscular man, and he asked me to follow him to his office. It was clean, with family photos on the desk, and on the walls were detailed sketches of what must have been prototype combines.

"Please, sit down, Mr. Hetteen," he said, motioning me to the chair in front of his desk.

It is my tendency to get business over with. Get in, get out. Normally, busy people like that. But I'd learned that Mr. Sieger liked to chat a little. I told him about myself, about my family, my business, my hometown. He did the same. We talked about the local economy, and what we thought of the combine industry. He seemed a nice man, and I felt good about my chances.

In my initial pitch, I wanted to attack his possible objections, to dull their impact. If I could overcome his arguments before he knew them himself, I would be closer to getting the deal. It was a tactic that usually worked for me.

"Conditions are changing, Mr. Sieger," I said. "Combines, of course, are very popular. But there is a common problem with them. After a field is harvested, it is sometimes difficult to till the straw into the soil and to add the organic matter into the land."

He said nothing, so I continued my explanation.

"As it is now, if a farmer wants to get straw into the soil, he has to disc it in, which is a slower, more tedious process. And even then, it doesn't always work. Of course, we always can chemically fertilize our fields, but it is not nature's way. With only chemicals, the ground grows hard and isn't as productive.

"If he doesn't disc, the farmer can only do a few things with the straw. He can burn it. He can rake it, or he can turn it into bales. But I don't want him to burn it, and I don't want him to rake it. If we can cut the straw and till it in during the harvest, we will mellow the soil and make tillage easier as the years go by."

Mr. Sieger continued to nod.

"When we take a soil sample, we can tell what the soil needs. We usually see there is a tremendous need to put organic matter back into the ground. With our product, we can do just that."

It was the biggest presentation of my life, and my heart thumped crazily. I'm not sure what I looked like on the outside, but I was nervous on the inside.

"Mr. Sieger," I said, finally, "I want International Harvester to approve our straw chopper attachments. Eventually, I'd like your company to buy them."

Judging by his response, I'd convinced him. Being prepared had won the day.

"We can start the ball rolling, but you should know, it's a long process," he said. "We'll have to set up a test, which will take the entire harvesting season. We'll run your choppers on our test combines as they follow the harvest, beginning in the south."

Nodding, I asked only one thing: Could I be at the test when the straw chopper was attached to their combine? I wanted to make sure it was working, so some little thing didn't go wrong. Mr. Sieger nodded, and said it would be fine.

The meeting finished, and I returned to Roseau. A few weeks later, Mr. Sieger called. The tests would begin in the South. It was an unbelievable high, and I set to work. I contacted the engineer who would be supervising the tests and learned a little more. In a week, he said, I had to be in Rolling Fork, Mississippi.

"But Mr. Hetteen, may I ask how you're getting there?" he asked.

"Flying."

The engineer wasn't looking forward to his long drive south. Few cars had the luxury of air conditioning.

"Would you be able to stop in East Moline and pick me up?"

"Sure, be happy to," I said.

What good luck! I could make friends with the fellow testing my chopper. So a few days later, I dropped down out of the sky and landed at the East Moline Airport. Whenever I had the chance to fly, I took it. I loved being in the air, away from all the troubles of the ground.

The engineer, a portly fellow, met me on the runway, and we shook hands firmly. I refueled and he loaded his equipment into the plane. All seemed fine, but the combined weight of his equipment and his large body would prove almost too much for my little Luscombe.

My plane seated two people, side-by-side, with a small baggage compartment behind. It had no electrical starter and no radio. With its 65 horsepower, it had to go far down the runway to get off the ground, especially on a hot, humid fall day like we had. The engine struggled to pull us and seemed to grunt as it finally achieved enough air speed to lift off.

I've kept that small story secret for many years, because it was a violation of International Harvester rules for their people to ride in small aircraft. They didn't think it safe. Telling what happened now, however, probably won't hurt anybody.

As we flew, we chatted. I learned more and more about the testing process, and several hours later we landed in Rolling Fork, the small town where International Harvester had shipped my chopper. Though it was 8 a.m., the temperatures had already risen to 85 degrees. The test began in a field of wheat, which serenely wafted back and forth.

The chopper performed as it should have, ripping up the straw and leaving it nicely on the soil. When the day was over, my shirt held huge pools of sweat. We soon found a nearby watering hole, ordered a couple of cold beers, and relaxed. At our table, the engineer downed his beverage and bent over a sheet of paper. It was his report on the straw chopper, the crucial report that would decide my fate. My head flushed – like watching a teacher fill out your report card. I glanced at it but couldn't tell what he was writing.

Every night, we wound up at the same watering hole. And every night, he mulled over his report.

"Edgar," he said one night, "what should I put in this report?"

"Well, it worked pretty good, didn't it?" I said.

"Yeah, it did," he agreed.

"Why don't you just put in your report that it worked good?" I said.

"I think I will," he said with a smile.

But a few days later, he grew tired of doing even that. He wasn't fond of paperwork, and I couldn't blame him.

"Edgar, you're telling me what to put in the report anyway, why don't you just write it?" he asked.

"I can't write it, it has to come from you," I said, laughing, though it was a tempting offer.

He did write it, and kept on writing them for a week or so. Then, as the combines moved their way north, it was time for me to leave. I had a little company in Roseau that needed revenue, and I had better things to do than follow the harvest.

Several weeks later, Harold Sieger phoned.

"Mr. Hetteen, your straw chopper has impressed my engineer in the fields. I've checked over his reports and have decided to approve your straw chopper as an attachment."

It was as simple as that.

"Now, that only means we in engineering have approved it," he added.

"I still have to win over marketing, sales and purchasing."

"Yup. You better get yourself back to East Moline. You have some people to meet."

The straw chopper had done its job; now it was my turn.

I returned to East Moline. I met first with marketing and sales. I told them how the straw chopper worked, and why farmers would buy them; it was essentially the same pitch I'd given Harold Sieger. They liked the idea, and said all I needed to close the deal was to convince the purchasing department.

It would be my biggest presentation yet. Though I'd cleared three big hurdles and was well on my way to the prize, the purchasing department didn't part with thousands of dollars without being darned sure. They needed to believe the straw chopper would earn money. With this in mind, I returned to my hotel. I stayed up half the night going over my presentation. What would I say? How would I act? How long should I talk?

I woke early the next morning, nervous and excited, and drove to International Harvester. I waited about 15 minutes and was escorted into a room where four men sat around a big table. After the initial greetings, I stood and began my presentation.

I told of our 15 hard-working, clever employees. I told of the beginnings of the straw chopper, and why it was the answer to the long-time problem of returning straw to the soil. I told of our distributors. I told of Minneapolis-Moline, and how well the straw chopper was selling for them.

When I finished, I said thank you. We shook hands, they politely said they would get back to me, and I returned to the motel. I waited, and waited, and waited. I sat on the bed and watched the phone. Suddenly, it rang twice, and my heart leaped. I breathed deeply, closed my eyes and lifted the receiver.

"Could you come back over here in about an hour?"

What a question. I was back in a shot, and they got straight to the point.

"Mr. Hetteen, we'll order about $100,000 worth, paid on delivery," one of them said.

My eyes wanted to bug, and I had to keep my mouth from turning into a gaping smile.

They handed me the purchase order. Never had I seen so many zeroes, and as I left, my heart seemed to lift me off the ground. Talk about a salesman's high. I zipped back to the hotel and then drove from East Moline to Roseau in one stretch. I don't remember ever touching the road. The elation of conquering International Harvester was incredible.

It was with that high that I went to the banker, confident I would get the money needed to fill the order. Without cash, we couldn't do the job. We needed new machinery, more men, perhaps even additional factory and warehouse space.

❧ ❧ ❧

So, a few days later, I sat in the local bank, the purchase order clenched in my hand, and waited for the loan officer. Had there been any choice, I would not have picked that particular banker. Several years earlier, our relationship had been formed when he and one of the bank's board members showed up at my struggling business. This was before David and Allan joined, when the business was touch and go, when I desperately needed money.

The two men in suits strolled into the shop. Could I spare a few minutes? they wondered.

"Sure," I said, "sit down." You should always be friendly to the people who loan money.

"Your bank statement shows your net worth at $3,000," the loan officer said. "That's not much, Edgar."

I smiled inside, because little did he know that I had done everything in my power to make it that high. I was probably worth far less.

He paused and got to the reason he was there.

"We like your little company and have a proposition. Think about this, Edgar. We both will put $3,000 into your firm, and you will have $6,000 cash to work with," he said. "Frankly, you need the money."

I nodded but said nothing.

"Then we will have a three-way partnership," he finished.

For me, $6,000 was a lot. I did need the money, but I wasn't willing to sell my soul. The reason I'd struggled alone was because I wanted my own business. And if I did have partners, I wanted to pick them based on their ability to contribute work, energy and know-how, such qualities as David and Allan possessed. It didn't take me more than three or four seconds to respond.

"No," I said. "I don't want to do that. I'll get the money a different way."

In a small town like Roseau, this was not the good, political answer. But then, I've never been known as a good politician and never felt the need to sugar-coat my feelings. Some people haven't liked this quality, but oddly, the people who criticize me and my independence the most are those who have become extremely wealthy on my endeavors – the same endeavors that would not have come to pass without that independence, stubbornness and tenacity.

Since our first meeting, that loan officer had turned me down regularly. But despite our poor history, I was sure a $100,000 purchase order from International Harvester would be more than enough to secure a loan. The bank couldn't turn down such business; it would be foolhardy.

The man arrived, shook my hand, and I followed him to his office. It was a good feeling; the years of hard work had been worth it. I was on a high, a high a salesman gets when he has closed a deal and has the payoff in his hands.

He took a seat behind his desk and I spoke quickly.

"International Harvester has given us an order for approximately $100,000. To build their choppers, we're going to need a loan of $10,000."

I gave him my treasured piece of paper. He looked at it, twisted it back and forth, and squinted. He looked up at me.

"Edgar, this is only a purchase order," he said.

"It's from International Harvester," I said, growing angry at his attitude toward my wonderful purchase order.

"I can't do anything about this."

"International Harvester is good for it," I argued.

"I'm sorry, Edgar. You're going to have to go back and ask them for a 25 percent deposit with their order. That's the only way I can help you."

Perhaps by turning down the loan officer those years earlier, I'd ruined my chance with the bank. As I faced the man who just torpedoed me, my heart sank. I stood and abruptly left. In a daze, I wandered back to the truck. My world had come to another end, as it so often did walking through a bank door. What would we do? What would I tell everyone at work, those who were so excited at our big order? The banker was wrong: Asking International Harvester for a deposit was out of the question. They were big and strong, and Hetteen Hoist and Derrick, not yet even Polaris, was small and shaky.

Things were serious. If we botched this, if we dropped the ball on International Harvester, word would get out that we weren't able to follow through on big orders. We'd be finished. To make matters worse, we appeared to have few options. Roseau had another bank, but it was even more conservative. The straw chopper seemed to be on its last legs.

Still, I never gave up; and it finally occurred to me that even the man at the bank worked for somebody. I learned his boss was a man named J.R. Chapel, who owned not only the local bank but also the Merchants National Bank in Winona, Minnesota. My only option seemed clear: I had to find Mr. Chapel and explain the predicament.

I drove to Winona, a seven-hour trip, and went directly to the Merchants National Bank. I was told, however, that Mr. Chapel was at the golf course. I didn't understand such a place is sacred ground. You're not supposed to run out there like a bull in a china shop. Yet, of course, it's exactly what I did. To heck with etiquette, my finances were about to collapse. I had to tell Mr. Chapel about it, whether he was playing golf or not, whether he liked it or not. At that point, I might have barged in on a wedding.

I made my way out onto the deep, green grass and asked for Mr. Chapel. Someone said he was out by No. 8, and pointed in a certain direction. I didn't know what No. 8 was, or what it pertained to, but I dashed across the ground. I must have looked a terrific sight, running in this old suit of mine, its flap flying up around my head.

Jogging and panting, I approached a group of men.

"Is Mr. Chapel here?" I asked.

"I'm Mr. Chapel," said a gentleman. He stepped forward, swinging a putter back and forth.

"You are? That's great," I said. I laughed loudly, which proved a terrible mistake because everyone turned to look at this goof who was disrupting the golf game. Mr. Chapel frowned. Undeterred, my mouth took over. In rapid-fire fashion, I described what had happened at the bank in Roseau. I told about the International Harvester purchase order and what I needed to make it happen.

"So you see, Mr. Chapel," I wrapped up, "this is a very good deal, not just for me but for your bank. I can't understand why the bank would decline the interest on a $10,000 loan. The purchase order is from International Harvester. They're good for it."

Mr. Chapel clawed his chin with the tips of his nails. He nodded. His decision came quickly, perhaps because he wanted to get back to the game.

"I'll take care of it," he said. "By the time you get home, the loan officer will know that he is supposed to help you."

Mr. Chapel was true to his word, and I soon had the money. It was one of the few times I felt good walking out a bank door. So, with the proper funds, we built International Harvester their straw choppers, and earned $100,000. Moreover, we paid back the local bank, with interest.

❧ ❧ ❧

The straw chopper taught me so much about persistence. It is essential to success. It was the reason I landed the deal with International Harvester, and the reason the choppers didn't die at birth. Persistence saved us after a huge mistake.

The difficulty had happened years earlier, in the late '40s or early '50s, when we decided to perform a trial test on our new device. It would be in Oklahoma. That year, as the test began, it was hot and dry.

The straw was a golden brown, and as the combine rolled over it, the chopper spewed the remains over the ground. Debris from the straw fluttered and seemed to levitate. The chopper worked wonderfully, and by the time we got back to Roseau, I thought we were ready.

We sold 350 for the following year, grossing $150,000 and earning $27,000. It was success we'd never before had, and I expected it to continue.

It didn't. The test in Oklahoma was our undoing. We hadn't planned well enough, hadn't thought ahead. When the straw was dry and easy to cut, the choppers had performed just as they were supposed to. But a year later, with normal rainfall, they didn't work at all. Due to higher moisture content, straw jammed the cutters.

Irate letters and calls poured in. It was the low point in my career. If we didn't do something fast, the whole thing could come toppling down. We couldn't afford to get a reputation of building poor products. No matter how much it hurt our pocketbook, there was but one thing to do. We had to fix those choppers.

It seemed we rebuilt a thousand choppers that winter, though the count was fewer than 300. By the time we were done, we'd spent approximately $35,000. It was a lot of money, but we'd made good on our word. During the next harvest, the new and improved choppers worked just as we'd hoped. Farmers wrote and called, this time with praise. Possible enemies had become staunch allies, and a sad negative was now a positive.

With the crisis over, we needed to market the choppers. We had distributors, but wanted to sell directly to combine manufacturers. However, because of the setback, we were cash poor. Without money, it was difficult to mount an extensive campaign.

Fortunately, we had something in our favor. By repairing the choppers so quickly, we'd gained respect as a company that would stand behind its products. A few cities began courting us, asking us to relocate Hetteen Hoist and Derrick. One was willing to toss in a $250,000 building. Others offered reduced tax rates and additional incentives. Word spread in Roseau that we were considering a move. I let the rumors persist, though I doubt we actually would have left.

With our implied threat hanging over the town, several businessmen said they would give us $40,000 as preferred stock. In addition to helping us continue with the straw choppers, the money could fund prototype machines and other projects. We didn't want to leave Roseau anyway, so I agreed to the offer. It was a great thing those men did. I am sometimes critical of the help we received from our community, but in this case, they came through, even though later, when we got to snow-mobiles, they would forget all about their faith in us.

The $40,000 deal came to this: As preferred stock, we had to pay it back, with interest, and the investors would not own any part of Hetteen Hoist and Derrick. They did however, ask for two positions on the board of directors. I agreed, and that would prove to be quite an error on my part.

But for now, the crisis was over. We were ready to market the chopper.

Throughout the 1950s, we would make deals with most of the large combine manufacturers. None of them however, would have come about had it not been for the private distributors. We had the Lindsay Brothers in Minneapolis, and they covered several states. Lindsay, like others, bought and resold the choppers. They got the ball rolling. Without them, it would have been impossible for a little blacksmith shop in Roseau to even approach International Harvester.

Without them, it would have been impossible to land our first deal with a combine manufacturer, Minneapolis Moline in Hopkins, Minnesota. Being only 360 miles from Roseau, it was only natural to go see that company.

Its chief engineer, Martin Ronning, eventually came to Roseau and watched the choppers at work. He was impressed and we struck a deal. Hetteen Hoist and Derrick would build choppers for Minneapolis Moline, painted in their trademark prairie gold, and tailored to fit their needs. Though Moline wouldn't buy them directly from us, they would help sell them to their dealers. It was a leap forward, and it taught me that in business, in life, you rarely get somewhere all at once. You must have patience and persistence.

After Minneapolis Moline, we landed International Harvester, and then went ahead with plans to tackle the other combine manufacturers. Over the next few years, we nailed down contracts with Case in Bettendorf, Iowa, with Massey Ferguson in Toronto, Ontario, and with the Oliver Corporation in Battle Creek, Michigan.

All seemed well until problems arose because of a certain arrangement we made with the manufacturers. We called it private labeling. We painted the choppers their color and they sold them as their own. It seemed a good deal, and we were earning decent money.

However, our distributor in St. Louis, Missouri, it turned out, was mad as hell. He claimed that by us dealing directly with the manufacturers, he'd been cut out of the loop. Selling Hetteen Hoist and Derrick choppers was impossible, he said, while International was selling the same chopper with their name and color only a few miles away.

At the same time, we weren't real happy with him. He wasn't a very good salesman. In his territory were hundreds of older combines he could have fit with a chopper. International would not have gone to the trouble of retrofitting those machines. Therefore, our man should have been fine.

But he continued to squabble, until we finally said, "Pay us what you owe or we'll take back our merchandise."

The man refused to pay his bill, which perhaps totaled $15,000. To us, that was an awful lot. Without it, things would have been real rough. We had no choice but to go south. I sent Roy Baumgartner, one of our intrepid employees, to St. Louis on a mission: Get a check or get our stuff.

Roy made his way to the distributor's warehouse. With no one around to pay the bill, he pushed open the large metal doors and backed up the truck. In the heat and wind of Missouri, with constant looks about, he began to reclaim our choppers.

He hustled and hustled, sweat pouring off his slight frame. But just as he was putting a third chopper into the back of the truck, he heard a low grumbling noise, that of a car engine. Stepping in front of him with a badge on his chest was a deputy sheriff. A friendly deputy.

"My boss is coming down here and he will have some kind of re-straining order to prevent you from doing this," he said. "I would suggest you not be on the premises when he gets here."

Roy was smart. He quit loading and hopped in the truck. He gunned the engine, but in his haste, he revved that old Mack truck too hard. He heard a snap and a terrible racket in the engine, that of the fan going through the radiator. A cloud of steam rose from the hood.

Roy cursed. If the sheriff came, he'd be dead in the water. With the engine still hissing like a snake, he managed to pull away. The old truck grunted and popped but made its way onto the public street. To safety. Roy wiped his brow with relief.

We sued the distributor for what Roy couldn't get. He in turn sued us, alleging that he had exclusive rights to the straw chopper for his area. It was the second time in my life that I was in court. The first time was in Roseau, defending myself against a man who alleged I owed him a handful of dollars. It was devastating to be sued in my own hometown. However, in that case, the judge ruled in my favor; in fact, my ex-friend was ordered to pay all court costs.

Unfortunately, this federal judge in St. Louis was something different. My attorneys, whom I found in the phone book, argued as best they could. They cited many companies that did private labeling while also selling the product under their own name. But when the judge started questioning me, it was obvious: We were lost.

"Mr. Hetteen, don't you think it's difficult for your distributor to do business when much larger companies have the same product in his area?" the judge asked.

He waved his pencil in the air, virtually shoving it on my nose. It was unnerving for a farm kid from Roseau. To the judge, I was a Yankee, perhaps a damn Yankee who was hurting a good southern boy. He ruled against us, and our financial balancing act received an unexpected blow.

ଙ୍କ ଙ୍କ ଙ୍କ

We bounced back. We always did. We would continue to make deals with the combine manufacturers, and we would paint choppers in their colors with their labels. The distributor in St. Louis may have won the battle, but we would win the war.

Yes, as a bunch of uneducated, untrained farm boys from Roseau, we had done no small job to get all of those companies to approve and buy our chopper. We also had to work hard to keep the choppers modern, because whenever a manufacturer changed design, our chopper had to change as well. In constant flux, we had to adapt to four or five different designs.

I could have, at that time, said, "We can take pride in what we've done." But I've never felt that way, and maybe that has led to some of my entrepreneurial success. I've never stood back and said, "This is a job well done. I'm proud of what we've done." No, I always felt we could and should do better. As a result, we never grew lazy and complacent, as some companies do.

The only real satisfaction I had came from the fact that those combine manufacturers placed their trust and confidence in us. In refining the choppers to fit their combines, they let me run around in all of their advanced engineering. They trusted I wouldn't tell a competitor about their new models. They let me work with their marketing people and trusted I wouldn't disclose those plans. More importantly, I learned how to divide up departments and how to make things run efficiently when you have more than a few employees. That knowledge would be important, especially as we grew.

We did grow, and the years ticked by. I found myself in my mid-'30s. There still was so much I wanted to do, and straw choppers were not the whole world. I felt torn; the choppers were taking too much of my time. To solve that, Orlen Johnson, who worked with us from the start, became my assistant in chopper engineering. Gradually, he took over most of my duties, and I could dedicate myself to other projects.

Like a funny contraption we called a Sno-Traveler.

Chapter 5

YOU BUILT WHAT?

It must have been fate. Edgar Hetteen's future may have been deter-mined at age 6, when in 1926, he gained a business partner and a lifelong friend, a fellow who would lead him to the snowmobile.

Not far down the dusty country road from where Edgar was growing up, his grandmother was at work. As a midwife, she helped the country women give birth. At the time, a doctor was a luxury the rural community didn't have, and Grandmother Hetteen was an excellent replacement. She had a gentle touch, and the women she cared for felt content in her charge. Of those, one was Mrs. Wafford Johnson, pregnant with her fourth child.

One dark night, Mrs. Johnson, with Grandmother Hetteen at her side, gave birth to a son, David. Shortly after, she developed scarlet fever; she was dying. Before she passed, she called for Edgar's grandmother. She asked the woman in a quiet voice, "Would you take care of the little one?" The midwife nodded. Of course.

The little one was David Johnson. Growing up nearby, David was like a brother to Edgar. As teen-agers, they bounced around the country roads on their motorcycles, and they played and tinkered with engines.

In the mid-'50s, David had a revolutionary idea.

ॐ ॐ ॐ

"David, David, David," I said. I shook my head and looked down, to the hulking machine on our shop floor.

Anger isn't the proper word to describe my emotions, but I certainly was miffed at my long-time friend and brother-in-law. I was feeling many emotions – confusion, bewilderment, perhaps dismay. Only earlier that day, in the winter of 1955, I'd returned from a long-needed vacation to California, where my wife's sister lived. Refreshed and at relative peace, I was now back at our factory, which we'd recently expanded. From the success of our straw choppers, we'd climbed to the point where we had a little money, though we still sweated out each pay day. We'd put on wood and concrete additions, plus bought the church next door for additional space.

But now what the heck was David doing? How had he managed to build this thing in the few days I was gone? Vanished was my peaceful feeling.

"Edgar," he had said. "I built something."

David, my brother Allan, and I were three-way partners. The two certainly could do anything they wanted, although that freedom didn't mean I wouldn't get upset if it were something silly, something that lost money.

"All right," I had said agreeably. Perhaps he'd improved the straw chopper, perhaps he'd built a new combine attachment. But what I was shown was not a chopper at all, nor farm related, but a big, bulky metal thing with tracks and an engine bolted on top.

"It's a snow machine," David said.

I had figured that out. But why? Rudimentary snow machines had been around since the turn of the century, but you didn't give them much thought. They were built in garages with parts from a junkyard. Some worked, some didn't, but none had any practical sale value.

Why was David wasting his time like this? Our factory built farm equipment. Furrowing my brow, I asked him why. His answer was something I guess I already knew. He loved the outdoors, and simply wanted to get around in the snow. So, he more or less had inverted a grain elevator track and attached it to an engine. He'd then fashioned some skis out of a car bumper, built a scooped front end, and put it all together.

Well, I ignored the machine for a week. If David wanted one for his own amusement, so be it. It wasn't as if he'd cost us much money, just his time, and he more than made up for that by working day and night, as we all did. Let him have his toy.

The days passed, and David continued work on the machine he called a Motor Toboggan. More and more, in spite of myself, I was drawn to it. A week later, I noticed that it was no longer around; and I missed the thing.

"Hmmm," I thought. "David must have taken it home."

Except he hadn't. He'd done what I thought impossible. He actually sold it. Pete Peterson, who owned a lumber yard across the street, had bought the first Polaris snowmobile.

I had recently changed the company's name to Polaris Industries. Polaris was Latin for the North Star and was descriptive of our product as well as our location. Moreover, it was not a confining name like Hetteen Hoist and Derrick. Under the new umbrella, we could build more than just farm equipment; we could build snowmobiles.

Anyway, back to Pete Peterson, a very nice fellow with one little quirk. The guy had an uncanny ability to break things. We knew with him buying No. 1, it would need lots of work. We were right. From the tiny window of my office, I'd gaze onto a nearby field, and I'd watch Pete rumble through the snow. The machine would bog down and it would die. I'd shake my head and wonder: What on earth had we unleashed?

But the more we fixed that sled, the more I became intrigued. I grew interested in the possibilities such a machine presented, especially in the snow belt, and especially for us. It was to be the beginning of a 23-year romance, which was sometimes violent, sometimes emotional, but never dull. The machine became the catalyst for meeting some of the finer people in this world, some in government, but mostly private citizens. It would take me places I never would have dreamed of. But I am getting ahead of myself. We'd built only one.

Enthused by David's machine, Allan constructed one of his own. Much to my surprise, another guy wanted to buy a snowmobile. That fellow was Harley Jensen, who lived on an island in Lake of the Woods. He needed the thing to go three or four miles to cut pulp during the day and then return in the evening.

Harley wanted to meet at the Northwest Angle, the farthest point north in Minnesota. We would hand him the snowmobile, and he would hand us $700. This was before the Angle had real roads, and it was a rollercoaster in my old pickup, trying to find the trail through the thick woods. The snowmobile rattled and rolled in the box. We arrived at dusk; a gentle snow dusted the land. Harley stood in our lights, with a wool parka covering his face.

We said our greetings, got the snowmobile out of the pickup, and it wasn't long before David told Harley to climb on for a test ride. Harley obliged, and they puttered off into the distance. Just as they went out of sight, I thought I saw David jostling with the throttle. The throttle had stuck open and, of course, when it sticks, you can't slow down. It was a common occurrence with those early models. It would stick, and you had to bang on that sucker until it gave. Thankfully, David got it under control. He circled around to where we stood.

There now seemed little chance Harley Jensen would buy. But as he got off the sled, snow falling fast and whipping up even faster, he scratched his chin. "I'll take it," he said.

This was good news. It was Thursday evening, and with Harley's check soon to be in our hands, I was plenty glad. Though it was one sale, it would go a long way to covering the payroll due the next day. My elation, however, was quickly doused.

"I don't have a check with me. I'll have to send you one," Harley muttered, and turned away to the snowmobile.

Great, I thought. I'd flown mail up to those islands, and knew full well there were only two mail planes a week. The earliest a check could possibly get back to us in Roseau was the following Wednesday, far too late for the coming payday. Besides, by next Wednesday the doggone machine probably would have broken down and he wouldn't want to pay.

The first sleds at Polaris were called Sno-Cats and Pol-Cats, but finally Sno-Travelers.

But what else to do? We couldn't tell him the deal was off. He was one of the few even interested in our machine. So, with the snow still falling, we nodded our agreement, and he got onto the snowmobile. As he went out of sight, the engine puttered softer and softer, fading away, just like our spirits.

A week later, however, Harley proved true to his word. We got his check. I don't know how we covered the payroll Friday, but it wouldn't have been the only time we fudged the books a little.

Upon selling No. 2, I started to really like this snow machine. I thought about its potential. While it was true our straw choppers were doing well, the upside of the snowmobile seemed too great to ignore. The machine finally won me over, and it wasn't long before I divorced myself from the straw chopper side of the business and worked full time on our motor toboggans, which we were having a hard time naming.

We called them Pol-Cats (Polaris Cats); however, that raised images of an animal that smelled rather bad. They became Sno-Cats, but I was concerned about borrowing 'Cat' from the huge Caterpillar company. Finally, I changed it one last time to Sno-Travelers, and Polaris stuck with that until the mid-'60s.

We got started; the early machines needed lots of work. I remember hanging out in that little plant late into the night, all dirty and grimy as we built No. 3. I remember my head and body under the frame for hours, screwing and twisting and hammering.

Through that winter, we improved the way No. 3 ran, and started on No. 4. We put a windshield on that one, and designed it better, so it looked like it came from a regular factory rather than a garage. It had a radio, cigarette lighter, self starter, and a compass. We even added head-lights, which wouldn't be standard for several years. I wanted it to have a big impact with potential dealers.

Meanwhile, the straw choppers, our main business, kept us afloat as we tinkered with this crazy idea only David, Allan and I thought had merit. The two other members of the board, who I won't name, did not. They thought the Sno-Traveler was nutty, as did many of our employees.

Despite initial negative reactions from most everyone, we kept at it. We knew we were onto something, and nobody could tell us differently. All the experts in the world are wrong when you know you're right. As president, I kept pushing the machines, and we kept improving them. We knew you didn't give up on a good idea, as I had years earlier with the hoist.

We built five that first winter. Before it was over, I decided that we had such a fine snowmobile, it was time to seek out dealers. We'd learned from the straw chopper experience that, for the snowmobile to take off, we needed such people. We should go, I thought, to a place where they really had snow, where they really ought to welcome us.

We'd start in Alaska, partly because of the snow, and partly because I needed an excuse to get up there. It was my favorite place in the world outside of Roseau, and it always beckoned me. I loved the people there, their spirit of adventure, their individuality, the stuff that made up my soul.

I called a good friend, Denny Dunham, in Anchorage. I asked if I could send a machine up to him and then retrieve it at his place in about a week. Denny, who became an incredibly successful Arctic Cat distributor, agreed, as I knew he would.

To Denny I sent that specialized fourth model, which was nothing like today's machines. It was many times heavier, mostly because it had a 12-horsepower Onan on it, a twin cylinder opposed engine. Though we'd added a radio, lighter, compass, electric start and headlights, it had no cushions, and no brakes. Such drawbacks never caused any problems, however. The lack of cushions made up for the lack of speed, because the hard hits on your backside made it seem as if you were zipping right along. And brakes weren't necessary because in our flat country, the machine had enough internal friction that it slowed quickly when you reduced power.

No, we hadn't reached perfection. We'd come a long way since David's first model, and it was time to build a dealer network; but there remained several glitches. That old snowmobile would bog down, it would break, and the throttle would stick. It had tons of quirks. Even so, I fooled myself.

"Gee," I thought. "If we go up to Alaska, where the snow is deep and it's really winter, it ought to work just great."

My wife and I flew into Anchorage, where we hooked up with Polaris employee Steve Rugland, who was in Alaska trying to earn some extra money. The three of us then went to see Denny. The snowmobile had arrived safely and sat on a trailer in his driveway. Denny is about my age and so we talked over old times. I told of our efforts to build the snowmobile, and my hope to find a dealer. I said I wanted to get to Fairbanks to visit another old friend, Rudy Billberg, who also was from Roseau.

"Problem is, Denny," I said, "I don't have a good way to get to Fairbanks. Any ideas?"

"Edgar, take my car and my trailer and you drive to Fairbanks," Denny said, because that's the type of guy he is. "Use it as long as you want."

I thanked Denny, and we took his brand new Chevrolet, trailer attached, and headed to Fairbanks. It was a long way, down that winding, snowy road north, and it took us most of the day. Had we been in the southern 48, we might have stopped for a rest, but in the mountains there were no opportunities.

We drove into Fairbanks on the airport road but stopped several hundred yards from the terminal. I unloaded the Sno-Traveler and prepared to drive it the remaining distance. I thought it would make an awfully big splash, that everyone would gather around and say how wonderful the machine was, how wonderful I was, and inquire how they might purchase one.

I revved the engine and headed for the ditch, because I wasn't going to ride on the road where it was nice and easy. I wanted to go into the snow, show everyone what this little sled could do. It was a granular snow, and the snowmobile traveled quite well – in a downward direction. I was riding a sinking ship, and it reminded me of the scamperings of a frightened Minnesota gopher heading for his hole. The snow machine dove deep and stalled. There I sat, more than a little red-faced and quite discouraged.

*My wife and I on our way to Fairbanks in Denny Dunham's car
with that early No. 4 model Polaris.*

I stepped off and sank waste deep into the grainy stuff. I called to Steve and my wife, who stood on the road.

"Need a shovel," I said with dismay. Steve pitched it down to me, and I began digging, tugging and pushing. I had wanted to make a splash, with everyone excited about our new design of a snow machine. I didn't want to dig it out of a ditch, load it on a trailer and slink out of there like a whipped dog. It's not what I had in mind, but it is exactly what I did. Leaving that place, I wondered if coming to Fairbanks had been such a good idea. For a moment, I wondered if the snowmobile was such a good idea.

Quite unhappy, we went to see Rudy Billberg. I knew he would have ideas, being by now a full-fledged Alaskan, and a bush pilot as well. He would know possible dealers, or at least could point me in the right direction.

He lived about 15 miles from Fairbanks. We arrived and unloaded the sled onto the road high above Rudy's house. His home was nestled at the bottom of a hill and tucked quietly in the trees. I hopped on the sled and took off down the hill. With no problems, I zoomed into his yard. Super, I thought, and climbed off into deep snow. Perhaps the incident at the airport was an unfortunate accident. I turned the machine around and pointed it up the hill. I revved the engine. Now, for a true test. Very, very quickly, however, it bogged down. I threw my fist against the steering wheel and let out a curse. To say I was disappointed with our performance in Fairbanks was to put it mildly – real mildly.

Rudy and his wife, Bessie, who four years later would join me on that spectacular trip across Alaska, now were outside looking over the machine. They said nice things, though they'd just watched me dig it out of their hill. As we spoke, a man drove up in a Jeep. He hopped from his vehicle and landed with a plunk on the snow. The guy was wearing great big bunny boots, GI flight pants, a GI parka and gloves. He strode over to us, slapped Rudy on the back and began talking to my friend. He paid no attention to Steve, me or my wife, and I resented him because I'd come a long way to visit Rudy. Now here was this auto mechanic, or whatever he was, taking over the conversation.

We soon moved into the house, and this guy plopped on the couch. He whipped off his big bunny boots and took off his military garments. He looked a little better, but I still didn't like him, because he'd taken my friend away. As I listened on the edge of his conversation with Rudy, I heard him talking about flying, and though I was still angry, my ears perked up. There were three things in my life: the opposite sex, airplanes and snowmobiles. Maybe the guy wasn't all bad. Then he told a story about how he went to Switzerland, where he apparently bought a new airplane. I scoffed to myself. Nobody I knew went to Switzerland, least of all to buy an airplane.

He turned to me.

"You've got that machine out in the yard?" he asked.

"Yeah," I said.

"What are you going to do with it?"

I began to like him a little better. He was interested in my snowmobile, and it was flattering, even from this big talker.

"Looking for dealers, if I can find any," I said.

"You ought to take it to my friend Tommy Brower in Point Barrow. The snow is windblown up there, and the machine should be right at home."

"What's your friend do?"

"Owns a general store. If anyone in Alaska might buy one, he'd be the one."

That was great; I knew, however, that no roads went to Point Barrow, which sat on the northern coast, some 500 miles away. The only way to transport the machine would be by plane. Trouble was, our bank account back home was overdrawn. We had no money and couldn't afford to hire a plane or a pilot.

"How could we get to Point Barrow and to your friend Mr. Brower?" I asked.

He had an answer.

"You come and see me at my office tomorrow morning and I'll take care of you," he said.

I really started to like this guy.

Morning arrived. We said our goodbyes to Rudy and Bessie, promised to see them soon, and went to the man who had promised to help us. His name was Sig Wien, and he was one of the founders of Wien Air Alaska. His office was bigger than our whole snowmobile factory, and we certainly had no carpeting. The guy sitting behind the desk was the same fellow from a day earlier, but in a suit he now was quite respectable. I had misjudged him, just as I sometimes misjudged others in those days. It was all part of learning how to size up people, and I actually grew quite good at it during my journey through life.

Sig Wien shook my hand and asked us to sit. He said he could get me, my wife and the machine into a DC-3 cargo plane (Steve planned to stay in Fairbanks). It's a whirlwind in my brain some 40 years later, but we hastily agreed. He made the arrangements over the phone in a matter of minutes.

"Now, Edgar," he said, "when you see Tommy Brower, you tell him you are a friend of Sig Wien."

"Thanks, Mr. Wien," I said. "If you're ever in Roseau, be sure to call."

And really, Sig Wien sure was great, because before we knew it, my wife and I rattled and jiggled in the cargo hold of a DC-3 on our way to Point Barrow. What an adventure! The pilots asked me up to the cockpit. It was the first time I'd spent any time in the office part of a twin-engine plane, and I was thrilled.

We landed that night near Point Barrow, snow whipping up around the windows and clouding our vision. We opened the plane's door, and a gust of wind smacked us hard. A nighttime blizzard was under way in that far corner of Alaska, and the wind practically blew us backwards. On the ice, we hunched over, arms folded firmly across our chests just to remain upright. It would be difficult to find our way to Point Barrow. Though only a few miles away, in the snow and the dark, it might as well have been a hundred.

***The Polaris Sno-Traveler is placed on the DC-3. My wife and I
would follow it into the plane, and we would enjoy a bumpy
ride to Point Barrow, where I would try to set up the first
dealer.***

Unfortunately, there appeared to be little choice. We were just about to risk the drive, when up came a twin-tracked army vehicle rumbling through the snow. It was there to meet the airplane, and it was our savior, because when the plane took off and the army machine turned around to Point Barrow, we hopped on the snowmobile and followed. We stayed close behind, because otherwise we'd have been lost. At last, we saw the lights of the small town.

We drove to a place called the Top of the World Hotel, where we registered and went upstairs. Our room was eight feet wide and the beds were bunked. It was heated by a stove down at the end of the hall, and the warmth entered the room through the door, which started two feet from the floor and finished two feet from the ceiling. Needless to say, we wondered if anyone would peek in on us. And yet, it was clean and comfortable and we enjoyed it.

The following day dawned bright and blue. My wife planned to stay in the hotel, so I pulled on thick winter clothes and padded out across the hard snow to the machine. With the engine revving nicely, I went to find Mr. Brower's store. In such a small town, it didn't take long. Though the store wasn't large, he had a nice variety of products. That was clear by the number of women plucking things off the shelf and bringing them to the counter, where this man, whom I assumed was Mr. Brower, totaled it all up. He made change out of what looked like a shoebox. My stomach tensed as I watched; for I had reason to be nervous. This was to set up a dealer. If he said yes, we were on our way. If no, it would be back to square one.

I also was apprehensive because I'd never talked to anyone who lived this far north before. I wasn't sure how to start a conversation. I waited a few minutes, mustered up my courage and stepped to the counter.

"Mr. Brower," I said as confidently as I could. "I'm a friend of Sig Wien."

Sig Wien suddenly had become a very good friend.

"What do you want?"

"Sig suggested I call on you in regards to this snow machine I have outside. I'm wondering if you'd be interested in becoming a dealer."

I didn't beat around the bush. That's how I approached business. Straight to the point, get it over with. He looked me up and down and made a quick decision.

"A moment," he said. He beckoned for his son. A young man had just entered, and he came over to work the counter while his father went with me.

"I'd like to take you for a ride," I said. We stepped outside and our eyes fell on the machine. He nodded without speaking. I started the sled and he hopped on behind. We took off across the wind-driven snow near the Arctic Ocean.

Eventually, it came time to slow the throttle, only, it wouldn't slow. It was Harley Jensen all over again. The throttle, that annoying throttle, had iced up and, though we were on flat barren land heading to the ocean, we still had cabins to avoid. Even with a snowmobile that didn't go too fast, it was plenty fast when you couldn't shut it down. Suddenly, a cabin came all too close, and as I struggled with the throttle, I swerved. We weaved in and out, in and out. The demonstration was not going well.

I hit the throttle and wrestled with it, and finally it closed and the machine stopped. We found ourselves on a high drift that covered someone's cabin. What a mess. There are times when everything goes wrong. In those moments it is best to stay calm, and in those moments, success is born. It is one thing to perform in good conditions, it is quite another to do so when the pressure is on.

It took time, but we got the machine off the drift and got everything working. I asked Mr. Brower if he wanted to continue his ride. He gave a slow, slow nod.

I just knew I'd lost this customer before I ever had him, but at least he climbed back on the sled. We made our way around the village and returned to the store. We soon were sitting in his office. It didn't take him long to speak, and I cringed waiting for the bad news.

"How much do they cost?" he asked, leaning back.

Well, you could have knocked me over with a feather. That's not what I expected, that's not what I expected at all. I gave him the retail price, and then I gave him the dealer discount. He pursed his lips, deep in thought. Much to my surprise, he reached for his checkbook. He laid it on the desk and grabbed a pen.

"Who do I make this out to?" he asked.

"Polaris Industries," I said.

"OK."

He wrote a check for the dealer amount and slid it across to me. I stared at it, and could barely speak. In the matter of an hour, I had my first dealer.

I took the check, and then my heart dropped. It was drawn on a bank in Seattle, which was a long way from Point Barrow. How could his bank be in Seattle? How did this man make his deposits? What had I gotten myself into? Maybe the check wasn't any good. Half-heartedly, I slipped it into my pocket.

The situation went from bad to worse.

"I'd like to keep the machine here," Brower said.

Oh boy, I didn't want to leave it. I needed it to see the crash site of Wiley Post and Will Rogers, those who had died in Post's airplane near Point Barrow on their way to Asia in 1935. Post was the first person to circle the earth alone, doing it in 1931, and I was interested in his accident. I hadn't expected Brower to take possession of that snowmobile. I'd hoped to ship him another. But no, with the check in my pocket and he most insistent, I had to agree.

Resigned to the fact that I probably was giving away the snowmobile for a bad check, and that my bank account desperately needed real money, I gave him some last-minute instructions and trudged to the hotel. I marched head-down, because of my failure, and also because I knew the next plane out was two or three days away. We would have to wait in that tiny hotel room with half a door.

I fell asleep that night in the bunk bed, sorry I'd ever gone to Point Barrow. My sleep was fitful, and when I woke, I heard more bad news. There was a knocking at the door. It was a hotel employee who said a man was waiting in the lobby.

My heart sank, absolutely sank. Again. I knew exactly who it was. I just knew the machine had broken, or he didn't like it, or he wanted his no-good check back. Or something. I walked downstairs and saw Mr. Brower.

He spoke first.

"Mr. Hetteen, I've run this machine overnight, and I think I can sell them," he said. "I'm going to the 'outside' on a speaking engagement, and I'll be gone for 30 days. In that time, my son will sell the machine. I'd like you to ship up some more."

Wow. I hadn't known he was important enough to have a speaking engagement; but I still doubted his check. He handed me another, this one worth a few thousand dollars. I took it; and it, too, was written on a Seattle bank. Great. Just great.

"I want you to give me credit for that amount," he said. "As my son orders them, you can charge my account."

I didn't know what to say. I now had two bad checks. But still, I took them, shook the man's hand, and said goodbye. A few days later when the plane arrived, we gladly were on it. It was a long way back to Roseau, and I talked little on the return trip, thinking about all I had to do. The instant I got to Roseau, I had to run to the bank and deposit the checks. If they were bad, I would send Rudy or Denny to retrieve my machine.

And yet, sure enough, when I went to my little bank in Roseau, and they called the bank in Seattle, that check was good.

Over the next 30 days, we shipped enough machines to take care of the deposit, and there is no question: Mr. Brower was the first legitimate snowmobile dealer in the world. In fact, many years later, when I began Arctic Cat, I called on Mr. Brower in Point Barrow. He was still selling Polaris.

Early snowmobiles on display on Main Street in Roseau. David Johnson, Allan Hetteen and I show the public our machines.

"Mr. Brower," I said, "you probably won't remember me."

He looked up from his counter and nodded.

"Yes, you are the snowmobile man," he said.

"Well, Mr. Brower," I said, "I know you're a Polaris dealer, but I am up here now to convert you to being an Arctic Cat dealer."

He shook his head no, and I knew I'd made an errant trip.

"Mr. Hetteen, when you were here the first time, you said people like you would come and try to convert me to some other dealership. I remember that, and I'm not going to drop my Polaris line. Period."

Some of the things I said to him in 1955 worked against me. He did not become an Arctic Cat dealer. Period.

❦ ❦ ❦

The upshot of making him a dealer was this: I thought, "Gee, this selling, this setting up of dealers, this should be simple. People love these machines. Wow! What a thing we've got."

Gone were the heartaches and problems with the machine I'd had in Fairbanks, gone were the thoughts of it acting like a gopher. We'd found it a home, on the wind-driven snows of the Arctic, the compact snow you could walk on. Those people wanted our machines, those people liked them.

Flushed with such success, it was reasonable to assume all we had to do was expose the public to our machines and they would buy them. We only had to choose the next location and our next dealer. We were in control. We would call the shots. And what more logical place to do so than Sault Sainte Marie, Michigan, where the snow is heavy and where people love the winter? The boys and I spent the next few months improving our product and then made plans to hit Michigan. Steve Rugland and I would go there. We thought we'd quickly set up a dealer, then move to the next lucky city.

We began at a Sault Sainte Marie Bank. And we questioned the middle-aged man in a fancy suit who sat us down at a desk and offered us coffee.

"Who in this town has the best credit, the best showroom and the best service department? Who would make the best dealer?"

With a list comprised of car dealers, farm implement dealers and sporting equipment dealers, we set out. We just knew they would love our machine. They'd understand the Sno-Traveler could make winter easier. Dollar signs would light in their eyes, and they'd be eager to buy.

We first approached a car dealership. We walked in and I pointed outside to the snowmobile on my trailer. The salesmen furrowed their brows and shook their heads.

"No," they said. "We're not interested."

They promptly turned around and went back to business, as if Steve and I were vermin. They might as well have punched us in the gut.

Each time we walked into one of those places, the men we spoke to furrowed their brows and shook their heads. When they agreed to go outside and look, they would shake their heads some more. It was discouraging, because we'd been so confident and so sure of what would happen. Instead of great success, we were suffering great failure.

The salesmen we'd found didn't believe anyone in their right mind would play in the snow. They thought we were insulting their intelligence by even suggesting it. We got two orders from those men: Get out, and stay out.

By the time we'd gone through all the names the bank had given us, we were feeling many emotions: discouragement, frustration, and uncertainty. We'd sought out all the businessmen in Sault Sainte Marie who had a showroom and experience selling machinery. And we'd come up with a big fat zero.

As it turned out, the car dealers, with their showrooms and their dressed up salesmen in Oxford shoes, weren't about to go outside and demonstrate the snowmobile. They would not bundle up, they would not convince anyone how much fun winter was. They wanted to stay inside, where it was nice and warm and comfortable.

Nor would the sporting equipment dealer hear us out. He sold fishing tackle, clothes and equipment; he wasn't interested in some snow machine. There were the implement dealers, who came close to fitting the bill, but they weren't interested either. We tried the marine dealers, but since it didn't go on water, they shook their heads and pointed to the door. We tried them all, and none of them gave us hope. Most agreed there was a need for winter recreation, but the snowmobile wasn't perceived as an answer.

With these defeats, our noses were bloody. We felt like putting our briefcases on the curb, sitting down, and crying. We might have done so, only we reasoned that, being grown up and all, we'd be conspicuous crying on a corner. We wouldn't get dealers that way either.

Frustrated, we drove down the road for 15 minutes or so, until we arrived at a little country tavern in Brimley, Michigan. We sauntered in and sat at the bar, wanting nothing more than to drown our sorrows in a couple of beers. We hunched over our drinks and tried to keep to ourselves, but there was a guy standing behind us, and he wouldn't go away. We grew annoyed.

Here I am on an early Sno-Traveler.

We tried to ignore him, but the guy still didn't leave. He wore denim overalls and a white shirt. With a twinkle in his eye, he stepped up to us. We cringed. We did not want to talk to anyone, much less a local who might tease us.

"What is that on the trailer outside?" he asked, his voice rising strong out of the air behind us. We swiveled on our stools.

"It's a Sno-Traveler, drives on the snow," I said. I was gruff, but you couldn't blame me. They'd beaten us up all day long, and this old-timer probably was going to do the same.

"I thought so," he said, pausing for a time. "Is it for sale?"

What a foolish question.

"Yes," I said with a tired chuckle. "It's for sale."

We began to talk, the guy no longer annoying. He said his name was Henry Smith, that he was a retired gunsmith and that he lived right there in Brimley. We took him for his word.

Not an hour passed before Henry volunteered that he would like to be a dealer. At the end of a day like we'd had, he was a heck of a guy. He gave me a check for $700, and gone were all thoughts that we should qualify this man, that we should have the bank check on him, that we should request background information, that we should do all the things an upstanding business is supposed to do.

We didn't care who he was. We'd found a friend, one of those fantastic people who would make up the sport of snowmobiling. We didn't realize the significance of Henry Smith, but as it turned out, he would be one of the people we needed to sell the early snowmobiles; somebody who believed, who would work hard, who would demonstrate. We didn't need the man with his fancy showroom. Henry would do everything, because he liked the outdoors and loved our machine.

We left Brimley fairly satisfied. To our knowledge, we'd established the first snowmobile dealer in the continental United States.

And yet we said to ourselves, "a retired gunsmith as a dealer? That can't be good." Even though we'd found this special person, we didn't realize what fate was telling us. We continued to try for the car dealers, implement dealers, marine dealers and motorcycle dealers. We canvassed most of Wisconsin that way, but nobody would look at us. Finally, because we were smart or because of necessity, we went with the people who believed, people like Henry Smith.

About to haul a shipment of snowmobiles in our semi-truck.

Sure there were doubts, many doubts, and for good reason. By and large, the early dealers were not business people. They were not savvy about banks. They didn't know how to borrow on a serial number, or how to manage large amounts of money. There were so many things they didn't know, and we viewed them with concern.

Such concern, that even after we'd set up a few people like Henry Smith, I sent Steve Rugland west to try once more for the professional dealers. Weeks passed, and still Steve hadn't found an established dealer willing to sell snowmobiles. He did, however, find a Greyhound bus driver in Billings, Montana. When he told me of our new dealer, I kind of smiled and threw up my hands. I'd learned my lesson. So much for getting experienced dealers.

In those days, if you wanted to be a dealer, all you had to do was say the magic word: "Yes." If you as much as indicated an interest in us, we would dress you in bunny boots, pants, the whole bit. We would plop you on the snowmobile and take you into the winter. If we could get you on the Sno-Traveler, we usually could make you a believer. That was important. Only the believers would go to the trouble of selling our machines.

We found friends. We found guys willing to put in the time. We found men who used their brains, their sweat, their ingenuity. They saved us, and moved the industry ahead. On the backs of many Henry Smiths, Polaris and Arctic Cat were built.

Nearly 40 years later, my recollection is a blend of two companies, but between them we had many non-traditional dealers. We had an insurance agency in Marquette, Michigan. You could buy insurance and then a snowmobile. In Ely, Minnesota, real snow country, we signed up a barber in a hotel. Don't laugh. What do you do when nobody else in town will talk to you?

We had Sparky Meyer, a saloon keeper in Neenah, Wisconsin, who perhaps was the most successful of all the early guys. We had a mail carrier, who lived near Mahnomen, Minnesota. We had a game warden named Paul Asper from Pennsylvania. We had Pete Wass, a mine fore-

I spent so much time honing and improving the early snowmobiles. It was my life.

man in Grand Rapids, Minnesota. Pete and I would sit up for hours at his kitchen table eating biscuits, drinking coffee and talking snowmobiles.

They were great fellows. They might not have had business experience, but they were gritty and gutsy, everything we needed. What would structured business have said about them – a bus driver? a barber? a mine foreman? They would have hated our dealers, but I defy them to have found any at all.

Yes, those men were saviors, but eventually we'd have to say goodbye. Because of their work, big business caught up with Polaris and Arctic Cat. We'd go through an age of canceling many of the guys who got us started because, as we grew, the accountants and the attorneys and the experts told us to get rid of them. They looked at our dealer structure and saw barbers, insurance agents and mail carriers. They saw this hodgepodge and said, "This can't work." They advised us to go to established dealers, who by then, in the '70s, were eager to join us. We listened.

And so we became more structured, more refined. In ways, the experts were right, but they also didn't fully understand what they were doing. The evolution may have been necessary, but I believe we hurt ourselves. The world was not quite ready to buy a snowmobile over the counter, not quite ready to accept the fact that snowmobiling was fun. Customers still needed to be taken out into the snow, and shown. The professional dealers wouldn't always do that.

While our guy might have been a barber or a saloon-keeper or a gun smith, and on paper didn't look like much, he had something the big shots didn't. He ate and slept and breathed snowmobiling. He often sold more than the "respectable" dealers. Those early men saved us and pushed snowmobiling into the modern era.

❧ ❧ ❧

Perhaps I've gotten ahead of myself. I mean, it didn't go nearly as fast as it might appear on paper. Our dealership network was built over a period of years, and it was long before they, and we, went gangbusters.

That would take some time, though production did increase from that first year. We built 75 in 1956-57, then increased it to more than 300 in 1957-58. However, much to our dismay, they weren't selling well. In our desperation, we tried building other kinds of snow machines. We fashioned a device with long augers, side by side. As you sat between them, the machine screwed its way through the snow. Theoretically, it would turn by speeding up one auger and slowing down the other. It didn't, however, work the way it should've. While the augers were spinning, one would go forward while the other went sideways. Then maybe after going sideways, the other auger would catch hold of something and zip the other way. We nicknamed the thing Screwing Lena, but didn't try building any more.

Despite such failures, we were convinced that Sno-Travelers would be our future. We had faith, even though most had little idea what snowmobiles did, or what they were used for. I often said we had the difficult task of selling something that didn't really work to people who didn't really want it.

In 1957 or 1958, I was at something called the Sportsman Show in Minneapolis and was faced with the hard realization that the snowmobile was a long-term project. I worked the show for 10 days with no staff. I had a booth and my snowmobile, along with brochures of the machine's dimensions and capabilities.

Those old Sno-Travelers had a pointed snout turned up, slightly resembling a boat. People would walk up. They'd wander around, stand back, and hover. They'd sit on the sled. They'd stare up at me.

"How fast will it go?" they'd asked.

That was always their first question. According to the brochure, the old machines went 24 miles per hour. Though honestly, because of low horsepower and weight, they did only if you were going downhill with a tail wind.

They then would ask the second most popular question.

"Will it go on water?"

I spent a number of frustrating days answering the burning question of whether that huge glob of steel could float. Finally, I developed a suitable answer.

"Yes," I'd say. "If the water's frozen."

It was annoying, but these people were saying a few things without coming straight out with it. They were asking an important question: "What is this? I don't know. I don't understand. Teach me, educate me."

Ten days was a long time for a show. It was a long time to answer questions of the same caliber, and I finally got so I wasn't real nice to everyone. And yet, the experience taught me about dealing with customers. I first had to understand them, and I began putting myself in their shoes. If you know where the other guy is coming from, you can play to that knowledge, and that can make all the difference.

Just as we didn't always understand the customers and their exasperating questions, they didn't understand us. They called us strange and crazy. But I wish they could have put themselves in our shoes. The Westinghouses and the Fords were the rugged individuals of their day. We don't see that enough in society. Society is teaching us to conform. If you're not like everyone else, you're an oddball.

We shouldn't laugh at someone trying to be different. We should understand where he is coming from, what he wants to do. If we did that, we'd have more progress. More people would work toward their dreams, and society would benefit.

As much as I hoped people would understand me, some never did. It was a shame, and it's why I now want people to understand the entrepreneur, what makes him tick. It's important to support those people; they are our future. Even as we went about going to shows and doing anything to push the snowmobile, a lack of support would lead to a point in the late '50s when I had to consider leaving Polaris.

Chapter 6

OH, TO FLY

Edgar Hetteen is a man with interests beyond the snowmobile. Take his machines, his countless machines built long before the Sno-Traveler. And take his love of flight. It, as much as anything, molded and shaped him. Hetteen became an accomplished pilot and developed a passionate attachment to his airplanes, the ones that saved his life so many times.

I was airplane crazy. As we sold straw choppers, as we went about the task of designing and selling our snow machine, as we struggled weekly to pay our employees, I was flying, as was David Johnson. It was a company obsession.

Airplanes were a love that served a great purpose, at least for me. The pressure of keeping our little company afloat was intense, and flying relieved the pressure. Just being afloat in God's skies allowed me to look at the world with perspective, to get a handle on my problems, and to think more clearly on what should be done. It gave me a great outlook on life and how it should be lived – to the fullest.

We'd use the planes just to get away for a quick weekend. Such was the motive David and I had on an excursion with our wives to the Northwest Angle. Everything was fine, until we decided to leave the Angle. We then came face to face with our own mortality.

That morning, my wife and I got into our rented Piper Cub, a little thing with a top speed of 74 miles per hour. The skies were bright and the wind gentle, but there was a heavy feel to the air, like a storm was brewing. Still, no reason to stay, so we picked up speed and left the Angle behind. We also left David and Eleanor, who were planning to stay a few extra hours.

Within 15 minutes, the wind turned strong. The cockpit rocked, gently at first, and then it shook. I rattled in the front, where there was only one seat, and my wife rattled in the back. It soon was a constant struggle to keep the plane level. We later learned gusts were clocked at 90 mph.

Now remember how weather works. In our country, it usually moves from west to east. This particular storm had been moving east, into the angle. So when I took off, the winds weren't bad, but the more I flew west, the worse it got. Fortunately, David left later in the day, after the storm had passed.

By the time we reached Roseau, the wind snapped around our little plane like it was made of paper. With gusts that exceeded the airplane's top speed, we actually would move backwards, only to bounce ahead when we came out of a hard wind. My wife's face was an ashen white, and I, too, was worried.

I spotted the Roseau runway and reduced speed, but against the wind, we barely made headway. The slow speed was threatening our very lives, and there was only one thing to do: I had to approach the runway at nearly full-speed. It was dangerous, but had I tried it any other way, we definitely would have blown away.

As I touched down, the wind practically held us still. I wanted to kill the engine, but just couldn't. If I tried, the wind would grab the plane and smash it. Battling the controls, I twisted my head and shouted to my wife.

Here is my first plane, the PA 12 Supercruiser, with Clifton Brandt and Lloyd Olson somewhere in Texas.

"You're gonna have to jump out and get help!!"

She nodded with grim determination.

Suddenly, a hard gust of wind came up and hurled us backwards and up. I was constantly on the throttle either increasing or reducing power, just to stay hovering over the same spot. At last, I touched down, barely skimming the surface, long enough to institute our plan.

It was touch and go. My wife climbed out the door, and I quickly looked back. I worried for her. It'd be tricky, because when she leaped, the plane would become lighter, and, therefore, use less air speed. I'd have to adjust power. To make matters worse, at any moment a gust could have taken the plane and smashed us over the ground.

We were a foot off the runway when she climbed down onto the tire. She held on for a second and then jumped. Her dress and hair whipped wildly in the wind, reminiscent of Dorothy in the Wizard of Oz. On the runway, she ran about 40 yards to the office and phoned Polaris. She told them I needed help at the airport and to have a bunch of boys come out. Quickly.

As she ran, I still had a plane to save. I ran the engine hard in a stalemate with the wind, hoping I wouldn't run out of gas. Had I, it would have been the end of the airplane, and maybe me. Sometimes I gained a little, sometimes I was picked up and set to one side or the other. Never had my heart beat so quickly.

Eventually, the boys arrived. It had taken them only about five minutes, but for me, it seemed like one heck of a long time. They dashed to my plane, the only one on the runway. Nobody else had been as foolish. With them hanging onto the wings, they walked me to the hangar. My guardian angel, who I'm sure I always had when it came to flying, took care of me that day, as he so often did.

❧ ❧ ❧

I bought my first airplane in 1947, the PA 12 Supercruiser 4045M. For weeks, I'd heard talk that Doctor Harris of Roseau had ordered a new plane from Dan Carver, my instructor and Piper dealer. The price of the plane was $3,600. Rumor had it that, for reasons of his own,

August Borg and Norman Flagstad joined me on a flight into Canada for some ice fishing.

Doc did not want to take delivery. I knew the reasons behind the rumors. I suspected his wife frowned on the whole thing, and it gave me an idea.

For years I'd flown any doggone airplane I could lay my hands on. If I could talk somebody out of 15 minutes of flying time, I did. I'd do anything to get in the air, so I jumped at the chance to have my own.

"Doc, if it's true that you'd just as soon not take that plane you ordered, I have a solution. If you could see your way clear to loan me $1,200 for the downpayment, I would accept the new plane and take it off your hands."

Doc agreed to my offer, and I got the rest from the Marquette National Bank in Minneapolis. Lo and behold, I'd bought my first airplane. And a new one at that.

I picked it up at Fleming Field in St. Paul. It shimmered in the sunshine, the yellow and soft red shining off the fuselage. I knew I'd made the right decision. I was in love.

Going home in that airplane, at 105 mph vs. the 74 mph I'd been used to in the Piper J3, was quite a difference. The gas tank held 36 gallons compared to the Cub's 12. I was king of the air. I could have flown to Roseau, returned to Minneapolis, and still not have run out of gas.

The acquisition of the PA12 was the continuation of my love affair with flight. It brought me to a new world, a world of adventure, a world I'd only dreamed of.

Today, as I sit here these many years later and again contemplate these events, I would like to be flying. It's the one thing that bothers me about getting older. I'm not concerned about growing old, I don't even want to go back to yesterday. But man, I would like to have my love with me, that airplane. And people say, why not just fly? Well, I really can't do that. The airplanes that I had and the things they did for me were so great, that now it would be wrong to fly when I can't pass a physical. I'm going to fly illegally? It would be a shabby way to treat my love affair with airplanes.

I was to fly my PA12 a great deal, using it during our straw chopper testing program, which began in Texas and Oklahoma and then worked its way north with the harvest. I regularly flew to check on those machines.

One late November, I was returning from Montana. It was toward dusk, and as I flew west to east over North Dakota, I overtook a violent weather system. I pushed the stick forward, forcing the plane down. It was a heavy snowstorm, and I got low, because visibility was near zero.

Even from powerline height, the ground was a hazy mass, and navigating was guess-work. Snow fell hard and was whipped up by a heavy wind. Moreover, night was coming. Had it been day, I probably could have flown out of it. But continuing in the dark was not an option.

The power poles whipped by, and my plane tipped left and right. I had to get down and get down fast. According to my map, a strip was fairly near. If I could find it, I'd be safe. For five or 10 minutes, I saw nothing, and I began to fear I might have missed it, might have overshot it. If that were the case, I was in serious trouble. But soon, below me was the strip I'd been looking for, sitting there like heaven. I put the airplane down and, fortunately, the snow was loose enough so, even without skis, I didn't nose over or suffer any problems.

I tied the airplane down, and then somehow got a ride into town to a hotel, where I retired for the evening. Before going to sleep, I stared at the ceiling, contemplating the day's events and everything that was transpiring. Polaris was finally starting to go, and I had great hopes for the straw chopper. Suddenly, I thought I smelled smoke. I sniffed and sure enough, it was. Heavy smoke. I threw on some clothes, opened my door and stepped into the hallway. It was full of billowing smoke coming from a room that had its door partially open. I dashed inside and there, surrounded by empty, half-pint whiskey bottles, was a smoldering mattress. It looked ready to burst into flames.

What to do? I quickly got downstairs to the desk. I ran to the clerk.

"Hey, you better come with me. I think we've got a problem upstairs."

The guy ran with me and we went into the room, into the smoke. We threw open a window, each grabbed a side of the mattress and tossed it out into the snowstorm. A catastrophe was averted.

The next morning when I went down to check out, my bill was marked, Paid In Full.

And they say flying is dangerous?

୧୦ ୧୦ ୧୦

We acquired a number of planes through the company, but I always considered them my own. Some I fell in love with, some I didn't care for. That was the case with an old 65 horsepower Luscombe. It was a two-seater, side-by-side plane with no electrical equipment or radio. Though I didn't want it, ironically, the little plane would save my life.

It was late in the afternoon, and a line of thunderstorm squalls ran in front of me. As I stared into the swirling black clouds, there climbed a big thunderhead blocking my way. I quickly realized that if I were to circumnavigate this big one, it would take too long, and would put me too far off my flight path. If that happened, I wouldn't be able to find Roseau's small strip in the dark. Before runway lights or radio navigation, I was in a spot of trouble.

Perhaps I can fly under it, I thought. It seemed the only solution, and I began my descent. The plane tilted forward and I flew under the cloud. Suddenly, a huge waft of air grabbed me. That giant vacuum cleaner picked the Luscombe up. Up and up we went, caught in a massive thermal created by the thunderhead. We were riding the fastest express elevator in the world. My body shook as I pushed on the stick in an attempt to ride out the storm. The little Luscombe with the weak engine practically stood on its nose as I tried to fly out of it.

With turbulence shaking me hard, I had little time to think of anything but keeping the plane pointed to the earth. My shoulders and arms grew sore. I kept struggling, and a few seconds later (it seemed like an hour) I flew out from the clench of that thundercloud. I sighed heavily to have evaded the gigantic monster, and gave my little Luscombe a pat on the wing when I landed.

 familty familty familty

Yet my Luscombe was too small; I needed a new plane. I began searching and found a much larger one in Wisconsin. It was a 1947 four-seat Stinson with a 165 horsepower, six cylinder Franklin under the hood. The NC number was 9274K. It was a model 108-2.

I flew the Luscombe over to Wisconsin. The Stinson sat on the ramp as I touched down. It looked so eager to fly. It was almost wagging its tail like a faithful dog. I had to have it. The owner leaned against his plane, and I began to deal with the fellow. The negotiation was quick, perhaps because we both wanted a deal. When our business was finished, we shook hands and I owned a plane. I asked if we could go for a check ride to make sure I could fly it. I wanted to know where everything was, and if it had any strange quirks.

He shoved his hands in his pockets and shook his head. No way.

"We made a deal for the airplane, now take it and go," he said.

I was stunned; check rides were common. His attitude should have told me something. But once again, I looked at that plane. It begged me to become its owner. Left with only one option, I climbed in and began learning where the gauges and switches were. It was a strange setup, I even had to learn where the starter was. Eventually though, I taxied and lifted off toward the Twin Cities. According to its logs, the engine had been used a lot, and I decided I'd better fly straight to Flying Cloud Airport in Eden Prairie, Minnesota, to American Aviation, and have the engine looked at.

They checked it all right, and thank goodness! It had gotten there with four broken valve springs. Shouldn't have flown at all, they said. True, I hadn't been entirely pleased with its performance on the trip, but not knowing what that beautiful six-cylinder Franklin engine should sound like, I hadn't noticed it wasn't up to par. I decided to have the mechanics do a major overhaul. That took several days, but when I left with my perfect engine, I knew the difference. Wow. That plane was to be the nicest, best, greatest airplane I ever owned. The Stinson was my pride and joy. I flew it all over the United States, and it always protected me.

Even in business, I couldn't get away from the lure of the airplane, so intoxicating was it to me. By now you know that we had lots of products. So many, indeed, it grew to be somewhat of a joke. But when I let my love of airplanes get in the way of better business judgment, it was too much.

Throughout the '50s, I was flying. I flew just about everywhere as we worked to build our name. It was my escape; I think everyone should have an escape. But you shouldn't let your escape come into your business. Let me explain:

On a trip down to the Twin Cities, I stopped at a hangar, where a couple of guys were building airplane skis. I ambled over and chatted with the fellows. It turned out that they were struggling to keep the business afloat. Too bad, I thought, what a great product. They were a combination wheel and ski, and were called Fli-Lites. They were nice and good, and I wanted a pair. By having them, I could land on snow with the skis or land on a runway with the wheels.

When I excitedly asked what they cost, I was disappointed. I couldn't afford them. I couldn't spend that kind of money; neither could Polaris.

But perhaps, just perhaps, this little shop was a business Polaris might acquire. Perhaps we could get this whole little outfit and build the skis ourselves. Don't laugh, please don't laugh. I admit now, my interest was motivated by emotion, and that's usually not a good thing in business.

Being president of Polaris, I got my way, and it wasn't long before we acquired the Fli-Lite Corporation. We moved it to Roseau and, for a period of time we built aircraft skis. No, this did not help Polaris. We postponed several new ideas just to get ready to build skis. We had to get acquainted with the rules and regulations of making aircraft parts

My wife Ruby and my son Ron next to my Fairchild PT 26.

and components, testing them and getting certified, and we had to train our men. And yet, despite leaping into it blindfolded, I had high hopes for our new product.

There was logic behind my hopes. Airplane skis, until that time, had been heavy and cumbersome, and took away from the airplane's ability to haul payload. Our aluminum skis were extremely light and strong. Of course, as it turned out, they were like so many of our products – ahead of their time.

We sold few, mainly because we hadn't evaluated the market. We came to know, unfortunately, that even if we sold skis for every single plane in the snowbelt, we wouldn't have made much. You live in Roseau, you have snow, you think the whole world has it. We thought that of the snowmobile, too, but more people could use a snowmobile than airplane skis.

Though airplanes would serve our purposes at Polaris, allowing us to connect with the rest of the country, I really was a man for hire. On only the slightest pretense, you could get me up in a plane. Through the late '50s, I ferried aircraft to Alaska for a man name Charlie Hallock, a wiry Italian who was a Piper Aircraft dealer at the Anchorage field. I usually picked up planes from the Piper plant in Lockhaven, Pennsylvania.

"Edgar," Charlie said once. "I have a plane that needs to be picked up. It's a tri-gear, I hope you can fly it."

I'd have to go by commercial plane and then bring the Piper back. A tri-gear is an airplane with its wheels in a triangle, while the back of such a plane remains about five feet off the ground. Charlie was right, I'd never flown one, but it didn't matter. I was grateful to get in the air, and I agreed.

"OK, Edgar, now when you get that airplane, go into the parts depot, get the parts I've bought and load them into the airplane."

"How much will the plane carry? I asked.

"Quite a lot. If you can shut the door, it's OK."

I made it to Lockhaven and took possession of the plane. Moving back and forth from the parts depot, I then loaded it with paint, crankshafts, cylinder heads and other items.

"Don't you think you have enough stuff in that plane?" the parts man asked.

"Nope, not yet. Besides, if I can shut the door it will be OK."

He nodded and smirked but allowed me to continue.

Finally, I finished. I pushed the door and it shut. Great. I wiped my hands on my pants and climbed into the plane. I did a preflight of the instruments, fired up the engine and began to taxi. But within seconds, about 30 feet from where I started, the main gear on the airplane actually spread apart from the weight, and the tail, which had been bouncing in the air, smashed to the ground.

It was not supposed to do that. I sat in my seat, like an astronaut, staring up at the sky through a slowly rotating prop. I had a problem. I shut off the engine and managed to climb out. I lifted the tail, and moved the airplane forward until the gear snapped back into place. I shifted the cargo forward, some with me in the cockpit, and the tail stayed up. Now I'd be in good shape.

I got in and moved no more than 30 feet again, when the gears spread and the tail hit the ground. I stared up at the sky. I was beaten. I climbed out, got the tail back up where it was supposed to be and began to unload the plane. As I did, I came to realize a lot of people were standing on the ramp, and they were staring. They'd been watching all along. No doubt I looked like a bush pilot who thought he could ignore the laws of physics.

Despite the embarrassment, I had to carry the parts back to the depot. As I did, I noticed feet and legs around the airplane and around me. I never lifted my face high enough to see what the people looked like. I was too humiliated, too embarrassed. I never looked up when I returned to the plane, never looked out when I began to taxi out of there. Fortunately, the tail stayed up and I could make the trip to Anchorage.

❧ ❧ ❧

Flying was a release from a hectic life, but I think it did something else. Sure, the episode on the ramp at Lockhaven was humbling, but flying itself wasn't. It was an exuberant, wonderful feeling, and it gave me perspective. You look down and you know there are people all over, and they're not even big enough to see. It lets you know you're just a small part of it all.

You can have confidence in life and still be humble. You can have confidence and not be cocky. You can have confidence and not be boastful. Flying taught me what I hope is a degree of humility that has served me well in business and in life.

Chapter 7

GOODBYE, MY CHILD

For nearly 40 years, Edgar Hetteen's decision to leave Polaris in the spring of 1960 has been filled with rumor and head scratching. Why do it? Why leave a business that clearly was on the rise? Why leave a company he built with his own hands? The answer is not a simple one. Understand that Hetteen does what he does because it is fun, it is something he loves. By 1960, being at Polaris no longer was fun.

Yes, Polaris kept struggling to make ends meet, but the late '50s were exciting. It was a time, it seemed, when nobody missed a day. If you did, you probably missed something great. It seemed only a matter of time before Polaris shook the shackles of a small struggling company and blossomed. Of course, for that to happen, the snowmobile needed to lead the way. This much we knew.

We also knew things had to change. We simply could not continue year after year, selling a few models here and there, setting up a few dealers now and then, and still run around the country making sure the straw chopper didn't die. The pressure was intense, and I felt it daily from our board of directors. They seemed to hate the Sno-Traveler, and every year that went by without a breakthrough was another year they could shake their heads and say, "See? This isn't going anywhere. Why are we wasting money when we have so many other products to support?"

They were driving me crazy. I thought about it days and through sleepless nights. It was tough on my family, but I couldn't get it out of my head. I complained at the dinner table, and I complained in the car. Why couldn't the rest of the board see what David, Allan and I saw? We knew the snowmobile was the future, but it was hard to take the insults. It was tough to sit in a cafe and get winks and nods and points, and maybe some joker coming up to the table with his pals and teasing, "How's your snow machine?" Then laughing. I think David and Allan took it better than I, though it wasn't easy for any of us. It meant so much, but to some we were a joke. It was a lesson, a lesson to anyone struggling to achieve a dream. As long as it's in your heart, you need to focus on it, no matter what anyone might say.

Allan, David and I ran the ship. We were partners, but they let me make the decisions. I wore many hats. I worked in sales. I worked in the shop. I designed, I sold. I was in at 4 a.m., or leaving at 3 a.m. I devoted my life to Polaris.

But we had two men on our board of directors who by 1960 were making me miserable. They were not there by my choosing, but because those Roseau businessmen who lent us $40,000 wanted to keep an eye on us. What could we do, owing them all that money, but agree?

So we were three, and they were two. They were two too many. Despite what probably were good intentions, they didn't seem to understand manufacturing, didn't seem to understand things take time and money to develop, and more time and money to market. They were accustomed to retail business, where you sell a product, and then order more.

In the years following the deal, the board and I had our ups and downs. We were a mismatch from the beginning, but I must admit that I learned from those two men. They contributed to my knowledge. They taught me to do my homework before presenting an idea. After a few meetings of getting stumped by them, I wanted it never to happen again.

However, such a relationship could not exist indefinitely, and things were bound to come to a head. In 1960, it happened. I'd recently proposed the trip across Alaska, not only to test the machines but to generate regional and national attention. The snowmobile had a long way to go, and I knew national publicity could push us over the hill we constantly were climbing. But the biggest hurdles, as always, were those board members. It looked to me like they just knew the snowmobile would never make any money, and that they just knew it would destroy the company. When they saw me testing the machines, kicking up snow and making noise, they cringed, and seemed ashamed. They wanted me in a suit, sitting at my desk, making calls, selling choppers, being respectable. They wanted me to be everything I wasn't.

They didn't understand me. I was a maverick, a guy who wouldn't conform. They always wondered, "What the hell is Edgar thinking?" They never knew what I was going to do next, and, I suspect, they hated that. They seemed to struggle with the fact that I wanted to make calculated risks for possible great rewards. They, on the other hand, wanted to sit nice and safe, without risk.

The Alaska trip was the last straw for all of us. I wanted to spend $3,000, which we admittedly didn't have. The trip, they said, was the biggest folly, the most tremendously stupid thing I could do.

Of course, I went; and you know the results. It was a great success. The Fairbanks Daily News extensively covered our 21-day odyssey. The news was picked up by the Associated Press and United Press International. Later, the Minneapolis newspaper published the account, as did the Fargo Forum and papers around the country. Polaris was flooded with phone calls about the Sno-Traveler. The trip pushed snowmobiling ahead at least five years.

Amazingly, after all this attention, the board members with whom I'd battled came to my shambly office. They paced.

"You do something like that to sell snowmobiles?" they asked. "You think that is going to help? This is so crazy, Edgar."

"You fellows don't understand," I said, trying to keep calm.

As we argued however, I grew angry. I don't remember the whole meeting, but everything said certainly implied I wasn't doing a very good job.

Soon after that, I decided to leave Polaris. Even after our success in Alaska, things hadn't changed. If anything, they'd gotten worse. The pressure of a decade had reached its boiling point. It was time to get out.

But why? Why after 15 years of struggles, disappointments and triumphs would I leave the company, a company spawned in my heart and by my hands? Why not fight it out?

I'll tell you why. Though we had other products, making the trip across Alaska had reinforced in my mind that the snowmobile was here to stay, and that it would become a popular machine.

But when I discovered my board was up in arms because of this trip and indicating that I was incompetent, it was too discouraging. I'd gone through 15 years of creating an enterprise in my little town of Roseau, taking on the public and financial institutions, taking on everything. I didn't mind those kinds of battles. But to have division within my own ranks was one thing I couldn't cope with. When I realized the trip had done nothing to change the board's position, I decided to take the initiative.

Because of Alaska, people knew what Polaris was, and at least some found us exciting. In addition to customer calls, I received calls from companies interested in buying us out. Wow. It wasn't just David, Allan and me being crazy. I was in prime position to drive my point home to the board and to leave Polaris with dignity. In May of 1960, I hopped in my car and went to Minneapolis to track down those companies interested in Polaris. I needed ammunition, and in the Twin Cities the future would be forged.

I wound up at the Superior Separator Company in Minneapolis. I met with its president, Mr. C.F. Pierson, and we discussed the snowmobile. He was fascinated by the possibilities our machines presented, and it wasn't long before we came to an agreement. We scribbled it on a piece of paper. For $150,000, Superior Separator Company would buy the rights to build Polaris snowmobiles. Polaris would keep its name and build whatever else it wanted. The deal would give us operating capital, something we'd never had before, and it also would provide a royalty for snowmobiles sold. It was a memorandum of agreement be-tween Pierson and me, signed as the presidents of our two companies and subject to ratification by our boards of directors.

This was good news, but my trip to Minneapolis wasn't finished. Over those few days in May, I also made a deal with Minneapolis Moline to buy the snowmobile line. Moline, you recall, worked with us on straw choppers but was excited by the snowmobile as well. A day later, I lined up another company called H.R. Block. They, too, were willing to go six figures for rights to the Sno-Traveler.

I'd found businessmen who believed the snowmobile was viable, that it was worth money, just as I'd always argued. Here was proof that all of our research and development and expense had been worth it. With the future of Polaris in my briefcase, I returned to Roseau knowing one thing for certain: I would not be there beyond June of 1960.

I first talked to my brother and then to David, and then I called the other members of the board. I said we would have a special meeting the next evening in my office. There, I sat at my desk, and they pulled up chairs in a semi-circle. I leaned back and took a deep breath.

"For a long time now, people have laughed at that snowmobile," I said. "You have told me it is not dignified for the president of Polaris to ride the stupid machine. You have made fun of it. You have mocked me because of it. But I can tell you one thing right now: It is here to stay."

From my briefcase I removed the documents that guaranteed the sale of Polaris. I laid them on the table.

"Here are three companies, three successful companies, that think the snowmobile has a great future," I said.

Anger and sadness mixed in my voice.

"You've always said this machine we've monkeyed with has no value, criticized my trip to Alaska and my promotional work, criticized it all," I continued. "But take a look. Here is what people will pay for that stupid machine, the one we could never capitalize, the one we could never support, the one that caused all the problems. You can have all this money and the company just the way you want it. Do whatever, but come June 1, I will be gone."

MEMORANDUM OF UNDERSTANDING BETWEEN SUPERIOR
SEPARATOR COMPANY OF HOPKINS, MINNESOTA, AND
POLARIS INDUSTRIES OF ROSEAU, MINNESOTA

This memorandum of understanding outlines the basis of agreement between
Mr. Edgar Hetteen and Mr. C. F. Pierson, presidents of their respective companies.

This memorandum of understanding is subject to approval of the boards of
directors of the respective companies and subject to being reduced to appro-
priate contract by counsel.

Mr. Hetteen has developed an over-the-snow vehicle and proposes to turn over
to Superior Separator Company the following:

> All literature, price lists, engineering drawings, motion
> picture films, pictures, stories, inventory, exclusive
> world-wide manufacturing and sales rights, a no-competition
> agreement between him, major stockholders of Polaris, and
> Superior, patents and patent applications, all modifications,
> new models or changes on said over-the-snow vehicle.

As a consideration, Superior Separator Company agrees to the following:

> 1. A one percent (1%) sales over-ride on all business
> secured by Mr. Hetteen in Alaska, or from the military,
> payable to Mr. Hetteen personally.
>
> 2. An agreement to buy all new, unused, and applicable
> snow-traveler inventory at cost.
>
> 3. A royalty based on the following schedule and based on
> the lowest net manufacturer's selling price:

First 3,000 machines	7%
Next 3,000 machines	5%
Next 4,000 machines	4%
After 10,000 machines	3%

Mr. Hetteen has agreed to secure and turn over to Superior initial orders which
he estimates will amount to approximately 600 to 800 machines. Superior agrees
to advance fifty percent (50%) of the royalty that will be due against such bona
fide orders at the time the orders are received by Superior.

Dated_May 6, '60_

Edgar Hetteen

C F Pierson

**Here is the original memorandum between Superior Separator
Company of Hopkins, Minnesota and Polaris to sell the snowmobile line.**

The mood was tense and silent. They recognized I was past the point of no return. They could read it in my stony face.

The board members who hated the snowmobile slowly picked up the documents. Their eyeballs grew and blinked fast, seemingly baffled. Reality had confused their long-held view of me. Words were few, but what were they supposed to say? In just a few minutes, they'd been proven wrong.

The only action taken that night was to name Allan president pro tem, which temporarily made him the head of Polaris. I guess in the back of their minds, they didn't think I was serious, but of course I was dead serious. I'd learned that as long as your troops march with you, you can take on the world. But when some march sideways or backwards, you just can't do it. Or at least, I couldn't.

Eventually, those two board members would realize the Sno-Traveler's potential. "Hey," they decided later, "we can't sell the ENTIRE snowmobile line. It's got value. We'll just drop those other things Edgar was working on."

They never gave up the snowmobile, and in 1995, sales topped $1 billion. Through the years, Polaris has sold thousands and thousands of sleds. The board came to the right decision. However, by the time they did, I was long gone. I left Roseau on June 2, 1960, the day after my daughter, Nancy, graduated from high school.

As I look back, I do not do it with regret or say I shouldn't have been that impetuous. I have my convictions, I believe in them, I follow them. I left Polaris a winner, because my Alaskan trip helped put together the deals to sell the snowmobile line. My point was proven, and I left satisfied. David and Allan would now have to deal with the board. My family and I were as good as gone.

I jumped in my old Stinson, which I purchased from Polaris, and flew to Fairbanks, where I found us a little place to live. I returned commercially to pick up my family. We bought a travel trailer and began the 10-day trip to Fairbanks. On the storied Alaskan Highway, we drove through the dust and gravel, up mountains and teetered on cliffs.

Finally, we arrived and began the long process of unpacking. I also began the process of getting back into business. I wasn't in Alaska on a whim. I had a plan, a good one I thought, and Steve Rugland was going to join me. We planned to set up a representative organization, and before Steve arrived, I started things moving. I became a factory representative for many things – outboard motors, aircraft batteries and front-end loaders, to name a few.

I tried, I tell you, I tried. For a month, maybe two, I tried. Yet I discovered in my heart I just couldn't run around and sell aircraft batteries and outboard motors. It wasn't me, and I couldn't drag Steve into it. I called and said, "Steve, stay at Polaris."

So OK, those plans failed. I was at a loss. I didn't quite know what to do, but then I talked to Rudy Billberg. A few months earlier, while chugging across Alaska, we'd stopped in Ruby, in the interior, and stayed at a hotel owned by a widow. She was a fascinating lady, living all alone in the middle of nowhere. Her husband had been prospecting for gold and had brought in bulldozers, core drills, portable welding machines and all kinds of mining stuff. He'd done all the prospecting and core drilling – the hard work – but died before getting out much gold. To keep her husband's claim, the woman had to work it every year or lose it. She'd hired a bunch of men, but she just knew they were stealing her gold. She made us an offer. For $5,000, she would sell us everything, and we would have a gold mine.

As Rudy and I discussed this over the phone, we grew excited. Rudy had recently panned for gold along the Yukon, and I believe he had the bug, as did so many. But we weren't crazy. We didn't want to buy the mine without first looking it over. And yet, how would we do that? Though we both had airplanes, the mine was in a place you could get to only by helicopter. We had no helicopter, and renting one would cost $1,500.

I met Rudy at the Westward Hotel in Anchorage, the same place in which I stayed the night before leaving on the great Alaskan journey. I found my friend in one of the rooms. Another guy was there, too, but Rudy failed to introduce him.

"Hey, Edgar, sit down," Rudy said with a big grin.

I looked past Rudy to this older fellow. He had gray hair, a beard and a nice suit. For all I knew, he was the carry-out boy at the local grocery store. But anyway, Rudy and I started talking about the gold mine, saying we ought to take a look at it.

The stranger's eyes bored in on us.

"Fellows, you should do that," he said.

By now I knew his name was J.C. Morris, but I still didn't know who J.C. Morris was, or where he came from. But here he was, giving us advice.

We don't have the money to hire a helicopter, we said.

"I'll pay the $1,500, I'll give you the $1,500."

Jeepers, I thought, what a bag of wind. Then he pulled his checkbook from a pocket and began writing a check. He handed it to Rudy.

"You guys go and take a look at that mine," he said. "If you're interested in buying it, why don't we have a three-way partnership? I have a corporation that isn't being used, and we can make it cover us."

That made sense, but I still thought he might be a con artist or at the very least a big talker.

"I'd put in $250,000, a quarter of a million in that gold mine," he continued. "We'd own it three ways."

At this point, I knew the guy was absolutely lying, because why would he do that? He didn't know me, and I didn't know how well he knew Rudy. A quarter of a million? It seemed preposterous.

Yet the man continued.

"If you or Rudy use your own airplanes with this mine, I want to make sure you have insurance on them," he said.

Now that made sense, and I began to think maybe he wasn't such a blowhard. A guy trying to impress wouldn't be worried about being sued for liability.

I finally had to ask the question that hung in the air.

"Just who the heck are you?"

Rudy and the man grinned at each other.

J.C. turned out to be Rudy's brother in law. He originally was from Bemidji, Minnesota, and as a young man went up to Alaska, where he was a section hand on the railroad. He became fabulously wealthy by buying land and then reselling it.

The conversation concluded with an agreement that Rudy and I would go look at that gold mine. Days passed, however, and we never went. We canceled the plan because we knew how that mine would work. All summer long we would dig in the dirt and pile it up. In the spring, when the snow melted in the mountains and the water ran down, it would go through our sluice boxes and the gold would wash out. But it wasn't the thing for us. It would be our luck that it wouldn't snow the next winter and that we wouldn't have any water. We never spent the $1,500, and J.C. got his check back.

Maybe we can look back and say it was a missed opportunity. Maybe. It certainly was an opportunity, but had I done it, a lot of things would not have happened.

Still in Alaska and desperate for work, I answered a series of blind ads in the newspaper. One of them was to sell encyclopedias. That's right, selling encyclopedias door to door. The representative for all of Alaska met me in a hotel room and pitched me the scheme. A vast majority of the population of Alaska were people leaving the military, and the man said it would be a good deal for me. Those military folks would practically beg to buy the books for their growing families, he said.

"I don't know if I can sell encyclopedias," I said, shaking my head.

"I'll tell you what we'll do," the guy said. "We'll go out to the Air Force base and we'll make a few calls. Just see if you like it. You owe yourself that much."

"OK, I'll go along."

We went out to the living quarters of the base, and we knocked on a few doors. We found a little corporal at home with his young wife and six-month old baby boy. The encyclopedia salesman gave the guy his canned spiel and, before I knew it, the corporal was signing a document to buy $600 worth to educate his young son. The books would be obsolete by the time the kid could even walk, so I said, "I don't want to do this." I couldn't be that type of salesman.

I continued to search for something I could do, something that would make me happy. I went to school for a weekend to learn how to sell stock market funds. But like the encyclopedia, I just could not sell a piece of paper. It wasn't me; not after years of building and selling machines.

I kept trying to find employment. I answered an advertisement to be a private detective but didn't take the job. I could just see myself getting hired by some guy thinking his wife was stepping out on him, then getting shot by an irate boyfriend or husband.

I worked as a mechanic at an airstrip, but that didn't seem to be my calling either.

I tried many things to fit into the world's structure, all of them failures. I had left behind the only thing I had ever known, and now I was floundering. My family was supportive, but I grew discouraged and a little depressed. I'd come to Alaska as part of a plan, and now I was going nowhere. I had mouths to feed, but little money.

Walking down Fourth Avenue in Fairbanks, I saw a sign in front of the Alaska State Employment Agency – Aptitude Test Given. It rang a bell with me, because I thought what I'd done in life was not right. I should be in some other occupation. And here was an aptitude test that would tell me what I was good for. I walked in and made an appointment to take the test the next day. I practically skipped home.

I arrived early the next morning, very excited. They put me in a room, gave me a pencil, and I began. It took most of the day, but that didn't matter. Finally, I would find out about myself. Life would be much easier when I did the things I was qualified for – whatever they were.

Early the next day, I returned for the results. I waltzed in and stepped up to the counter, where a young woman in her 20s was filing papers.

"Name's Edgar Hetteen. I took the aptitude test yesterday and would like the results."

She looked down at what I assumed were the test results, and paused. She looked at me and her eyes glazed over. She hemmed and she hawed.

"Please excuse me," she said, and quickly took off for an office across the room. She knocked on the door and disappeared. I waited.

A man in a suit came out of that office and tentatively approached. I asked for the results, and he hemmed and hawed, too, said I would have to see the manager. So again I waited. And waited. Finally, another man came and asked me to his office. He motioned for me to sit down in the wooden chair in front of his desk, and he climbed into the soft one behind it.

"Mr. Hetteen," the man said. He, too, paused. "I'm sorry to have to tell you this. But we can't find that you're qualified for anything. You have no particular qualifications. I don't think this has happened before."

The results were so bad, the little gal hadn't wanted to give them to me. Without much more to say, I got up and left. I walked the streets. Though I now find it amusing, this was a devastating blow. I'd counted on that test to answer all my problems.

I let that bother me a long, long time. The months passed, and I scraped up enough work to get by. But eventually, I could no longer continue with that kind of life. I needed out.

In December of 1960, it happened that I had a choice between two very different futures. One of them was to return to Minnesota and build another snowmobile. At least I'd proven I could do that, regardless of the aptitude test.

I sat down at a table in our little house and began to write an important letter. It was addressed to L.B. Hartz of Thief River Falls, Minnesota. Hartz, a civic-minded man, owned about 400 grocery stores in Minnesota, North Dakota and South Dakota.

I wrote him for good reason. A year earlier, Mr. Hartz, accompanied by a group of Thief River businessmen, had arrived in Roseau. On a chilly spring evening, they came in two carloads and piled out to greet me in the plant. We shook hands and sat down to discuss the future. They had a plan for me and my company, and it didn't involve remaining in Roseau.

The men, who included Lowell Swenson, a name you'll come to know, had heard of my troubles at Polaris. They thought they had a solution. If I would move the company to Thief River Falls, they would back me with cash. With controlling stock, I could have done it. I could have forced the other board members and likely convinced David and Allan to move, though they might not have liked it. I could have done it. But finally, I told those men from Thief River, "No." In the end it was loyalty, perhaps misplaced, to Roseau. Though they often laughed at me, I couldn't take employment away from the residents of my home town.

But in the winter of 1960, I again thought of those fellows from Thief River. I thought of L.B. Hartz. I thought of the factory he'd talked about, an old seed building for rent by the river. It might be perfect.

A week later, L.B. Hartz responded. Yes, the building was still for rent, and yes, the cash backing might still be available; he would check on it. For the first time in months, I grew excited. I decided I would leave Alaska.

But remember, I still was considering a different path for my life.

I'd met a fellow named Joe, and we had an idea. Anchorage was fast becoming the crossroads of the world. Airliners came in from everywhere. And when they landed, they had about 120 people on board, but there was no catering service. So we planned to sell breakfasts – scrambled eggs and toast – for $3 a piece, or $360 a flight. We'd buy an old restaurant by the airport, cook there, and cart it over piping hot. In addition, we figured we should contract to do all the baggage handling, so each airline wouldn't need their own trucks and crew, who often just stood around waiting for flights.

Of all the ideas I had in Alaska, this one made the most sense. None of my other schemes had offered any real future. How far could I go selling encyclopedias? What were the chances for advancement as a private eye?

"I'm going back outside," I told Joe. "I'll stop by Los Angeles, maybe San Francisco, and I'll check out Minneapolis. I'll see how they do this. If it's viable, we might be in business."

I had no commitment to Thief River Falls, or to the snowmobile, and I really did consider teaming up with Joe. But driving out on that gravel highway down to Canada, I had time to reflect. The snowmobile, though it wasn't that big yet, was romantic and exciting. At Polaris, my horizons had been limitless. Nothing in Alaska, not even the airport plans, could compete with my past.

Therefore, in the car, I turned to my wife and declared I again would build snowmobiles. Admittedly, the catering and baggage handling did not get a fair hearing; because I was conditioned to the excitement of my former world. That world had once beaten me down, but it now looked very appealing. I had to give it one more shot.

Thief River would be my new home. I was 40, and it was time to do what I was best at.

Chapter 8

TRY, TRY AGAIN

Edgar Hetteen was like so many of us, and yet unlike any of us. In moving to Alaska, he began questioning himself, began to doubt his own abilities. In leaving Polaris, he had proven he was right about the snowmobile. But to come to a dead end in Alaska was a terrific blow, like that of a bludgeon. Quitting, however, has little to do with Edgar Hetteen.

He had struck gold once in the snowmobile business. The answer to his failure in Alaska was simple. He simply would have to strike it again.

I left Alaska with no job and no prospects, other than the wish to again build snowmobiles. True, I had a building, but no detailed plans of how to capture my dream. It was a difficult time because no one likes to fail. And yet, losing and winning usually go hand in hand. It was time to move on, to win again. So, during the Christmas season of 1960, we bundled up our boxes and bags, tossed them into the camper trailer, and headed down the Alaskan Highway. We went through hairpin turns, and we drove through snow that swirled in the wind and hindered our view. As we drove, I wondered what would happen in the next few months, and if I'd be able to feed my family. There were no certainties.

It was 10 days back to Minnesota. We drove into Thief River Falls and found a cheap hotel. Then I went to find L.B. Hartz.

Just being in town made my heart swell. It would be the perfect place to build a second snowmobile company. I was so eager to begin.

This is the building where I began Polar (Arctic). I lived up-stairs with my family for 14 months.

And yet, as always, there would be sacrifice. In business, in success, there must be. You might have a dream, but if you're not willing to dedicate yourself to it, you might as well not bother.

In other words, what I'd done at Polaris no longer mattered; I had to build from the ground up. Maybe there were better ways than how I did it, but my way worked.

It worked partly because I chose Thief River Falls. I'd called around to other cities but always came back to Thief River. I found there what I hadn't in Roseau – I found people with an understanding of industry, and that was the biggest thing of all.

I tracked down Mr. Hartz, who took me to his property. The old seed building was situated directly on the Thief River, and I liked that. There, I could test my future snow machines. Mr. Hartz and I made a deal by which I would pay him monthly, and he handed me the keys.

The building was an ugly, 30'x70', concrete thing that had just been sitting empty. Standing on an overhanging ledge were huge letters: Math Barzen Co., and they would remain for at least a year. I slipped the key into a rusty lock. The door squeaked as I shoved it open. I stepped through the dark, and a cobweb hit my face. I floundered for a light switch, found it, then lit the place. It was disheartening. It was a mess of grease, dirt and seed bags, and I had a moment of doubt. Could I turn this abandoned building into a functioning factory before I went broke? Could I clean out the seed bags, throw out the boxes and make it shipshape?

Well, within a matter of hours, I was at work, cleaning and throwing out boxes. I spent days tossing out debris and making plans for the future. Dirt and grime filled the wrinkles of my hands, and my face was a dusty mess.

With no discretionary money, all of it going into the business, my family – me, Ruby, and our four-year-old son, Ron – moved into the seed building. Nancy, recently graduated, had stayed in Alaska, and Patty was already married. We moved upstairs, where there were two rooms. I put up a divider and made them three, then added a stove in the smallest one. They were cramped quarters, but we lived between those concrete walls for 14 months.

It was something we had to do for the business. I had to sacrifice and, many times, my family had to as well. So often, it is the family that ultimately pays the big price for such endeavors. As I look back, I regret that my family had to pay an exorbitant price for my drive. But I always had a good family who would do those things, who would live in a bricked warehouse.

But let's get one thing clear. I didn't put my family through all of that because I had a big ego, or because I wanted to show Polaris up, or prove to Roseau what I could do. I didn't really care what they thought. My actions have always said so. This is me, take it or leave it. Yet admittedly, for whatever reason, I was driven.

So we now have the very humble beginnings of what would become Arctic Enterprises, though I initially called it Polar Manufacturing, a take-off on Polaris. I used that for the first year, but after a while, the name became too confining and too confusing. I planned to build a variety of products, so we needed something expansive. We came up with Arctic, because it was descriptive of both our product and our location. We settled on Enterprises because under that umbrella, we could do whatever we wanted. It was a heck of a lot better than calling it Edgar's Garage.

I still needed money. Fortunately, I was in Thief River Falls. L.B. Hartz lined up those men who many months earlier had wooed me at Polaris. Ten of them went to the bank and co-signed a note, each guaranteeing the repayment of a thousand dollars.

But it wasn't enough. If I wanted to build snowmobiles, I needed more. Scrambling, I borrowed whatever I could on my insurance policy, then sold the small stock I had left in Polaris.

It was a good start, but I knew reality. A little more than $10,000 wasn't much for a new business. Before I could even think of building snowmobiles, I needed cash flow. I had to have patience with my dream.

※ ※ ※

Before leaving Alaska, I'd gone to see Burt Johnson, a good friend of mine who owned a surplus store. He had a junk pile out back. In the debris, I spotted something that looked like a printing machine.

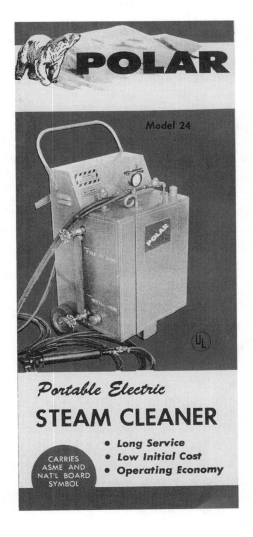

Our first product at Polar (Arctic Cat) was this model 24 portable electric steam cleaner. This is the cover of the brochure.

"Burt, can I have this?" I asked, lugging it inside.

"Sure, take it. It's not worth much."

It turned out to be a stencil machine. In a practical sense, it was a printing press, even had an electric motor. I threw it in the back of our trailer, and it became Arctic's printer. It was my first piece of equipment, though it is not my advice for those beginning in business to first get a printer from a junkyard.

With part of my $10,000, I bought shop equipment and some office furniture – a drawing board for me. I then contemplated my next step. I didn't have enough to build snowmobiles. Finally, I settled on something I'd designed at Polaris – an electric steam cleaner that cleaned with a jet of hot steam. We had built only prototypes in Roseau, but I thought they had promise. I was confident that they would raise enough cash so I could again build my motor toboggans.

With the family upstairs and me on the factory floor, I built the first few steam cleaners. A few employees then came on and we started to market them. Unfortunately, despite my high hopes, it turned out they were extremely hard to sell. I had a man pushing them from Minnesota to Nebraska to Texas, but sales never grew beyond mediocre. Strange, because once sold, people couldn't get along without them. If one broke, the customers were beside themselves until it was fixed. If it ran out of its special soap, which we packaged, they couldn't wait to buy more.

Over months of hard effort, we sold them to hotels, typewriter shops, marine shops and grocery stores. Because they worked so well, I wanted to stick with the machines but, ultimately, I said to heck with the steam cleaner. If I put the same amount of time and effort into other things, I decided, I'd get much better return on our efforts. To give a product a good try is determination; to keep plugging away when it just isn't selling, that is stubbornness.

We spent the first year digging for funds. We built anything that would sell, whatever would put a little money into our operation. It was a struggle, and once again, meeting Friday's payroll was the biggest thing in my life. Sometimes, thankfully, providence smiled on me.

Once, while I was in the shop tinkering and worrying about money, in walked two men. It was 1962. I wiped a dirty hand on my pant leg and shook their hands. One guy introduced himself as being Allen Eide from Grand Forks.

"I'm selling this thing that, for lack of a better term, is an insect light," Eide said.

The employees standing nearby looked at each other and scrunched up their faces. A bug light? But I politely nodded to Eide, and he continued to describe this crazy invention. It was a circular neon tube, he said, with a black light and a fan stuck inside. Air was drawn toward the light, then diverted downward into a perforated plastic bag that let the air out. The black light attracted night flying insects such as mosquitoes. As they got close to the light, to the center of it, they were sucked in by the fan, blown into the bag, and captured. It really did work.

Eide had been buying the units from another firm and acting as a distributor across the United States. Recently, he said, he'd lost his supplier and was looking for someone to build them. Needing the business, I said, "Sure."

Over the next week, I designed my own version and called it the Bug-O-Vac. I built those for Allen, and he sent a couple men on the road. Long before snowmobiles defined Arctic Enterprises as a place devoted to winter recreation, the company in Thief River Falls built little machines that caught bugs.

The Bug-O-Vacs sold well, and our production increased to 400 units a day. We sold many to local hardware stores. But in spite of everything Allen could do to promote the Bug-O-Vac, the market gradually deteriorated. People quit buying; it had been a fad. I'd walk down main street and see dusty Bug-O-Vacs sitting in store windows, but fortunately, we'd made enough money. After six months, Polar Manufacturing had done $70,000 in sales with a $14,000 profit. We had cash flow.

And if I could sell the several dozen Bug-O-Vacs remaining before I built my first snowmobile, the extra money would help a lot. With that in mind, I called Burt Johnson up in Anchorage.

This was the first Arctic Cat. It was originally billed as the Polar 500 but became the 450 Arctic Cat.

"Burt," I said, "I've got these fantastic lights that attract insects. About 50. Do you want to buy them?"

"Sure, Edgar, I'll take 'em," he said quickly. In the surplus business, he could get rid of the Bug-O-Vacs.

I shipped them, and it was a week later that Burt called back.

"Edgar," he said, "you son of a gun. Those lights..."

"Yeah, Burt, they're nice, aren't they?"

"You know it doesn't get dark in Alaska," he said. "How is that light supposed to attract anything when it doesn't get dark?"

⅋ ⅋ ⅋

I'd waited nearly a year, an incredibly long year filled with sleepless nights thinking of this day, the day I could begin the rest of my life. Building steam cleaners and Bug-O-Vacs hadn't been that rewarding. It was time to dig up all the drawings and gather all my thoughts and turn out a prototype snowmobile.

A few weeks later on a business trip, I found myself in Chicago, at a little hotel outside Midway Airport. I knew then that I would start on the snowmobile in a week or two. "But Edgar," I thought to myself, "what the hell are they going to look like?" I wasn't sure, though I certainly wanted them different than those at Polaris.

I sat at a little desk and sketched. I thought of what the snowmobile was and what it would become. In those days, Polaris had long wooden skis reaching way back to the end of their machine. The operator rode on those skis, while the engine and track floated between the runners. My brain whirled and my pen zipped over the page. I got rid of the runners and put short skis forward. Even though my engine was still behind the driver, I'd developed a completely different concept and look.

I returned from Chicago, and we began building the first machine. I haven't yet mentioned the employees at Arctic, but they were important. Bob Johnson, my wife's brother, and his wife, Mary, both worked for me at Polaris and were my first employees at Polar. Mary ran the office, and Bob was a welder. I still can see him out there, welding smock on, leaning over the metal and that intense blue flame. Dave Erickson, a brilliant mechanic, came down from Polaris, as did Steve Rugland to do the sales work.

It was like those early days in Roseau, with all the camaraderie as we tossed ideas back and forth and built that thing. We stayed late and came early. We watched it take shape under the flame of a welder and the wrench of a mechanic.

I'd made up my mind that the snowmobile should be an all-season vehicle, so it could run in the summer as well as winter. It sure would be easier to sell if it had 12 months of service rather than three or four. We built it with heavy, cleated tracks that would dig into grass and dirt. We built it with skis each equipped with a rubber tire. We powered it with a ten-horsepower Kohler 4-cycle engine driving through a gearbox with forward, neutral, and reverse. It weighed around 600 pounds. Finally, after a few weeks, we'd finished a prototype.

In December 1961, we came out with the Polar 500, an all-season, all-terrain vehicle we advertised for $1,210. We planned to sell to utility and oil companies, hunters, or whoever needed to get into the back country. We had high hopes, but it didn't work all that well. We built only 20, and sold even fewer.

The track mechanism was not the kind that lent itself to the bare ground. It just couldn't stand the constant pounding of rocks and dirt. We gave up my dream of building an all-season machine and turned our attention to winter. The 500 would become the 450, which was followed by the 200 and the 250. They were similar in design, but smaller, and made exclusively for the snow.

We were proud of our machines. They would blaze a trail in the industry, but in 1962, boy, were they cause for ridicule. Because by then, the snowmobile, Polaris' snowmobile, was gaining acceptance. People just knew a snowmobile had to be built the way they did it in Roseau. They just knew my design would cause the machine to dig holes like a gopher. They just knew I was a lunatic.

This is a lesson to learn. Whenever you do something different than your peers, you're going to face ridicule. You must be ready for it and not let it bother you. You have to bull ahead and do what you know is

Here was the flyer on the first snowmobile we put out at Polar Manufacturing (Arctic Cat).

right. If you can't accept that, then you might as well go buy yourself a shoe store. I was not prepared for ridicule when I first went into business. I let it get to me. It was one of the reasons that some of my early inventions weren't developed. I couldn't take the insults, and I let others affect my thinking. But by the time Arctic rolled around, I was ready for it.

I knew what we had, and with the 450, we lowered our heads and marched on. Slowly, people grew to accept that Arctic knew what it was doing. We built the 450 for years – that rear engine, side-by-side seating, large machine. It wasn't fast, but it could pull a tremendously heavy load. The naysayers were proven wrong.

We made progress because we were stubborn, but also because we found the financial world of Thief River completely different from that of Roseau. It was much more open. I was treated differently, and I learned something I believe is true: You should never try to be a prophet in your home town, because you won't be accepted. You will be laughed at. Though I'd moved only 65 miles away from home, I had some credibility. Respect came more easily, even if I didn't deserve it. Things I did at Arctic, arbitrary things, would take on sacred status.

As an example, years later in Sweden, I met a young engineer working to design a snowmobile. His name was Ole Carlson, and he wanted to do everything just right. I walked into his shop, looked at what he was doing, and noticed he was putting on a plastic slide rail.

I peered over him, and I scratched my beard. His head was pointed downward, blond hair tousled.

"Ole, why is that slide rail an inch and a quarter wide?" I asked.

"That's the way they're supposed to be," he said. "At Arctic and Polaris and at all the other companies, slide rails are an inch and a quarter. That's the way it is, Edgar. You should know that."

Well, I did know that. I also knew how that sacred dimension came to be. On the 450s and the 500s and the other early sleds, we used wooden slide rails treated with wax oil. We boiled the wood in oil graphite and cut the strips two inches wide. It was quite a project, and there just had to be a better way. One solution was to have them made of plastic.

Thinking about this, I called a plastic manufacturer. They sent a representative to Thief River Falls, and we met at Tilly's Cafe, a quaint, little restaurant that has since closed.

We sat at a booth and sipped our coffee. I don't remember much of the conversation, but we talked about slide rails and, eventually, got down to business.

"Edgar," he said, "what dimension should the rail be?"

I had no idea. I hadn't done any tests to suggest one size would be better than any other. I grabbed a table napkin, pulled out a blue pen, and started sketching. I planned to fasten the plastic to the frame by using a square, three-quarter inch tube. I sketched the tube, then I sketched a half-inch of plastic to the bottom that would act as the sliding surface to the track. I added quarter inch wide lips on each side of this to extend upward on the tube and become a guide for side loads on the track. Thus, the inch-and-a-quarter width of the plastic was born. I handed the napkin to the man, and he eventually built it.

It was designed as quickly as I drew it – in about a minute. Yet the whole world has accepted it as an absolutely sacred dimension. The upshot of this is that sometimes you have to debunk what people take to be sacred. Just because the competition is doing something, that doesn't mean you have to. The point is to be better, not the same. For all I know, the slide rail really works well at two inches, or maybe it works really well at three quarters of an inch. Who knows? Nobody's done any major research because it's a sacred dimension designed at Tilly's Cafe.

Those first years were a frantic time. We built a bunch of different models, all rear-engine machines, like the 450. They were fine machines, but I had an idea for an even greater breakthrough. I thought a market existed for a light snowmobile with the engine mounted in front. Throughout 1962, David Erickson and I worked on the model. The winter stretched into summer and summer into fall. As the snow hit the ground, we nearly were finished.

Once, my family asleep, I was down in the shop, kneeling and covered in grease, putting the engine into that light little thing. As I finished, I wiped my brow with a dirty hand and knelt near the back of the machine to add the hitch. Just then, in walked Pete Wass. The door was always open, even late at night.

Pete, a sturdy man with solid forearms, was a superintendent in one of the mines on the Iron Range, and he was a great guy. As our dealer in Grand Rapids, Minnesota, he sold sleds out of his garage.

Before he said, "Hello," or anything else, he watched what I was doing. He stuffed his hands in his pockets and pursed his lips.

"Edgar," he said, the words punching out like a gun, "you're putting that hitch on the wrong end."

Very funny. The implication was that the snowmobile would never pull anything, and that indeed, it would have to be pulled. Coming from Pete, however, it was perfectly acceptable conversation. I respected him. Yet in spite of Pete's opinion, the Model 100 turned into a great success, and the line grew to include many models.

Pete and I became quite good friends, as I did with many dealers. When he had a problem, which happened often in those days, I'd drive to Grand Rapids. We'd sit at his kitchen table the better part of the night, drinking coffee and eating fresh biscuits. Snowmobilers like nothing better than having good conversations, especially if it's about snowmobiles. Years later, when I finally left the business, it would be nights like the ones at Pete Wass' kitchen table that I missed most.

Whenever Pete needed machines, he would call and he would tell me he needed a 450 or a 250 and some spare parts. He would arrange to come to Thief River to pick them up on a Saturday night. It was always a Saturday night, because Pete had to work during the week.

In the mountains of Lake Tahoe, California, Steve Rugland tests the first Model 100.

I would build what Pete needed and, true to his word, he would show up Saturday night. He'd step through the open door, and I'd be working and dirty. The following became a ritual through the years:

"Edgar," he'd say, "go to the office and make up an invoice."

I would.

"Now how much do I owe?" Pete would ask. I would say that it was so many dollars and so many cents, and from his pocket he would take a wad of cash. He always had exactly that many dollars and that many cents. He knew what it was going to cost before he came. For as long as I knew him, that's the way Pete operated.

It was the little 100, ready for the world in 1963, that set Arctic Cat apart. SkiDoo had built a front-engine machine since 1959, but ours was the first in America, and we thought it a good deal more functional than the Canadian model. To me, the 100 was the way to go for sports. It was all sheet metal, and became known as the tin lizzy, like Henry's Model T. The retail price was $549. It worked like anything new, with a lot of problems, but it worked. We could pull another snowmobile behind it. The hook didn't belong in front.

Sales had been relatively sluggish, but with the 100, the public came to realize a snowmobile wasn't only for work. It could be fun. Sales dramatically increased, and in November of 1962, we grossed $100,000. Between April of 1962 and February of 1963, we recorded $439,000 in sales with after tax profits of $17,467.

None of that early success would have happened without a strong work ethic, which they also had at Polaris. We were few, and so we had to work hard. They were long, long days. There was no such thing as staying home on a Saturday. You worked, whether you liked it or not, or whether your family liked it or not.

Even at home, the business took over our lives. When we finally moved from the plant, we had a commercial sewing machine in our house. My wife, Ruby, did all the cutting and sewing on the snowmobile cushions. For that, Arctic paid her 90 cents a snowmobile.

We had so many different models in the early Arctic days.

Eventually, as sales picked up, we went to double shifts. The men and women worked eight hours at a time, with a half hour for lunch. I'd open the doors at 5 a.m. In winter, I'd crunch across the snow in the black of night toward the shop, the 30-below temperatures whipped colder by the hard wind. I couldn't wait to get inside. I'd work all day and into the night, then close up after the second shift. With everyone gone, the place had a strange quiet to it, and I'd set to work doing time and motion studies. In other words, I would weld or run the turning lathe, so I could judge how long it should take to build a snowmobile. I had to know if we were making good use of time.

It was late when I finally left for home, and when I arrived, I literally tumbled into bed, only to do it all again the next day. Looking back, it was tough, but that's just the way it was. I did those things and I didn't think about it. Today, maybe we'd have fewer failures if people would give that much of themselves. Whether it was the Fourth of July or Labor Day, it was all the same. I didn't always have my crew with me, but I worked. I had to.

In the process, we developed a bond as strong as family. In the early days, there were 12 of us, and once after work, somebody had money for a six pack. Twelve of us sat on the floor against the wall sharing beer. We were all greasy and dirty, but it was a good feeling. If only for a time, work was gone from our thoughts, and we were like brothers.

It was the same at Polaris, where my brother, Allan, was now president. People have often asked, "What was it like to be in direct competition with your brother?" It's an easy question, because when I was a kid on the farm, right across the road was my dad's brother, who also owned a farm. They grew crops and then sold them. Admittedly, it wasn't quite the same as selling snowmobiles, but they were competitors, make no mistake.

Allan and I had a very good relationship. We had the same mother, and we broke bread with her at Christmas, Easter, New Year's and at any other holiday that brought us together. We were good friends and good brothers. But the very next day, if I could take a deal away from him, I did, and if he could take a deal away from me, he did. If I could build a better snowmobile, I would get more of the market. If he could make a better one, then he would sell more. Consequently, we had a friendly war. And as a result, both companies benefited by getting better and better. As an aside, I think Arctic built the better snowmobile, though today, I'm not sure that's true. Today, you might like the feel and the handling of an Arctic, or you might like the feel and the handling of a Polaris. They're both good. Today, you buy what fits your desire.

We had similar goals, but Allan and I really weren't alike. He was a different kind of leader. At Polaris, Allan and David stood in my shadow. They let me do all the talking and the majority of the decision-making. It wasn't fair to them, but they seemed to go along with it. But when I left, they moved front and center. They came out from under my shadow and they blossomed. It was good for me and good for them. As I built Arctic, they continued to build Polaris, and both companies became giants in the industry.

Some years later, on Nov. 24, 1972, it was with deep sadness that I learned of my brother's death. Allan had gotten a call from a neighbor. "Hey," the man said, "I have some trouble and need a big, front-end loader for some excavating." My brother was a soft touch for people who needed help. He stepped outside and got on his rig, a machine so big you could barely reach the tops of the tires. He soon was on the road. Along the way, he ran into a stretch of ice. The rig spun and spun and finally flipped over. It crushed him. He died answering that call.

Two or three years earlier, Allan had sold Polaris to the Textron Corporation. He stayed on for a time in the managing end, but got away from that, too. When he died, he had a cattle ranch and we were talking about starting a business. It's a shame, because no matter what we would have done, it would have been a success. He brought a lot to Polaris. Like David Johnson and myself, he understood all about hard work. He knew what made a company grow.

Today, I see the heritage we built at our companies. It's that legacy, I believe, that has allowed them to survive and thrive. Creative people are allowed to create, are allowed to come and go, and are encouraged to use the snowmobile. They have freedom and are recognized for whatever innovations they bring to the sport. That's what we tried to instill in our people, and it has carried on.

It was that heritage, plus those long days, that helped Polaris and Arctic. By the early '70s, there were approximately 139 snowmobile companies. Outboard Marine, Johnson Evenrud, Mercury, AMF, FMC, John Deere and Massey Ferguson all built snowmobiles. I could go on and on, naming the tremendous companies that tried and failed in that pursuit.

To see why they failed, you have to examine why there now remain only four – Arctic, Polaris, Ski-Doo and Yamaha. We don't know what Yamaha does in Japan, but we can see that Polaris, Arctic and Ski-Doo have a common denominator, which is their heritage. All three were family-oriented, born small, where nobody wore a watch. The watch was thrown away, and they went by the calendar. Let's say you're an engineer at a large company, like John Deere or Massey Ferguson. This is your drawing board, this is where you sit. You start at nine and you quit at five, and you go home to Mom and the kids. That's your world. You've probably never ridden a snowmobile.

That wasn't true in our companies. We had a group of dedicated, creative people who didn't care what day it was, who didn't care if they got home for supper, or missed lunch, who loved snowmobiling and worked hard. They always gave you the best snowmobile. Maybe the employees were paid for a 40-hour week, but I submit they worked 60 hours, and often times more. That is why, out of 139 companies that tried to build snowmobiles, four still do. Of those four, as of this writing, Yamaha is far behind in sales and production.

Yes, I would have done anything for Arctic. All of us would have. We proved it time and time again. But there is such a thing as going too far. In 1963, on a desolate glacier in Alaska, I may have. I thought I was going to die for the company, for that little Model 100.

Chapter 9

FORGOTTEN

At Polaris, Edgar Hetteen risked his life in a journey across Alaska to prove a point. At Arctic, he would risk it again, this time to test a machine on an isolated glacier. One observation: The man must have a dozen guardian angels working around the clock, watching and protecting him. So many times he faced death, so many times he beat it.

This story begins in an airplane and ends with me and my friends starving, sunburned and alone on the side of a barren glacier. We soon will return to my efforts in Thief River and making the business go, but just now, we have to go to that airplane, during one of the countless times I found myself in the air, away from the worries of bank agents, of boardrooms, of meeting payrolls. The airplane was my respite, the place I always felt comfortable, the place that revitalized and inspired me.

And sometimes, scared me ...

My God it was dark in there, and it was rough. So rough, I felt the way a cowboy must feel at a rodeo when he's got the toughest bull of all. I was in a small airplane in a cut of the Rocky Mountains, really getting shaken up. The clouds were black, and I just had to retrace my steps out of there. Only, there was a big problem. How could I find a place wide enough in the canyon to turn the airplane around, and save myself and my passenger, Bill Wiesser?

The storm shook us so hard, I couldn't get my hands on the throttle. I just had to slow down, but how? I looked at Bill, who had a blank look on his face, the kind you have when your life is flashing before you.

Why was I in a dark, tough place to begin with? Why were we flying around a mountain where it was so dark, that at times it was hard to see the silhouette of the plane's prop? It was all because of our Model 100, that first American-made snowmobile with the engine in front. In the summer of 1963, the 100 lacked snow time and needed testing – I sent it ahead to Anchorage. We were on our way there when the trouble hit.

We'd flown out of Grand Forks, North Dakota in a Mooney Super 21 that Bill Wiesser had rented. Bill ran his own finance company and often loaned me money when I had nowhere else to turn. In this case, he'd never been to Alaska, and wanted to see it.

Our plane was not equipped with low frequency radio equipment, which can help you fly in poor weather. But thankfully, the skies were clear all the way to Fort Nelson in the Northwest Territories. We followed the highways there, and put down for the night. The good weather unfortunately, would not last.

The skies were poor the next day, and only half of the many planes at Fort Nelson had the radio equipment necessary to fly. But because of the camaraderie of pilots, those with low frequency radio offered to guide those of us without. We divided up based on the airspeed of each plane. My partner turned out to be a man with a Cessna 180, a plane slightly slower than our Mooney.

We took off, and I hung onto my friend in the 180, flying right off his wing. But gradually, the weather came down. It grew dark and visibility became poor. The man at the weather office no doubt had erred, because the skies were too poor to fly, even with low frequency radio.

There was no question – we just had to turn around. My partner banked, and I followed. As he did however, I noticed he wasn't returning to Fort Nelson; he was deviating. A few minutes later, he dove into a dark hole between the mountains. It then dawned on me: He was trying to find the road to our next destination, and that road went through the mountains. I figured he knew what he was doing, so I dove in there with him.

The Arctic Cat 100, the first American-made snowmobile with the engine in front. This is what we tested on the glacier.

That's when the trouble began. The wind bashed the plane around and I couldn't get hold of the throttle. Each time I reached to grab hold, it seemed to have a mind of its own and darted away from me. I'm sure Bill began to wonder not if, but just when we would plummet from the sky.

Finally, I grabbed the throttle. I tried to reduce power, because the Mooney was going too fast and jostling too hard. It wouldn't slow, and I worried I would soon tear the wings off this poor plane. The situation was growing desperate. But maybe, just maybe, if I cranked it into high RPMs, in other words, flattened the prop, that might act as a brake and slow me. It seemed to be my last hope.

I did it.

It worked, thank heavens, but my worries were far from over. I needed luck to find a place in which to turn around and return the way we came. Finally, praying I wouldn't collide with that Cessna, which was somewhere in the dark, I found a spot just wide enough and did a 180. A few minutes later, in front of us was the same bright hole we'd dove into when the whole thing began. We emerged into the clear.

But which way was Fort Nelson? I had no equipment that could home in on it. I had no idea where I was, so I got on my radio. I found other planes in the area, and followed them back. Eventually, my partner in the Cessna 180, who I'd lost, also returned.

The next day thankfully dawned blue, and Bill and I were off to Anchorage. We arrived a day later, but it was not the end of our problems. No, they were only beginning.

❦ ❦ ❦

I had to test that snowmobile. I had to do it in a place with plenty of snow. Where could I find that in the summer? Even in Alaska, it is somewhat difficult. But I decided that if we went to Ruth Glacier on Mount McKinley, we'd have plenty.

Because McKinley is quite a few miles from Anchorage, I figured we could send the snowmobile up on the railroad to a small town called Talkeetna near the glacier. Once the snowmobile was there, I hoped we could get the famous pilot Don Sheldon to take it the final few miles to Ruth Glacier. By ham radio, we contacted Sheldon, who agreed to fly up the machine, and then us.

The next day, Bill and I joined forces with Burt Johnson, a good friend of mine from Anchorage, who was originally from southern Minnesota. We rose at 5 a.m. that Monday morning, and drove a rental car to Burt's. He threw some stuff in our car, and on the front porch, hugged his wife, Mickie, goodbye.

"Mickie, we should be back sometime this afternoon," Burt said as she looked on with a fair amount of concern. Flying into the guts of Alaska was never routine. "Don't worry, we'll be OK."

Had Mickie known what was about to befall her husband and me, she would have grabbed on tight and held on. But she could not know. None of us did.

We made it to the Anchorage Airport, climbed into the Mooney, and soon were in Talkeetna. We found Don Sheldon. He'd already dropped the snowmobile off and now it was our turn. Our Mooney, without skis, simply couldn't land on the glacier, and that's why we needed Don.

He welcomed us with a big meaty handshake, and showed us his plane.

"Well, climb on in. We'll have you up there soon enough."

We lifted off, and soon were flying through the mountains; it was quite a view. As we approached the glacier, I noticed it sloped uphill. Before leaving the snowmobile there earlier in the day, Don had marked a place to land with spruce bows, so he could find the old spot. As we touched down, the plane bounded before finally coming to a stop. It was a strange sensation landing uphill, but with an experienced bush pilot, it was a joy. We hopped out and landed in a granular snow comprised of ice crystals. We made our way to the nearby snowmobile, crunching all the way.

"Don, we'll have enough gas in the machine for about four hours," I said. "You should probably pick us up around noon."

Sheldon nodded and grunted that noon would be fine. Leaving us standing around the snow machine, he marched back to his plane. Halfway there, he turned, as if he'd forgotten something.

"Say, fellows. Do you see that little mound of snow over there on top of the glacier?"

We looked and spotted it about 70 yards away. In unison, we nodded.

"Well, there in that mound is some corned beef hash. The Royal English Marines were up here and were climbing Mount McKinley. They left that stash of food."

He began to walk toward the plane and stopped. He turned again.

"I wanted you to know in case I don't get back on time. Just to be safe."

His little information should have been a dire warning, but we only nodded. Had we analyzed it better, we would have said, "Hey, you better take us back right now." It wasn't the kind of place you'd like to be stranded, corned beef hash or not.

Anyway, we watched Sheldon climb into his plane and take off in a spray of ice crystals. We turned to the business at hand, driving that snowmobile, testing it, and learning what I wanted to know about weight balance and steering response. It wasn't long before the tank was empty and we sat around the machine, looking out over that big valley covered in ice. It was noon, time for Don to return.

But soon, it was one o'clock and then it was two. It was three and then four, and then six and then seven. He never showed; not the whole evening.

I had brought one sleeping bag and one loaf of bread. That's not much for three men. It was frustrating, especially as we grew hungry. We gobbled up the bread, but it wasn't enough.

"You fellows still hungry?" I asked.

They nodded slowly. Bill was chewing the last of the bread.

"I think we better crack open that corned beef hash, because your Mr. Sheldon isn't coming back tonight," Burt mumbled.

We hiked the 70 yards and started digging on hands and knees. Sure enough, resting there under the snow was a case of corned beef hash. We lugged it back down to the snowmobile and slapped it onto the sled. I don't know for sure if we had anything but pocket knives, but we managed to get it open. That night, with no forks or spoons or much of anything, we dined on frozen corned beef hash. And, for a time, were full and happy.

To this day, I don't recall how we slept, or if we slept, but I do know this: It was hard to sleep, and it grew boring.

"I need to get up and do something," Bill said. "You know, I used to be an Army drill sergeant. Why don't we do a little drilling?"

Bill was the drill sergeant, and Burt and I became the drill squad. We could do the snappiest about face you ever saw. We marched late into the morning, anything to keep from thinking about Don Sheldon and his missing plane.

Tuesday morning came, and our pilot still hadn't shown. We watched the sky and shook our heads, breathing a little faster as we worried. To keep our minds busy, we went back to drilling, and back to our corned beef hash.

By Tuesday evening, he still was missing. Without anything else to do, there was more drilling throughout the night, because after all, the sun was up nearly the whole night.

He hadn't shown Wednesday morning either, and so it was more corned beef hash, more drilling and more orders barked by our drill sergeant Bill.

By Thursday, we'd finished the corned beef hash. Hungry and with little sleep, our brains grew punchy and our bodies felt like empty husks. My stomach flipped upside down, empty and tired. Moreover, the bright sun and its reflection off the snow was burning us up. The weather was what pilots call severe clear. Our faces turned red – it hurt miserably – and we knew it'd only get worse.

We buttoned our GI parkas as far up as we could, but it was impossible to escape the sun's rays. We looked like boiled lobsters. We began to doubt our own sanity.

I took a walk and noticed a black speck in the snow. Leaning over, I discovered it was a fly. I went back to Bill and Burt and said, "Fellows, you know what? We have flies up here."

They looked at one another and nodded slowly. "Sure, Edgar. Sure." My pals thought I was hallucinating, and that we'd better get off the glacier before they had trouble with me. But, I wasn't crazy. I really did find a fly on that barren ice. I mean, I think I did. I believe it fell out of the parka I'd gotten from Burt's surplus store.

 প্ত প্ত প্ত

The story of that fly would return to me a year later, when my brother phoned.

"Where can I go and test my snowmobile," he asked.

I chuckled.

"Gosh Allan, I know just the place. You go up to Alaska and get Don Sheldon to take you to Ruth Glacier."

"What gear should I bring?"

"You go see my friend Burt at B&J Surplus in Anchorage."

Allan went up there and Burt fixed him up with a pack of stuff. On the glacier, Allan began to unpack, and there, in the gear from Burt, was a case of DDT. A few days later, he asked Burt about the poison.

"Why'd you give me DDT?" Allan asked.

"Because," my friend replied. "Edgar said there's flies up there."

প্ত প্ত প্ত

Burt had a tremendous sense of humor. We needed it trapped on that glacier. Don Sheldon already was two days late. Worse, he wasn't there Thursday night, and he wasn't there Friday morning. We could do no more drilling. We were spent, and we grew despondent. Bill had to get back to Grand Forks, and I had to get back to Thief River. We didn't know what had happened to Don. Maybe he'd crashed, and nobody knew where we were. Maybe nobody was coming.

We were hungry. We were in trouble. If he didn't show Friday, or at the latest Saturday, our lives would be threatened.

But lo and behold, Friday, before noon, four days late, coming up the glacier, was an airplane. Its engine purred through the cold air, and it sparkled in the sky like a diamond. It came down gently and landed between the spruce bows. As it slid our way, we saw that it indeed was Don Sheldon.

"Edgar," Bill said, "you know what I'm going to do with that so-and-so when I get to him? I'm going to punch him out. I'm going to fix him for leaving us here."

"Bill," I said, grabbing him on the shoulder. "you can do that, but why don't you wait until he flies us to Talkeetna. You can do anything you want to him then. OK?"

Don walked up to us, hands in pockets. He seemed nonchalant, almost carefree.

"I'll take your snowmobile in first and then return for you fellows," he said. We smirked. He was crazy if he thought we'd agree.

"No, Mr. Sheldon," I said. "No, no, no. You will take us in first. Then you can come back and get the snowmobile."

We happily piled in, one on top of the other, like puppies going to their mother. We lifted off and left that terrible glacier. On the way to Talkeetna, I wanted to know how much this would cost us.

"Don, how much do we owe you?"

He named a figure.

"You know," I said pausing, exasperated, "I'd be willing to call this even if you just go pick up that snowmobile and you can have it. We will have had the experience." It would have cost me more than it was worth to haul it back home; and Don agreed.

As we flew, gazing at glorious Mount McKinley, we friends exchanged looks. So far, Sheldon had said nothing about leaving us on the glacier.

"Mr. Sheldon, I'm curious why you left us up there all those days," Burt said. "Did you forget us?"

"The weather was bad at Talkeetna," Don said quickly. "I couldn't get out."

We again glanced at each other, and Bill shook his head. Don's account seemed unlikely. It had been clear all four days at our end. A little while later, we touched down at the base of the mountain in Talkeetna. I quickly got out of the plane and walked briskly to the flight service station.

"Hey, what kind of weather have you had this week?" I asked.

"It's been good," the man said. "Clear as can be."

I think Don forgot us. Worse yet, he might have continued to forget us had it not been for Burt's wife.

Imagine Mickie in Anchorage. She expected us back Monday afternoon. And then we didn't show. We didn't show Tuesday, we didn't show Wednesday, and we didn't show Thursday.

She grew concerned. She knew how Alaska is, and she knew you can be delayed when you're traveling, but still she worried. She decided to get hold of Don, except there wasn't any direct telephone line into Talkeetna. Through a ham radio operator, she got him the message: She'd like to have her husband and his friends back.

Her call set a chain of events into motion. Apparently it was too late Thursday for Don to come get us, and so he set out Friday. We might still be there – our bones – had Mickie not called and reminded Don of the three men he had stashed on a glacier.

Chapter 10

GOODBYE AGAIN

When Edgar Hetteen returned from the glacier in 1963, shaken but still alive, Arctic Enterprises would provide a different kind of adventure. Three years old, the company was a growing concern, but every day was a worry. As always, funding was the problem. And as always, Hetteen would find a way.

Before long, however, he would say a fond farewell.

ॐ ॐ ॐ

Despite all of our hard work and dedication, and though we knew we'd eventually succeed, we often were dreadfully short of money. Sales were fine, but there were 30 to 40 people to pay every week, debts to service, and products to design, build and bring to market. Moreover, the banks, not even the good Thief River ones, would loan us money.

Arctic Enterprises, starting with $10,000 borrowed, wasn't bankable. Thief River Bank President Jim Womack, who often came to the plant, helped all he could, but just couldn't loan us money. He did, however, go to the trouble of getting a finance company, Western Acceptance of North Dakota, to take us on. Their interest rate was 18 percent, payable monthly.

Even at that high rate, however, the money from Western Acceptance wasn't enough for all we wanted to do. So, through Allen Eide, the Bug-O-Vac man, I met Bill Wiesser, who spent those days on the glacier with me. Whenever I didn't have enough money, often just to pay the employees, I'd run to Bill in Grand Forks, North Dakota and sign a note for three or four thousand. Bill's rate was 24 percent, and some days it felt as if I were signing over my eternal soul. I worried, but never missed a payment.

We made ends meet by walking the edge of poverty and sometimes falling in. We were forced to reach into a bag of tricks to save ourselves, tricks that were unconventional at best. On many a Friday night, without enough money in the bank to cover payroll for the week, and having already borrowed too much, I would make plans to see Allen Eide, who by then was a good friend.

Allen lived in Grand Forks, and I in Thief River. We would get into our cars and we would meet, maybe in Crookston. We'd go to a darkened, empty parking lot, our headlights intersecting like swords. The cars would stop. He would run out of his and I out of mine. He would hand me his check, and I would hand him mine. They both were written for the same amount, $600-$700. Sometimes we didn't even talk. There was one cold, miserable Halloween-type evening: He didn't say hi, I didn't say hi. We exchanged checks, pivoted and stepped briskly back to our warm cars.

Early the next morning, I would deposit his check and he would deposit mine. It gave us a few extra days in which to get real money for payroll. Both our companies always worked backwards to cover what we'd done the day before.

Yes, this was somewhat sneaky, but when you're desperate, you'll try most anything. We did it for a long time, until finally, we were caught. A little clerk in the Thief River Falls bank had been going over our checks and noticed something strange. "How come all these checks are exactly the same?" he wondered to himself.

I can tell you, we were scared. But the clerk said he wouldn't turn us in, as long as we quit doing it. Only, we just couldn't stop. We needed the time the checks bought. Our businesses depended on us meeting payroll, so we started writing them for different amounts. One week, he would make his bigger, the next I'd make mine bigger. We gambled that if we got two or three days covered at the bank, we'd have the cash for the checks; and ours never bounced. I couldn't do that to Allen, and he couldn't do it to me.

I certainly do not encourage anybody to copy us. There are limits to what you should do to make a business go. What we did demonstrates how desperate things were, and it seemed innocent enough at the time. I wouldn't do it again today, and I feel embarrassed by what we did.

You must understand, paying employees was a relentless grind. In Roseau, the boys often went without pay, but at Arctic that was never the case. Still, I always looked forward to time, time for the extra money to roll in, time when you prayed you would have enough by Friday, time when you would do anything to raise a buck.

Holidays were the best – boy, did I look forward to them. It was one more day when the mail didn't go through, one more day when the bank didn't get the check. Two holidays in a row were cause for real celebration.

We worked around not having money. When I incorporated as Arctic Enterprises and became a corporation, I had to have a board of directors. Not liking to spend time with finances and all of that, it was my theory that, "Hey, if I put a banker on the board, I'm going to get his financial advice." So I put Jim Womack on the board.

I hated insurance, so I put an insurance broker, Les Ihle, on the board. I asked L.B. Hartz, who owned my building and for whom nothing was impossible, to join. Bill LaFave, president of the Bridgeman Creamery, also came on. I hated things of a legal nature and couldn't afford to see an attorney, so Bob Wurst, a lawyer in Thief River, was asked to be on the board.

When I was finished, I had a good cross-section of different talents and abilities and skills. I had the benefits of all of their knowledge and I paid nothing. It was my way of dealing with our lack of money.

In our wage structure, my salary as president and CEO was $6,000 a year. Steve Rugland, my vice president, earned $7,200. No, I didn't make much, because Arctic didn't have much. The only reason I gave

From 1963-65, Arctic was the first with two-wheel and four-wheel drive machines that worked extremely well. They were discontinued, however.

Steve more was because he was worth it. Understand, I had faith in the future. I wasn't just working for that paycheck. I was working for all those to come.

We didn't take home much, and that helped the company grow. It was one of the sacrifices we were prepared to make. You have to be ready to do those things if you are going into business. If you think, "Well, I can draw a big salary right off the bat," you're probably not going to make it.

The company grew, because we made it grow. Each year we came out with new models, and sales increased. In the public's eyes, we now were an alternative to Polaris.

By 1963-64, we had a growing group of hard-working, clever distributors. They all made us grow, but no one person helped us as much as did Sparky Meyer. Sparky, remember, had been with Polaris, but then moved over to Arctic. He perhaps was the most successful of all the early dealers. Sparky had a tavern at Highway 45 and G Street near Neenah, Wisconsin, on the eastern side of the state.

At his tavern, he had a 5 o'clock crowd. When the factories and offices closed for the day, the folks always stopped by for a drink. During his days at Polaris, he had ordered about six snowmobiles, and when he received them, he lined them in front of his saloon. He just knew he was going to sell those, probably sell them fast. But a few days went by, and then a few weeks. He didn't sell any. The 5 o'clock crowd had a good time at Sparky's expense.

The Arctic Kitten was built the last two or three years I owned Arctic. It had two big flotation tires in back, with a track attachment available.

"How simple, how stupid could you be?" they said.

Well, you just didn't do that to Sparky Meyer. One night after the saloon had closed, Sparky went to work. In the pitch black of a winter night, he dragged one of the snowmobiles from where he had it on display to a barn behind the tavern.

Note the wooden replica of an Arctic Cat. This is how early dealers advertised.

Over the next couple weeks, he hid two more. The crowd wasn't laughing quite so much, because they'd noticed a few of the snowmobiles were gone. Finally, one of the regulars eyed Sparky from across the bar.

"Sparky, did you sell those?" the man asked.

Sparky nodded, and smiled.

"Yeah, yeah. They're starting to move."

He created an illusion. Such was the ingenuity of the early dealers. Pretty soon, he sold one for real, and soon after, he sold a second. Then he got them out of the barn, and, of course, told his customers that he'd just gotten in a shipment.

Later, with Arctic, Sparky Meyer would go to fishing derbies and whatever else attracted people in winter. Being very astute, he contracted with Miss Wisconsin to represent the snowmobile. Her job was to never leave the machine far behind. When she was photographed, an Arctic Cat was photographed. Tremendous ingenuity. It shows what man can do when faced with a real challenge. Sparky didn't want to tell the world, "Hey, I can't sell these things. They're no good." So he did it his way.

We owe Sparky much. He taught us to never give up. He even accompanied us to dealer meetings out of his territory. If a dealer at one of those complained that he couldn't sell, Sparky would stand up, and in a booming voice say, "How come?" They would answer and Sparky would say, "There's nothing to it. Here's what I do."

Sparky knew how to promote our sport. He helped organize the first snowmobile race in Eagle River, Wisconsin, in 1963, which our employee Roger Skime handily won against 70 competitors. Because of his brilliance in promotion, we made Sparky the distributor for all of Wisconsin. He eventually sold the tavern and built an expensive distribution headquarters. Sparky reached the heights of success. He flew a Mooney MU2 turbo prop twin engine plane that must have cost at least half a million dollars, and in the late '70s, he sold his distributorship back to Arctic Enterprises for an amount measuring in the millions. When he sold out, one of his final acts was to come to Thief River in his MU2 to pick up Hannah and me. Hannah is my second wife. (We married in 1967). He took us to Alaska and flew us all over that state, as I had done with him a few years earlier. It was his way of saying, "Edgar, thanks for helping me."

Yes, our growing distributor and dealer network helped us greatly. And as they sold, we were hard at work developing new models. In 1963-64, we increased the number of models from six to 13. Our largest engine went from six-and-a-half horsepower to ten. We added a fiberglass version of our popular, steel-hooded 100 model, and you could choose between electric or pull-start engines. The 100 led all sales, though the 450 with its rear-mounted engine wasn't far behind.

The year 1963 marked a turning point. Arctic Enterprises had incorporated in the spring of 1962, but a year later, we had our first public offering for 100,000 shares of common stock at a price of $1.15 a share. We had to raise at least $50,000, or the money would go back to investors. No worries; we raised $60,000, which was a nice boost, and allowed us to do more things. Before the stock offering, we had less then $2,000 cash.

In 1964, we built more than 800 machines, and the company did $750,000 in volume. By 1965, we had approximately 50 employees. We had a number of new products, including a four-wheeled drive all-terrain machine and our exciting Tom Cat snowmobile, which boasted a powerful two-cycle engine. We'd developed a motorcycle, becoming the first snowmobile manufacturer to come out with summer vehicles.

And yet for all the success, a funny thing was happening to me. As a company prospers, an entrepreneur has to transform and grow with it in stature and knowledge and sophistication. I didn't particularly like that. As I examine my past, I was much happier when we were struggling and things were rough, than when we started to boom and I had to wear a suit to board of directors meetings. That was not my nature. But such is what happens when your product takes off.

The environment for my departure was in place, and as it turned out, I only needed a nudge. It came from Lowell Swenson who dropped in to help me get a handle on the books. Lowell was an accountant and had been running a company called Dow Key that made electronic components. When his audit was finished, he sought me out.

We sat in my office. Paper was scattered on the desk, and around the floor lay gears and tracks and pieces of snowmobiles.

"Edgar," Lowell said without much preamble, "I would like to buy half of your company."

This wind-driven machine was built at Arctic. It was the only one built.

His deep voice rattled, and he floored me with the thought. I didn't know what to say. I stared at him. With all the hardships at Arctic and making it grow, I hadn't stopped to consider the future.

I clasped my hands and leaned back. The more I thought about it, the more I liked it. Arctic had really reached a turning point. It was now at a maintenance level, and could exist without me. When that happens in a company, people change. It gets big and you don't know everyone. When it's small and struggling, there's a camaraderie, and that was important to me. With 50 employees, that was no longer true.

Even worse, I was having trouble learning to be a team player. I wanted to do everything, but just couldn't, not to the degree that was necessary. Arctic was picking up momentum and needing specialists. I did not want to adapt to the changing times.

Lowell was quiet as I thought. A few minutes later, I decided something that, in retrospect, was a mistake.

"No," I said. "You can't buy half the company, Lowell. If you want to buy it, you have to buy the whole thing."

That was a terribly foolish thing for me to say. But at the time, I hadn't become acclimated to organized business and how it worked. I was too much of an entrepreneur. Had I played it right, I could have gotten the same amount of cash for half the company as I got for all of it. And today, I would be independently wealthy.

I don't mind the fact that I lost money, but it was a decision based on the transition an entrepreneur has to go through to become a more sophisticated businessman.

Lowell agreed to buy the whole company. We would go to an attorney later to make it official, but just then, I pulled out a sheet of Arctic letterhead and scratched out a contract. Its terms were simple. He was to give me a small amount down and then pay me the rest as Arctic prospered. It was all done in 45 minutes. Yes, had I been more savvy, I could have shared the path Arctic took. But I never looked back with regret. I never said, "I wish I could do that over."

Had I stayed at Arctic, certain good things might not have happened. I had tremendous respect for Lowell's ability. While I would quake in my boots talking to bankers about $500, he'd talk to them about $50,000 with assurance. That made all the difference. For the good of the company, perhaps selling was the best.

Anyway, I honestly didn't think it was that big of a deal. If you have any confidence in your own ability, you say, "So what? So what if I left Polaris and sold Arctic? The world is mine, the whole world is a challenge." I always had the feeling that, "Hey, it's no big deal. I can do it again if I want to."

ൟ ൟ ൟ

Lowell Swenson and I walked through the offices, and, as memory serves, asked everyone to join us in the plant. Only a few minutes earlier, the rattle and shake of work had created a joyous noise. Now, as the employees gathered in a huge semicircle around us, there was quiet. I wondered what to say. It wouldn't be easy for me, and I knew it wouldn't be easy for them. We were family. Many had followed me from Polaris, and my departure would come as hard, hard news.

I decided not to give a long speech, because that would have been emotional. I wanted it brief and to the point. I cleared my throat, and said it as quickly as I could.

"Hey, you're going to have a new boss," I said, looking around at all my dear friends. "This is Lowell Swenson, and you'll answer to him now."

It was good I'd decided not to give a long speech, because I was starting to choke up. I was curt. That's the easiest for me when I've got something tough to say.

I looked around and saw tears streaking faces. A few of the women came to hug me. My close friends gathered around and asked what had happened. My heart felt like a lead weight. This was hard.

We had toiled at Arctic for five years and were family. They were every bit as responsible for the success we'd shared, and my departure was like a divorce in many ways, though an amicable one. When I no longer knew what to say, I ambled to my office. I grabbed some personal stuff out of the desk. With that, I said a few more goodbyes and wandered into the plant.

Standing there was Art Stordahl, who owned a big truck line, and for whom I once worked.

"Edgar," he said, "is your driver on the road right now, your truck driver?"

"No, he isn't, why?"

"I'm short a driver, and I need someone to take a trip to St. Cloud."

"Hey, Art," I said, "I'll take the trip for you."

In the early fall of 1965, I walked outside and climbed into Art's big semi-truck. What the heck. I could get out on the road and look forward to my future.

Chapter 11

A NEW BEGINNING

It happens fast. Lowell Swenson steps into Edgar Hetteen's small Arctic Cat office and 45 minutes later the deal is done. Edgar then jumps into the front seat of a semi-truck and drives to St. Cloud. It all seems unreal, and yet, that is the essence of Hetteen. That is what drove him – the instinct to pull the trigger, the instinct to make decisions in the blink of an eye, and never look back.

True, the decision to sell Arctic to Lowell Swenson proved to be a wrong one financially for Edgar. There is no getting around that, but it was the same machine-gun decision-making that built Polaris and Arctic Cat. Without that ability to think quickly and act fast, Arctic would have fallen apart long before Lowell Swenson ever arrived.

The truck rumbled down the highway south. Perched high in the cab, I stared out over the bleak countryside. It was a lot like being on a snowmobile; I could look out over everything and let my mind drift. It was good knowing Arctic Cat was in strong hands, but there was a deep sadness knowing no longer would I parent the child I created. Melancholy came over me, but I knew for the future of the company I did it right.

As for my future, I looked forward to it. I wasn't scared. I had no reason to be. Though only hours earlier I'd left behind a period of my life I dearly loved, the whole world seemed open. Once again, it was

This little number worked like a charm. It was one of the last sleds I designed at Arctic. It was just a little run-about, and was never put into production.

summer vacation and I could do anything I wanted. Instead of hunting gophers in the fields of rural Roseau, this time I could do any kind of work. I was 45 and life was full of opportunities.

The trip didn't take long. Once in St. Cloud, I switched trucks with another driver and immediately returned to Thief River Falls. I had a long conversation with my wife that evening. We sat on our sofa. Though at first surprised, she was understanding. She knew I decided things quickly and never looked back; she knew I wasn't a normal 9-to-5 type person.

A few days later, the company threw me a party. There were plenty of tears and hugs, especially from Mary, Bob, Steve and Marilyn. I still have the gift they gave me, a large barrel that opened up, and inside were shelves with glasses and bottles, a miniature bar. It was an emotional time, and though I had tinges of regret, I knew I had to move on. There was so much to do in the world, so many challenges, so much to overcome.

I rested well with the knowledge that the Arctic employees would do well in my absence. Though I had sold the business to Lowell in only 45 minutes, we later came to a couple of agreements. Before I would make the deal, he had to promise two things: Employees would not be fired for a year without my approval, and he couldn't get rid of dealers and distributors without consulting me. The idea was that an employee or a dealer had a year to prove himself to Lowell, and it worked great.

For me, it was a time of new challenges, and I loved challenges. And yet, what does an entrepreneur do when he's out of work and needs to feed his family? I didn't get a lot from Lowell. In addition to a small amount of cash, I'd gotten 3,000 shares of stock. Arctic would go public in 1969, and through the '70s my stock would increase in value to beyond $1 million. But in 1965, it was worth hardly anything, and I needed work. I couldn't afford to wait long. My family wouldn't have patience for that, and neither would I. It's never been my nature to sit around and do nothing.

Thirty odd years later, I don't remember exactly what I did the few weeks after selling Arctic. Fortunately, it didn't take long to get back into business and, as usual, it wasn't your run-of-the-mill work. I started speaking to Allen Eide. In the five years since I had met Allen, we'd become staunch friends. We'd known for years that one day we would team up; we just didn't know when. In Allen Eide, I would find my new adventures.

Our escapades began one night as I sat at home, probably listening to the radio or talking to my wife. The phone rang. I picked it up. Allen sounded excited. Looking back, he may have called because he knew I had to put food on the table. Allen was, and is, a wonderful friend.

"Edgar," he said, "we've just bought 40 acres of unharvested potatoes."

Allen was a lot like me. A lot. He did things the normal person would never think of, that the average person would find slightly weird.

But potatoes? It wasn't the most interesting thing I'd ever heard. It took me a while to respond.

"Where are they?" I said.

"They're in Gonvick," Allen said.

Gonvick was about an hour from Thief River Falls in northwestern Minnesota. It didn't seem a real good deal to me, but I agreed.

"You're going to have to figure out how to get them out of the ground," Allen said.

"Allen, I grew up on a farm, but I've never harvested potatoes. I don't know a thing about them. We had oats."

"Well," he said, "you'll do fine. I won't be there, because there are a few other deals I want to look into."

I went to the site and looked at our 40 acres, which seemed so large. I pulled my car to a stop and climbed out onto the windswept field. It was a strange feeling. In only a few weeks, I'd gone from selling snowmobiles to digging potatoes. Quite a change, but I liked change.

The potatoes would rot if they stayed in the ground too long. I had to get started. I rented a potato digger, a machine pulled by a tractor that digs out potatoes, shakes off the dirt, and lays them on the ground. I then spread the word in Gonvick (a very small town) that I was looking for pickers.

It didn't take long to hire about 10 women. Their job was to walk through the field and fill their burlap sacks with potatoes. For every bushel they picked, they would earn so many cents. It seemed a simple process. Unfortunately, I hadn't counted on the dark side of human nature, and how it can sink a business venture.

I expected the picking to go quickly, but the women were slow. I began to watch them more carefully. They tramped through the field, a few wielding thick, smoky cigars. Then I saw what was happening. I hadn't noticed it at first – too busy to keep an eye on everyone – but they were putting little rocks and little clumps of dirt in their bags. Anything to fill out a bushel, anything to get paid.

Something had to be done. We couldn't wait on those women. I got in my truck and went to find Allen Eide's brother-in-law. He lived in North Dakota and owned a potato harvester, a machine that picks the potatoes, and keeps them on a platform while you have one or two people bagging them. I got the harvester and returned to our site. With that, I was able to reduce the number of people by about 60 percent. We soon finished, without the rocks.

While I dug potatoes, Allen was digging up more business. He was great at that. I liked him as a friend, I liked him as a business man, and I liked him as a promoter and a risk taker.

Unfortunately, the potato field was not a profitable venture. Likely the only guy who made out was the guy who sold them to us. That certainly did not deter Allen or me. We knew together we would do well. We made plans to keep in touch, and I left for Thief River Falls with only a few bucks in my pocket from the potatoes. Soon after, however, in November of 1965, Allen called again.

"Edgar," he said, "I have 11 semi-trucks full of toys I just bought from Montgomery Ward."

"Wow! Your kids are going to be happy," I joked.

"That's funny, Edgar, but we're gonna sell those toys. And we've got to do it before Christmas."

With folks gearing up for their Christmas shopping, we decided to sell the toys at public auctions. We would tour all over Minnesota and North Dakota. They were memorable trips, especially one in Circle Pines, Minnesota, a small suburb of St. Paul.

We got ourselves a permit and took out an advertisement in the local paper. We rented a building, as big as we could find. We set up a stack of bleachers inside and erected a stage for us to stand. By then the toys were stashed in a warehouse. We loaded up two vans and drove them over to Circle Pines.

We began the auction at 10 a.m. on a Saturday. Already, women stood ready with purses over the shoulder, holding tight to Christmas lists. Allen, a licensed auctioneer, began to bark out the sale. Meanwhile, Ed, a friend of ours, and I held up the toys.

In any good auction, it always takes a few minutes to get the crowd going. This was important. If those ladies could develop a rapport with Allen, the more likely they would buy. A little boy was in the front row, so we employed one of our favorite techniques.

Allen began taking bids on a toy. The boy held up his hand, waving it slightly as he sat with his mother.

"Nickel," the tiny voice rang out.

Allen dove to the front of the stage, crouching and pointing to the boy.

"Sold to the young person for a nickel!"

I grumbled and turned my mouth into a frown. In our little act, I was the bad guy, and Allen was the good guy.

The crowd loved it. They cheered.

I now held up a Barbie doll and I told the crowd what she had for accessories, whether she came with a purse or a dress or a refrigerator. The bidding began. Soon, we had a $1 bid. Allen turned to me.

"Can we sell it for that?" he asked.

I shook my head with a snarl, though as far as I was concerned, he could have sold it on the first or second bid.

"Too cheap," I grumbled. "We need more."

It actually was hard to keep from laughing, but it was all part of the show. We were sort of a vaudeville act, and I think the crowd knew we were a couple of clowns.

Pretty soon, we had them going. We were ready with the toys, because once Allen got going, he didn't let up on the tempo from one product to the next.

I grabbed another doll and held it high.

"I have a blond Barbie, and she comes with a purse and two dresses," I said.

The bids rang out, and finally we stopped on one. With that, Allen grabbed the doll from me and held it up over the crowd.

"Who wants one more?!"

Bang, bang, bang, several hands shot up. Allen had worked them into a frenzy, and we probably could have sold them anything.

"Give us your number!" Allen cried. We probably passed out 15 Barbie dolls on just the one bid, so even though they were small items, our volume per hour wasn't bad.

While this was going on, I had the next item ready, because Allen wanted to keep up the momentum. He was very good at auctioneer's patter. He made the toys sound so good, sometimes I wanted to buy. Midway through the auction, I held up a toy that proved how good Allen was.

It was a doll buggy missing one of its wheels. We had a bunch of them in the van. They were merchandise that had been returned to Montgomery Ward as being defective. I held up the three-wheeled buggy, and Allen made his pitch. He raced up and down the stage, extolling the virtues of the three-wheeled buggy.

"Just a wheel missing, not much at all! Three-wheeled buggies, something to have!"

Hands shot from the crowd to buy that buggy. They were caught up in the action. The final price was more than Montgomery Ward charged for a buggy that had all its wheels.

Allen held up the buggy and he screamed, "Who wants another three-wheeled doll buggy!!!?"

Arms went up, and he snapped his fingers. Boom, boom, boom. We handed them out. We were clowning, and the crowd was eating it up.

The auction went well, and by supper time, we still were going strong. Gradually, the original ladies left and a new crowd arrived. The new folks began to bid, and the sales kept on coming. An hour later, we noticed the women from earlier in the day had returned. They sat in the front row, purses on laps; but that wasn't all. They also had Montgomery Ward catalogs.

I turned to Allen.

"Boy, we're in trouble now," I said, and he nodded. Those women could ruin us if they told the crowd how the catalog price compared to what we were getting. Thankfully, they were no trouble, because every time we sold a toy for pretty good money, the women looked in the catalog and grinned and laughed. They were on our side.

It was early evening, and the crowds kept flowing in. Eventually, the women with their catalogs left, but still the people came. It was 9 p.m., and then it was 11 p.m. Allen kept crying out the prices, and Ed and I kept lifting boxes. Sometime after 11 p.m., Allen could go no longer. His vocal cords were raw, and he looked about to faint. Ed, who'd just brought in another box of toys, was nearby when Allen pointed to him.

"Ed, take it. Go!" Allen said.

Ed was not an auctioneer, but he didn't have time to say no. He struggled at first, but quickly developed confidence and was pretty good, because he had a good teacher in Allen Eide.

It turned midnight and cars were still pulling up. It was 1 a.m. and then it was 3 o'clock Sunday morning. Finally, we had to quit, even though there were more toys in the van. I couldn't lift another box and tell the crowd about it, and neither Ed nor Allen could cry another sale. It had been a tremendous day, and we made good money.

We held auctions all the way to Minot, North Dakota. We had one in Dilworth, Minnesota, where we did our act in a bar room. We held them in automobile garages and at car dealerships. From town to town, we hurried, because we had to sell the toys before Christmas.

When it was done, all the toys gone, Allen and I decided even though potato fields and toy auctions were fun, we wanted to do something permanent. We sat over coffee at Allen's car dealership in Grand Forks.

"Edgar, what are you doing now?"

"Oh, a few things here and there," I said.

"I have an idea that I want you to think about. Just consider ... I think we should build pool tables."

I sat for a moment and scratched my beard. I like new ideas, but need time for them to sink in. Pool tables? What did I know of pool tables? Did I think we could make money? I wasn't sure, but as I looked across the table at Allen, he seemed confident. Allen was great at taking calculated risks. Finally, I nodded.

"Why not, Allen, why not? But you better give me some specifics of what you have in mind."

Those would come over the next few days, and I liked what I heard. Everything came together so quickly, it's rather a blur these many years later. This much I remember: Allen located a big building in Antigo, Wisconsin, population 3,000. That done, in 1966, I packed up my family, and we drove the 10 hours to our new town. We did it fast, and there wasn't much complaining, because my family knew how I operated. It usually was quick, or it wasn't at all. There were no thoughts of failure.

Once there, I went over to our factory, which was quite large, probably 5,000 feet. It had been a window company and the old equipment was still scattered about the warehouse. To get some cash, we liquidated all of it and then bought what we needed.

Allen's main idea was to build specialized bumper pool tables. One was a desk that could be transformed. When you lifted off the top, a pool table would be underneath. We had plans for the first entertainment centers ever made in the world; they wouldn't be that big or sophisticated, but they'd have a radio, a phonograph, and maybe even a tape player, though it never actually happened. We also planned something called a Combo. It was a combination pool table, desk and bar, with a spot for glasses and bottles.

We named the business Allen Industries, after the man with the idea. I hired seven or eight people, and we went to work. Allen was busy running his car dealership, and I operated the plant. I set myself up a makeshift office off the factory floor, though I was never much of an office man. I spent most of my time in the plant, organizing and leading the troops. We had men and women who'd never made a pool table, and someone had to show them how. Someone had to buy the merchandise; someone had to draw the sketches, someone had to set up the machines. If I ever did go to my office, it was to get on the phone and find suppliers.

How did I know how to make a pool table? Well, building a pool table is no different than making a snowmobile. Whether it's made of wood or steel, it doesn't matter. If you cut the pieces right, it fits together. If you cut them wrong, they don't. I didn't view building them as miraculous or anything.

It was another business, with many of the same challenges, valleys and triumphs I'd found at Polaris and Arctic. Regardless of whether you make pool tables or snowmobiles, you have all the same problems General Motors has. You have engineering, you have production, you have sales and marketing, and you have financial hurdles. The only difference between GM and the companies I've been with is that we had fewer people to carry the load. That being the case, I often was too busy to even think. If I wasn't at the factory, I probably was loading up our old truck with pool tables and hauling them to our store on Lyndale Avenue South in Minneapolis.

I was so busy, Allen and I had little time to talk; but we understood each other. He had work and I had work. Though Allen spent much of his time at the car dealership, he also was out selling and promoting pool tables. He set up the store in Minneapolis, and he worked wonders. Our stores grew to several, running all the way from Sioux Falls, South Dakota, to Madison, Wisconsin. Had we continued producing pool tables, we might have had a line of recreational products that wouldn't have quit.

Things could have been great, but it was not in the stars. It wasn't in me; it wasn't in my heart. I just couldn't grow excited over pool tables, no matter how bright the future. However, I did enjoy my time in Antigo. Most of all, I liked the people. We had nice folks who worked hard. Unfortunately for them, I was infected by snowmobiles. Almost constantly, I felt myself tugged by an invisible thread leading straight to Thief River Falls.

I never told Allen I wanted to return to Arctic Cat, but I think he instinctively knew. At some point, we talked of closing the factory. Our retail stores could stay open by selling pool tables built by others, but the business in Antigo was destined to come to an end. When that day arrived, the employees were disappointed, and some angry. You couldn't blame them, and I felt bad about that.

But there was little I could do about my emotions concerning the snowmobile. Being 10 hours away from Thief River Falls was like being away from a loved one.

❧ ❧ ❧

My family and I moved back to Thief River, and I began consulting for Arctic and Lowell Swenson. I helped set up dealers and worked with the marketing department. Going back to the snowmobile, however, did not sever my relationship with Allen Eide.

Allen and I would continue for years, on into the '70s, even as I worked full time for Arctic. Though finances were touch and go in the mid-'60s, my Arctic stock and paycheck grew, until I was able to invest $100,000 with Allen.

We became partners in everything, including his car lots. Still, we didn't spend our time together. When we think of a partnership, we think of two guys, one with a shovel digging a hole and another with a shovel filling it. Allen and I were not like that. He did his stuff and I did mine, each of us trying to make money for the partnership. We had a car dealership on Lake Street in Minneapolis. We had one in Minnetonka, and another in Robbinsdale. I basically was a silent partner. I sometimes helped Allen move cars, but I never fixed or sold them.

My relationship with him helped me in ways I probably can't comprehend. It certainly changed me for the better. I've been fortunate in life to have been surrounded by successful, passionate people who have encouraged me. I have attracted or been attracted to that special breed, and they rubbed off on me. The more you can surround yourself with people who are optimistic and confident, the more you will carry those same qualities.

What Allen did for me, I could never repay. He was so unselfish. He did things that, looking back, seem almost unreal, and yet, they happened.

Even when things were tough and we were writing each other checks, he somehow would supply me with airplanes and cars. He was incredibly generous. It was his nature. If he liked you, he did things for you.

I remember one time, badly needing to get to Alaska on a sales trip, I asked Allen if he had a plane I might use. He said no, but that if he found one, I sure could use it, as long as I took along his father, who'd always wanted to go to Alaska.

As we chatted over coffee, he grabbed a copy of Trade-a-Plane, a newspaper with nothing but airplane classified ads. Allen paged through it and came upon a 210 Cessna in Indiana. It looked good, and Allen said he'd call the man. I listened as he did.

"Sir, could you have that in Grand Forks Monday morning?" Allen asked.

The guy said he could, so on Monday morning, I was in Grand Forks along with David Erickson, who worked for me at Arctic. The two of us, along with Allen and Palmer Eide, were at that airport when the guy touched down in his 210 Cessna. He stepped out of the plane, we shook hands and Allen and I looked the plane over. Barely 10 minutes later, Allen surprised all of us.

"We'll take it," he said with a quick nod to the pilot.

I shook my head. How would Allen pay for it? He was no better off than I. But before I knew it, the three of us – David, Palmer and I – got into that 210 and we fired it up. We taxied, picked up speed, and lifted off going west, leaving Allen and the other guy behind. We were gone, but Allen still had to pay for it. I never asked my friend how he did it. Neither of us were expressive people, and it was better left unsaid.

He once left me with a Beechcraft Bonanza, a nice single-engine plane with retractable gear. I had that for several months. He was extremely kind, way beyond the call of duty, even friendship. It is difficult to forget those things, because even though he was several years younger than I, he helped shape me. To a lot of us, he was a softy, but he covered it up by being a little gruff. So many people do that, even myself.

Allen Eide had a lot to teach. He became one of the most successful car dealers in the Midwest. He had tenacity, the kind of tenacity you need to succeed in business and in life. He was a guy who could calculate risks, and he taught everybody around him that it's good to take risks, as long as you understand both sides. He always asked himself, "If I do this, if I buy this, what is the worst that can happen? What is the real down side of this?" Then, "OK, if I'm a winner, what's the high side?" When he went for a deal, the high side usually won. I suppose he had a few setbacks, too. But when he did, he just tossed the experience aside and kept going.

He dared to take chances. He was not like people waiting for their ship to come in, because often those people don't even have a dock. He made things happen. He was the sharpest car dealer I ever knew and, since you're a product of your environment, I benefited from knowing him.

Yes, I have been fortunate in my life, surrounded by good people, and it should be a lesson to anyone wanting to do well. Surround yourself with success. Be with the Allen Eides of the world. You've already read of so many people who helped and inspired me. And I doubt I could list everyone; but it's important to mention four more, in addition to Allen, with whom I've had very special relationships. These men helped me become better than I would have otherwise.

There was Burt Johnson in Anchorage, Alaska, who had the surplus store. He did so many nice things for me, and was a dealer for both Arctic and Polaris before he died. We were great friends, and I feel I have exactly that kind of a relationship with Gary Lemke, with whom I am now involved in a company called ASV. There is Sparky Meyer, a former Arctic distributor and dealer, and who was largely responsible for us getting off the ground. And there is Lee Lynch, head of the Carmichael-Lynch advertising agency in Minneapolis, which handled Arctic's advertising.

Five important people in my life. To have had the good fortune to be involved with five giants – Allen, Burt, Gary, Sparky and Lee – was to lead me to greater things. I'd wish those relationships on anyone.

Chapter 12

BACK WHERE I BELONG

Was there any chance Edgar Hetteen was going to live in Wisconsin building pool tables the rest of his life? No, not a chance. It didn't fit with the excitement and occasional danger of the snowmobile world. But the thing is, Hetteen would try almost anything. He had the same knack children have. Unfortunately, most of us lose the ability to try new things. We have defeats and we decide we don't like to lose. We quit. However, the best among us, the Hetteens, keep on trying. He proved that time and time again.

The months passed. My time spent with Allen was waning. More and more I was consulting at Arctic. It was where I belonged. Pool tables had to be built, but not by me. No, surrounded by snowmobiles and snowmobile people, I felt at home. Thankfully, that feeling would grow even stronger.

It was a winter day in 1967 when Lowell found me in the plant. I was helping Arctic set up a new production line. He tapped me on the shoulder. I spun around.

"Why don't we just quit horsing around?" he said.

"What do you mean, Lowell?" I asked. I wasn't horsing around.

"Why don't you get back on the payroll and quit this consulting."

As usual, it didn't take me long to decide.

"If you feel that way, Lowell, OK."

I went straight to work. This time as an Arctic employee, not the boss. I'm often asked: Wasn't that difficult? Wasn't it tough to take orders instead of give them? Well, in the sense of an employee, I wasn't a regular one. I was basically a freelance troubleshooter, operating not much differently than before. The guys in the plant would build a snow-mobile, and I would look it over and say this could be different or that might be a problem. I did the same in sales and marketing, too.

My job description, however, changed drastically in 1970, when I became a vice president and head of marketing. Right away, there was a pressing job. The advertising had been handled by a local fellow named Ken Strandberg; he'd done a heck of a job. Yet by his own admission, it was time to find Arctic a larger agency. If we chose the wrong one, it could have serious repercussions.

With a list of agencies provided by Ken, I made my way to Minne-apolis. I went through the list, meeting man after man, but nobody struck my fancy. The final guy was a fellow named Lee Lynch. He picked me up and we drove to his agency, Carmichael-Lynch. We talked on the way and then suddenly, this Lee Lynch turned to me and said, "We missed the driveway." I smirked, thinking it a bit odd that he'd missed the entrance to his own business. But we began talking and about five minutes later, he turned to me again, this time with a sheepish smile. "We missed it again." I paused, speechless. This guy was going to run an ad campaign for a multi-million dollar company?

Lee might have been absent-minded, but he and his men knew their stuff. They impressed me with their creativity and their knowledge of snowmobiling. Only a year earlier, they'd tried to get Polaris, but the boys in Roseau chose another agency. My decision was finalized when Lee and I went out for drinks that night. We both had a few, and he still seemed as if he knew what he was doing. Carmichael-Lynch would crank out some of the best advertising any company ever had. We were going good before they came along, but with their ads, little could stop us.

Little, that is, except for our own explosive growth. Every day, it seemed, something was expanding. Production, sales, marketing, you name it. We really were growing too fast. They were the boom years and, though snowmobiles sold as fast as we could build them, we had problems.

The upshot of such growth was that the public was starting to hate us. Despite all of our sales, a tidal wave of anger was pouring over Arctic, Polaris, and the other snowmobile companies. If it continued much longer, we risked losing all of our gains.

We'd gotten a black-leather-jacket image like motorcyclists once had. As far as the public was concerned, we were bad. The snowmobiles of the day were terribly loud. Small children held little hands tight over their ears as we roared by. The people watched us drag-race down city streets. They saw us riding through back yards and through public parks. We rode wherever we could find a spot of land.

We'd discovered how much fun it was to play in the snow. We hadn't learned how to conduct ourselves in public. The press depicted us as marauding pirates on our scary machines.

Unaccustomed to fights with the public, we didn't understand the forces against us. But gradually, we grew worried. Barely a day passed without some mention in the papers of the terrible snowmobilers. Some of it was valid criticism. Speeds were increasing, and accidents were piling up.

"Edgar, we have to do something," Lowell said one day. "Have you seen the papers? It's getting ugly, and I'm afraid sales might get hit. I think you're the best man to calm the fears."

"I'll do my best," I said.

Things had to be done, or the very industry was at risk. I moved from marketing to public relations. We'd allowed it to get out of hand, now it was time to fight back.

A few years earlier, the International Snowmobile Industry Association had been formed. My brother, Allan, was its president for the first two years. It did a good job, but in response to public criticism, we formed a committee of engineers to study safety concerns. Of that, I was the chairman.

We analyzed the type of accidents we were having and asked what could be done. In a series of meetings, we developed minimum safety requirements for the industry. Among those: A snowmobile shall have brakes that will stop it in a certain distance; it shall have headlights and brake lights. I felt pretty good, having chaired the meetings that resulted in safer snowmobiles. We'd accomplished quite a bit in a relatively short period.

Unfortunately, it wasn't enough. The accidents continued, and not just in Minnesota. They were happening everywhere, and hysteria was setting in. Snowmobiles were dangerous; people who read the newspapers and watched television just knew it.

The first inkling that our industry was in trouble came from Ottawa, Canada, where a Dr. Campbell was complaining about the accident rate. He was advising the Canadian Parliament to impose restrictions on snowmobiles. He claimed our changes weren't good enough. That chilled us to the bone, because it's one thing to impose regulations on yourself, it is quite another to have the government impose them on you. From what we'd heard, the doctor's regulations could very well kill us.

He was proposing a law that called for roll bars on all snowmobiles. It would mandate seat belts and even a switch so that if a snowmobile came to a certain angle, it would immediately kill the engine and lock up the track. He wanted a thing called a deceleration light, which meant every time you let up on the throttle, your brake light would go on. He wanted so many darn things, he was going to make snowmobiling dangerous and more expensive – and, ultimately, obsolete.

We had to do something. If the Canadian bill passed, not only would it hurt us in Canada, but it could lead to similar restrictions in the United States. We didn't want that. Moreover, we couldn't build two separate kinds of snowmobiles, one for the U.S. and one for Canada. I decided our best strategy was to negotiate with Dr. Campbell. We quickly arranged for 50 or 60 engineers – all from the many companies building snowmobiles – to go to Ottawa and meet the man.

We got there, stayed overnight, and met the doctor in his office. He seemed nice enough, and asked us to a large conference room. I was encouraged by his demeanor. Perhaps we had a chance to convince him he was wrong. But no sooner had our discussion begun than we engineers began arguing among ourselves. Everyone spoke at once, trying to explain to Campbell that his safety ideas weren't safe at all. Fifty opinions shot into the air. The doctor didn't have to beat us; we were beating ourselves.

As chairman, I had to cut our losses. I asked if we could adjourn the meeting and reconvene in the morning. The man agreed.

I gathered the engineers together that night.

"When we walk in there tomorrow, we're going to have one answer for deceleration," I said. "We're going to stop arguing. Tonight, we're going to agree on everything, and we're going to have one answer. I want the bickering to end. We'll have one answer for the roll bar. We'll have one answer for the seat belt. We have to work as a team."

Everyone nodded, and we worked long into the night. There was some disagreement, but in the end, we hashed it out. Even so, I slept uneasily. So much was at stake.

When we arrived the next morning, it was easy, actually. For each rule Dr. Campbell brought up, we shot it down.

"I think we ought to have a deceleration light; that way, people behind will know you are slowing down," he said.

We had our answer.

"Dr. Campbell, if I'm going down the trail and I'm pumping my throttle all the time, and you're following, the light's going to be on and off, on and off. It will be meaningless. We don't want that light to come on until we hit the brakes. Then you'll pay attention."

We argued for a time, and he finally agreed.

He had more, however.

"OK, what about a seatbelt? People can't be falling off and getting hurt," he said.

"We don't want a seat belt because occasionally, you're going to tip your snowmobile over. We want you to be thrown clear. We don't want you trapped underneath the thing. A seatbelt would be far more danger-ous than nothing."

And he agreed to that.

For every proposal or regulation, he listened to our explanation. You want a roll bar? You want a roll bar to roll over you and crush you? We suggested either a better way or said do nothing at all.

There were, however, a few proactive things that came out of the meeting. Snowmobiles were falling off trailers, and Dr. Campbell was concerned, so we agreed to tie-down rods on trailers. Snowmobiles were being stolen; how could the police identify them? Until that point, decals were being used and could be peeled right off. We agreed to stamp in a serial number so even if it was buffed clean, the number could still be read with the use of dyes. Those agreements became federal law in Canada, and then later in the United States.

I was chairman of that engineer's safety committee for two years. Even though we'd cooled the blazes in Canada, we had many brush fires left. Soon after the Ottawa meeting, someone was seriously injured when a gas tank exploded in a collision. We came up with minimum safety levels for gas tanks. Each company had to prove its tank could be filled with water and dropped from a certain height to a concrete floor without bursting.

Despite these safety improvements, things were worsening back home. Our image continued to decline. We continued to be noisy and bother people, and the accidents mounted. With snowmobilers forced to ride wherever they could, the death rate climbed. Some of them were innocent people hit on city streets. It was not good. In 1972, 36 people died in Minnesota from snowmobile accidents, which is still the high mark. The outrage was real and hard. Something had to be done. It was like getting a girl pregnant and then marrying her to make it right. The snowmobile industry was pregnant all right. We had to make it right.

To me, we clearly needed a trail system, a place of our own. With no trails, we were putting ourselves and our image at risk. And yet, what could we do? Arctic Cat, Polaris and all the other companies couldn't build the trails. We didn't have the time or the resources. Yet with the recent onslaught of controversy, we knew if we didn't act first, the state likely would come down on us like a hammer with all sorts of restrictions. It was a pivotal moment in snowmobiling history. A wrong move and we risked our future.

It was important to do it right, because Minnesota produced the most snowmobiles. What we did with legislation and what we did with regulations would become the model for the rest of the world. I doubt we realized all of the ramifications, but we knew it was important.

I said to myself, "Why not get it so that the state charges every snowmobiler a license fee, and those monies will be used for trails and safety?" It seemed a good idea. I met with Arctic Cat, Polaris and other manufacturers, and we agreed it was worth pursuing.

But where to go, who to ask? We would fund the trails, but a state agency had to see that the rules and regulations were enforced. Some at Arctic wanted to go to the Minnesota Highway Department, because they were all set up for getting people safely from one point to the other. I argued against that, and for the Department of Natural Resources. The DNR were people in the wilderness; people at peace with winter. They would be friendlier, I thought. I argued and argued, and finally got my way.

The day came when we showed up at DNR headquarters in St. Paul. I can't imagine what they must have thought of us, a bunch of crazy people tearing into their office.

"Look, we're pretty nice people," we said. "But we need your help."

We became one of the few industries in the world who said, "We will pay, just help."

I had a number of meetings with DNR Commissioner Jarle Leirfallom. He and I became good friends because he was an outdoor type of guy. We wrote up most of the rules, regulations and laws governing snowmobiling in Minnesota.

We came up with a certain sound level that had to be adopted, but most importantly, we came up with a trail system, and we came up with a way to pay for it – license fees. We wrote the history, we wrote the book, with Arctic backing us up.

Arctic really led the way. Polaris and the other manufacturers had agreed on the course of action, but I was the mainstay, spending a lot of time in St. Paul working with the DNR. Polaris, anyone, had the opportunity to join us, but they never did. Much later, we were criticized for doing some of the things we did, for our unilateral action. But they could have been there if they'd wanted. The DNR was open to anyone.

Mr. Leirfallom pushed hard on the trail legislation and it passed easily. Snowmobilers were taxed through license fees, and a trail system was started. Though a smattering of snowmobilers disliked the fees, which indirectly raised snowmobile prices, I think most understood the need.

Those who best understood were by then forming clubs. Without their help, the trails never would have been finished. True, we had some state money and the DNR backing; but the funds weren't enough to hire people to build trails and warming houses. Getting us over the hump would be the snowmobilers themselves. They were the ones who went out and hacked paths through the woods. They put up the stop signs and caution signs. They made it happen. We likely were the only industry ever made by the customers themselves. We owed and continue to owe the clubs a debt of gratitude.

The trails progressed and, gradually, snowmobiles disappeared from city streets, back yards and public parks. Death and accident rates fell. We had a playground now, back in the woods. I recall hearing from the same people who used to complain about us.

"Hey, the snowmobile industry sure died," one fellow told me, rather pleased.

"How do you mean?" I asked.

"We don't see you anymore."

Well, of course they didn't. We had our own place. Back in the woods, there were thousands of us. These days, it appears we've outgrown that old trail system, and there's a need to enlarge it. But at the time, with speeds comparatively low, it was the perfect place and the perfect solution.

❧ ❧ ❧

It was a busy time. There was much left to do, because we still were under attack. While the Legislature was in session, I spent most of my time in St. Paul. I didn't particularly enjoy it, but I had to be there. As the industry grew, people came forward who wanted legislation that would bar snowmobiles from certain areas. We had to fight hard against such idiocy. I went to many meetings and so many hearings. I testified so often, I seemed to do nothing else.

In the mid-'70s, the environmentalists said snowmobiles were destroying the land. They said we ran up hillsides, caused soil erosion, and that we killed growing trees. They lumped us in with four-wheel-drive pickups, swamp buggies and dune buggies. They wanted us barred from so many different places, our trail system would have been completely compromised.

Worse yet, they were taking their fight national, to the Congress of the United States. If they got their way, I shuddered to think of the repercussions. We mounted a counter attack, and I became a member of a committee headed by Secretary of the Interior James Watt. Many were the times I flew to Washington, D.C., meeting with people and explaining all about snowmobiling.

Finally, I got the committee to take the snowmobile off their list of destructive equipment, to set it aside as a separate item. Why did they finally understand? Because I had said, "Look, we use the ground when it's dead, when it's frozen, when vegetation is dormant, when it doesn't grow. We use it only when the ground is covered with snow or ice. When the snow leaves in the spring, you can't find a mark where we've been. You cannot put us in the same category as four-wheel drives." They took us out, and we're still out.

I congratulate Brad Hulings on winning the Hetteen Cup in the early '70s, a race held in Alexandria each year. Brad drove a Scorpion to the win. For about six months, I was general manager at the Scorpion plant, which Arctic purchased.

But in those days, it seemed just when we'd fix one problem, another would come out of the woodwork. There were, and always will be, people who hate the snowmobile, who hate the internal combustion engine, who want everyone to ride bikes. In 1975, Congress was discussing a 20 percent excise tax to be levied against snowmobile manufacturers as part of energy legislation. Naturally, we would have added that to the price of the snowmobile. It would have been an insidious, punitive tax.

The International Snowmobile Industry Association quickly went into action. We had to. We set up a hot line and informed everyone of the vote to be taken. The alert went out from the ISIA to all state organizations: Get hold of your legislators. The state organizations then called every club, and every club had its own little system to get the word out. We had so many letters going to Washington, D.C., the politicians finally said, "Turn it off, turn it off, stop! You win, you win." I can't emphasize enough the wonderful things the club people did beyond the call of duty.

As the attacks came, I went anywhere to meet them. In a small town in Toronto, Ontario, a college of law was holding a symposium on snowmobiles and how horrible they were. Arctic thought I should be there. So I sat in the audience with professors and law students and listened to what a bad person I was. If you say bad things about snowmobiles, you say bad things about me.

A doctor concluded the symposium by describing how snowmobiles were a terrible device that hurt and ruined people. He wrapped up his speech by saying birth control devices should be furnished with the sale of every snowmobile. That way, the breed would die out.

As the next speaker, it was hard to have an immediate rebuttal. I did the best I could. I walked up and looked at all those eyes of disgust. I said the first thing that popped into my head.

"It is very apparent that the good doctor has never snowmobiled. Because if he had, he would know that when you spend the afternoon in the fresh, invigorating air, you go peacefully to sleep and you do not need a birth control device. He probably is worried that snowmobiling in the fresh air and being relaxed just might cut into his business of tranquilizers and sedatives."

It was a shot at him, but attacks like that used to make me mad – furious, in fact. It doesn't so much anymore. These days, more people understand snowmobiling. Anyway, I've learned to control my anger at people who do not understand us. There is a difference between being mad and being furious. If you can just be mad, you usually can come up with pretty convincing arguments. If you get furious, you lose control. It's all right to be mad, but for heaven's sake, be rational.

They were hectic days for me and, I daresay, lonely ones for my wife, Hannah. We didn't count how many days I was gone, we counted how many days I got to stay home. Hannah was wonderful, though occasionally angry with the situation. I couldn't blame her. Sometimes it seemed my real home was a hotel in St. Paul, Minnesota.

When not at the Legislature, I was Arctic's representative for all industry affairs and functions. That meant making speeches, taking cruises, and often being something I wasn't. In PR, I would go to the same meetings and meet the same faces and have the same drinks with the same people. I couldn't be myself. I had to be what the public perceived me to be, some kind of legend, or a celebrity. I didn't like portraying an image that wasn't true. I just wanted to be me.

Making up for those negatives was the fact that I loved snowmobile people, and loved working at Arctic. I was one of the few employees given an unlimited budget. If I wanted to go to Podunk, Missouri, I went to Podunk, Missouri. I got all the trips I wanted, and generally speaking, I did not abuse that privilege.

What I'm saying is that Arctic was good to me. And hopefully, I was good for it. Partly from my work through the '70s, our public perception had turned positive. Sales increased, and we had more money than we'd ever dreamed.

Unfortunately, though we didn't know it, the ride was coming to an end. Dark days were ahead, the worst time in my life.

Chapter 13

DEATH OF A CAT

It can be argued that through Edgar Hetteen's tireless work in the Legislature, the snowmobile industry was, if not saved, at least spared a shaky future. But even with all his work, even with all his ideas, he could not control the weather. He could not control the winters of 1979-80 and 1980-81, when according to the National Climatic Data Center, only a combined 70 inches of snow would fall on the state of Minnesota, which averages 50 a season. He could not control the economy. He could not control the high interest rates that plunged the country into recession. He could not control the circumstances that would lead Arctic to borrow $48.5 million from a consortium of banks. He could not control the slew of events that would lead not only to the collapse of Arctic but to the near collapse of Polaris. But through it all, even after personally losing millions, Edgar Hetteen would battle back. As he always did.

It was December of 1980, and I stared up at the sky. It was blue again, same as it been for the last couple months, same as it had been all the previous year. My heels scuffed across the blacktop as I moved to my car in the sprawling parking lot of Arctic Enterprises. In a typical winter, we'd have more snow than we knew what to do with, but now, beyond the dry pavement, grass stood out from under a layer of frost – a strange sight indeed in Thief River Falls, Minnesota.

To make matters worse, it was cold, perhaps five below. I shivered as I shoved the key in the door and climbed onto a frozen front seat. It was like a block of ice, and the car struggled to catch its breath. Finally,

---

the engine rumbled, and I began a teeth-chattering ride home. It had been a miserable winter, and as I listened to the weather report on KTRF-AM out of Thief River, things did not sound good. The forecast was for continued dry. I shook my head and sighed. When on earth would it snow?

The recent weather had been hard on snowmobiling. No snow meant few sales, and Arctic employees could sense the gloom. They knew things were not the same as they'd been only a couple years before. And yet, I doubt they realized the ramifications of what was happening. Even as a vice president, I didn't know how bad it was, or how bad it would become.

The reality was, however, that those two back-to-back winters of very little snow were coming home to roost. Each winter, some area of the world has a lack of snow; but in the winters of 1979-80 and 1980-81, snowfall was low throughout the North American continent. All the snowmobile manufacturers were suffering. Indeed, many had gone out of business. From the high of near 140 in the early part of the decade, only a handful remained.

Rumors swirled at Arctic, and I suppose at Polaris, too, that the very companies at the heart of the industry were in jeopardy. It wasn't just the lack of snow. Interest rates were high, and the country still was suffering from the devastating effects of energy conservation. The economy was stagnant, and inflation was tearing across the United States. To stay afloat, to survive the economy, the bad winters and lack of sales, Arctic borrowed millions. At the start of the new decade, we owed a consortium of banks $48.5 million. Yes, it was a big number, and yes, there were the rumors of Chapter 11, but I was fairly confident we could stay afloat. Long enough, I thought, to bounce back when snow finally arrived.

The impending disaster had happened so quickly. We'd actually set sales records of $175 million in 1979, but then came losses of $11.5 million in 1980, and unexpected layoffs. The bad news continued. In 1981, we were hit by a $10 million setback, and even more extensive layoffs.

Then came the crushing blow. In February of 1981, one of our lending banks got excited and blew the whistle. The officers of all the banks gathered, and after long discussions, they called in their loans, which I believe they did very prematurely. If only they'd left Arctic alone, the company would have recovered and the banks would have gotten their money. With one year of bad snow, we easily would have recovered. Even with two bad years, it could have been done. But after the banks called in their loan, there was nothing anybody could do to save our wonderful company. Eleven days later, we filed for protection under Chapter 11 of the bankruptcy act. It theoretically would give us some time to work things out. Unfortunately, not time enough.

We tried to find a buyer, but three companies – John Deere, Suzuki and even Polaris, which was having troubles of its own – looked and decided we were too risky. We also tried to find a bank, but again, nobody would touch us. It therefore was decided, with much disappointment and frustration, to liquidate the snowmobile division. As for the divisions we'd acquired in the '70s, such as marine and fabrication, those would be sold off.

These events are a swirl in my mind. It was like a death in the family. I existed in a disoriented haze, what I remember as extreme grief. It was a frantic time, with a lot of sad conversations, hugs and goodbyes. But through it all, I never sensed people laying blame on management. As far as I know, there was no attitude that somebody screwed up or did something wrong.

The world says, "Well, you should blame Arctic for going broke. Look at all the people it kept, look at all the money it spent, look at all the cruises and all the parties."

But when I confronted those detractors, I tried to get them to name the employees they thought were surplus. When they did, I would ask how much each of them earned? I would ask how much did those parties cost, how much were the cruises? I would add it all up, and I would say, "Does this equal the $48.5 million that we owed the banks?" No, of course not. It didn't even come close.

If anything, perhaps we lost sight of what it was like to fight and kick and scratch for every nickel. It was easy to think the company would grow forever. But it's my opinion that no one person or group caused Arctic to collapse, unless they had control of the weather and didn't exercise that power. No, it was just a terrible mishmash of circumstance, a chain of events that, once started, couldn't be stopped.

The result was a feeling of nostalgia, of overwhelming sadness. For so many years, Arctic was a beautiful place to work. There was a tingling, a vibration in the company. Employees didn't want to miss a day of work because they might miss something great. Like Polaris, it was a feeling of family and camaraderie. Then without warning, we'd fallen off the edge of the earth.

Before Arctic closed, a bunch of people were given a choice: Leave now and take some cash, or stay for a short time and get nothing. I had that choice, and I opted to stay as long as possible. Arctic was one of my children. I had to stay.

For my wife and me, our lives were falling apart. We'd enjoyed a world of travel. We had dealer meetings in places like Hawaii and the Caribbean and on cruise ships. To be a part of a company that owned five or six aircraft and to have access to those planes was better than any dream.

The only benefit to Arctic dying, that I could see, was that my night life would come to an end. We partied hard in those days, myself in particular. I could not have continued to do that indefinitely, probably would have collapsed in my beer one of those nights. Staying healthy, however, wasn't much consolation.

To make matters worse, not only were things falling apart at Arctic, but the same thing was happening at Polaris. Its parent company, Textron, was threatening to close things up. The winters had been just as hard on my child in Roseau; eventually, the employees there would number only 11. I had trouble sleeping as I thought of the possibility that both companies might die.

The days of 1981 ticked by, and I hung around Arctic, as did a few others. We didn't know what to do with ourselves. Though some worked to sell off merchandise, there was no production. It was all closed down and disheartening. But for a time, we still had our offices, and I kept going. After so many years, it was a hard habit to break.

I'd have stayed even longer, but I had to do something else. It's not in my nature to sit around. Given my background with Allen Eide, it was only natural that I checked out the used car business.

I did it for a number of reasons. I needed to become immersed in something else, to keep my mind off the events at Arctic. The other thing, just as motivating, was my lack of funds. Though it might seem odd, I did not have a great deal of money following the collapse. Because of it, I had very little. There are times when, despite all your hard work, all your talents and all your intelligence, things do not go as planned. That's not a time to get depressed, though I certainly felt terrible. At a time like that, it's time to try again. I was more than 60 years of age, and had to find work.

Why had I reached that point, why hadn't I set some money aside? Well, I've made some poor financial decisions over my lifetime. I want to tell you about these because they prove you can claw back from financial ruin. They prove that, no matter how many setbacks you might have had, you can still come back, under any circumstance, at any age.

My first poor decision came, of course, when Lowell Swenson wanted to buy half of Arctic and I said, "No, you'll buy it all or none." Bad decision No. 2 came when I was told in 1977 that I had to dissolve my partnership with Allen Eide. An Arctic lawyer walked up to my desk and informed me that I had to choose between Allen and Arctic. It was a conflict of interest, he said. I really should have checked into it, but at the time, I took the attorney at his word. A few months later, I dissolved my partnership with Allen.

Unfortunately, it wasn't long after leaving my friend that Arctic went into Chapter 11. Meanwhile, Allen Eide continued to prosper and do great things. From a practical standpoint, I would have been much farther ahead financially, with fewer worries, had I stayed with Allen instead of Arctic. In retrospect, there is not one good reason why I had to make any choice at all. The lawyer was wrong.

Still, even though I missed the financial opportunity with Allen, in the late '70s, I seemed set for life. By then, I'd accumulated well over $1 million worth of Arctic stock. On paper, I was a rich man. In a fair world, my money would have gone into the bank. I'd earned it. I'd worked hard and suffered through many difficult times. Unfortunately, the ruination of Arctic was coming, and I had no idea.

I didn't sell my stock because I didn't need the money. My weekly check was more than enough to take care of our needs. I couldn't conceive that anything would happen to Arctic and leave my stock worthless. I assumed, if anything, the stock would increase, and make me even richer. I look back now and say, "Edgar, there are two or three things you aren't so smart about. One of them is predicting the future." But today, when I look back, I say, "So what? I'm doing all right. I'd probably do the same things again." Anyway, being rich was never my main goal. Had it been, I'm sure I would have been.

The upshot of my decisions, however, was that at the age of 61, I went from wealth to mere existence. I had to get a job. But at my age, I wasn't very employable. Not that I would have made a good employee anyway. I hate the regimentation of a normal nine-to-five day with an hour off at noon. I can't do that. I don't mind working 12 to 15 hours a day, I just want to do it when I say I want to.

❧ ❧ ❧

I set up the car dealership at my home three miles south of Thief River Falls. I put the cars on my fairly good-sized lot bordering the state highway. I'd had an excellent teacher in Allen Eide, so I knew what to do. Soon, I started making more money than I'd ever made at anything.

Ironically, I did not like selling cars. I didn't mind buying, repairing and making deals; but I hated dealing with the public directly, as a salesman. I'd never had to do that before. Sure, I'd sold myself, and I'd sold products to dealers, but to have to pitch cars to customers wasn't me. I'm not the kind of guy who is good at retail and all the questions from customers, and I couldn't take all the derogatory statements that are made by people who buy from a used car jockey, which I was in their eyes.

As time passed, I hired a few salesmen, and Hannah, my wife, ran the business end. But every day I had to go out and sell cars was a day I hated. Gradually, the feeling grew in me that I wanted out. And with Hannah involved more and more in the business, it was only a matter of time before I'd get my wish. But sometimes you're stuck doing something you don't like. With Arctic down and out, I had little choice but to grin and bear it.

Through it all, however, I had ideas, I had dreams. They are what keeps you going; never give them up. I didn't. Even when they turned out wrong, I usually found something else to get excited about. As the car lot made me unhappy, I started thinking about Polaris.

In the late '60s, Polaris had struggled. It reached a point where it needed a heavy influx of capital, or likely would die. My brother, then president, knew the best thing for Polaris would be a buy-out. Inevitably, the decision was made to sell to Textron, a conglomerate that finally put an end to the constant worries about money. Textron saved the day and helped Polaris grow into a sizable company. It experienced growth similar to Arctic, and yet a little more than a decade later, Polaris was in bad shape again. In 1981, the same year Arctic declared bankruptcy, Textron announced it would close its snowmobile division. Both of my children were dying. Unless, that is, I could somehow stop it.

One day in the middle of this, I was at Arctic with Bill Ness, the firm's executive vice president. For a time, the offices were still available to us; and I'd often sneak to the old plant. Months earlier, it had been teeming with people, noise, and the pleasing sounds of industry. Now, it was a ghost town. As we sat there, Bill and I came up with a plan. "Maybe, just maybe," we said, "we should see if we could make a deal for Polaris." I knew its president, Bev Dolan, and I thought it possible for us to take over the dying firm. As long as Arctic was gone, why not?

"Bill," I said seriously, leaning up in my chair to look him in the eyes. "I'll call Bev and find out if it's for sale."

Bill agreed. We both were excited, especially me. Imagine, running Polaris again. I called Bev.

"Edgar," he said, "you're too late. I already have a group of people who want to buy the company. And I think we'll make a deal with them."

Those people were the employees of Polaris, and ironically, it was my old partner, David Johnson, who got the whole thing going. He arranged for employees Hall Wendel and Chuck Baxter and four or five others to make a deal with Textron. The group could not afford to buy it outright, but Textron, being an honorable company, agreed to be paid over the course of several years. They felt a huge responsibility for the employees and customers of Polaris.

Still, Bill Ness and I continued to talk. We saw a lot of each other; in fact, became pretty good buddies. We talked through the ugly summer of 1981, when bits and pieces of Arctic were sold off, and we waited through the winter and spring of 1982, when Arctic's tooling and parts were sold to Certified Parts Corporation of Janesville, Wisconsin. As the summer of 1982 approached, we heard talk of an auction that would sell off the remaining Arctic equipment. Again, Bill and I got together. We discussed how nice it would be to start Arctic up again, though we made no substantive plans.

In the meantime, enter Allen Eide, who was always there for me. He's never gotten any credit, but Allen was very much behind the reorganization of Arctic. We'd talked plenty since Arctic went under, often discussing its resurrection. We were on the phone in the spring of 1982.

"You know, Allen, that auction is coming up this summer," I said.

"Yeah, we've talked about starting it up again," he said.

"I know. We'd better decide pretty quick what to do. We'll need to bid on all the special equipment."

"What do you think it will cost?" Allen asked.

"For the equipment we'd need, I'd guess about $100,000."

"Gee whiz," Allen said, "why don't you get it? I mean, what's the downside? What's the most we could lose if we had to dispose of it?"

"Not much. Probably could get close to what we pay for it."

"Then get it. If you need any help at the bank, you can count on me."

So with a tentative agreement that Allen would be involved in the reorganization of Arctic Cat, I ventured over to the Thief River Falls bank. They were a lot kinder than the old Roseau bank, because it wasn't long before I made arrangements that would cover me for $100,000. Following the transaction, I met with Bill Ness, who was still interested in restarting Arctic. Over the next several weeks, he and I and others went over the auction list. What did we want? What did we need? How much would we pay?

The auction day arrived. It was August. It was steamy outside and warm in the massive warehouse where my child Arctic Cat had expired. I meandered about, saying hello to old friends. Soon, however, it was time. Along with Bill Ness and Bill Hahn, a purchasing agent at Arctic, I began to bid.

The auction would last two long days, and my arm was sore from raising it so often, but finally, after spending even more than $100,000, I'd bought enough that Arctic could once again make snowmobiles. Oh, there was plenty left to do, but we were on our way.

I spoke to Allen after making the deal, but he decided not to be an owner. He was having so much success in his other pursuits, he asked himself, "Why?" I thought that fine, but I now couldn't afford to pay the bank the $100,000. I went to Bill Ness and Ole Tweet and some others and said, "Fellows, I've got a note at the bank with $100,000 in my name. I need some help."

They came through, as did Allen, though he had no interest in Arctic. Bill Ness, Allen, myself, and several others, signed a note at the bank for about 10 grand each. We now were in it together and would raise Arctic from the ashes. With relatively little cash to work with, we would rely on experience. And somehow, we would do it.

Now let's be clear; I never planned to be Arctic's president. I was too busy at the car lot. Fortunately for everyone who wanted to see black snowmobiles again, Bill Ness wanted the job. Soon after the auction, Arctco Inc. was incorporated, and Bill got the fellows together. Time was urgent. With 1983 just around the corner, we needed to put things back together, and do it in a hurry. You've heard of Humpty Dumpty? Well, it was like that. We had to have new models ready for 1984, and that meant building them in the summer of 1983.

We worked on hurdles, such as manufacturing rights, financing, getting a building, and finding an engine for the new line. We worked to bring dealers back into the fold. Indeed, in the fall of 1982, Bill, Ole Tweet and I met a large group of wary Midwestern dealers in Alexandria, Minnesota. We needed their help. Our job was to convince them that the two-year layoff, while disturbing, was not a sign of things to come. They were a hard sell. We talked and we talked, and finally, they agreed to buy our new snowmobiles.

It was a significant moment, but not the end. Not by a long shot. By then, we'd lost access to our offices at the old plant and now worked out of Lowell Swenson's condominium on Highway 59. About 10 of us chipped in $500 and we added several phone lines. Though we had the Midwestern dealers, we needed to call across North America. Our objective: To obtain letters of credit from dealers, who hopefully would promise to buy snowmobiles on delivery. Those letters would be good at the bank and would go a long way to helping us rebuild.

I made only a few calls, usually when a dealer was playing hardball. It was my job to turn them around. Perhaps the biggest call, the most important one of all, was the one I made to Denny Dunham, our former distributor in Alaska.

Denny, who'd been so important to me at Polaris and Arctic, was the linchpin of our plan.

"Edgar, for you, I will guarantee buying 500 snowmobiles," he said. "I'd also like to invest in the new Arctic."

I sighed with relief. It was done. With his letter of guarantee, combined with the others, we could go to the bank and get a decent line of credit.

When the dust settled, we had orders to build 2,700 new snowmobiles. We had 42 investors, and we'd worked out a deal to build in the old factory. We also had money, because during all of this, we incorporated as Arctco Inc. Each investor had to put in $40,000, and despite the high cost of doing business, we raised $1.6 million.

I would have liked to put in the full $40,000, but could afford only $35,000, because during that same time, a pain ripped through my heart. I'd never felt anything like it. I was sitting in my recliner, late in the evening, and it hit. I doubled over. I made it through the night, but saw my doctor the very next day.

He sent me to Grand Forks, to a cardiologist who put me in the hospital. There I convalesced for nine days with angina. Gradually, I improved. Unfortunately, the attack had drained my checkbook. I simply couldn't invest the full amount.

Through Bill Ness' tenacity and perseverance, the whole thing came together. Bill worked out a deal with Suzuki to build us about 2,000 engines and, in a complex deal between Certified Parts Corporation, Minstar (Arctic Enterprises' new name), and our Arctco, we leased the center section of the old Arctic plant.

Moreover, during the two years that Arctic slept, former employees Roger Skime and Dennis Zulawski took it upon themselves to build some new models. They had the faith that Arctic would rise from the ashes. They worked on many innovative things, so when the company was ready to go, it really hadn't lost any time on technology.

On May 1, 1983, the Arctic crews were in the old plant and once again could concentrate on what they did best: building snowmobiles. Production of the new Panthers began August 1. What a day!

By then, however, I'd faded from the scene. I was older, and though I disliked selling cars, we were making too much money to just quit. Anyway, Bill Ness was running Arctco quite nicely.

They built only a few snowmobiles that first year, but there was great excitement. I remember those new models and how thrilling it all was. As the months drifted by and Arctco went on without me, I sometimes would sit on an old car and think about the old times, and how I loved snowmobiling.

I was getting the bug. More and more, I wanted to be involved in that world again. I'd helped get it back on its feet, and now I felt the urge to return.

I hated my life as a car dealer more than ever. By then, Hannah was doing all the paperwork and a great deal of the selling. I told her I could take it no longer. In 1984, a year or so after Arctic restarted, she agreed I should go back.

I'd hoped to return as a part-time employee, unfortunately, that wasn't in the cards. When I went over to Arctic, Bill Ness decided it would be best for everyone if we parted ways. I was angry at first, but later agreed that he'd probably made the best decision for Arctic. I'd never been a yes man, and I'd never been easy to get along with. I generally play the devil's advocate, and nobody likes people who challenge their ideas, who, as it were, makes them prove them.

Bill Ness and I had been good friends for many years, and I believe we still are. He probably did me a favor. Had I gone back, I would have become a vegetable, because I would have gotten into the old PR rut I was in before. In retrospect, I'm glad I didn't, because many good things would not have happened to me.

And let's make one thing clear. I love the people at Arctic, and I love their products. I have a lot of friends there, from management right down to maybe the janitor. After all, Arctic to me is a child, just like Polaris is a child.

However, I couldn't give up my dream of going back to the snowmobile. With one option left, I went to see Hall Wendel, president at Polaris. He was a good fellow, and I thought I could work with him. Much to my pleasure, we made a deal, and signed a letter of agreement.

Part of it was that I had to sell my Arctic shares, the ones I'd bought for $35,000. With some regret, I sold them and made a small profit, but had I waited a few more years, I could have been really wealthy. It was my second chance to get rich with Arctic, and it went up in smoke, all because of the agreement I'd made with Polaris.

To make matters worse, as Hall put his company together, employees were given an option to buy stock before Polaris went public. Unfortunately, I didn't get the notice to do that because I wasn't an official employee, only a consultant. Consequently, I missed the chance to invest whatever money I had. The snowmobile industry, as such, has not made me much money. Most of it's been my fault, but I feel having to sell the Arctic stock prematurely and not getting the chance to invest in Polaris were circumstances beyond my control.

I write this not so you'll feel sorry for me. Do not. Now in my late 70s, I am doing quite well. I've made it because I did not feel sorry for myself after losing millions at least four times. In my mid-60s, I had to start over, and I still climbed the hill. It's never too late to earn your fortune; it's never too late to make your dreams come true. Indeed, it wouldn't be until the mid-'90s that I finally earned some real money.

In the early '80s, I went to work for Polaris as a consultant, though I still lived in Thief River Falls. I spoke at company functions, and was on call to talk to snowmobile clubs across the country. It was nice to be back.

But a couple of years passed, during which we would close down the car business. And eventually, night after night of giving the same speeches and telling the same stories wore me down. I was spending my life on airplanes and in hotels. I missed my wife and I missed my home. Near the end, I went to a meeting in Oregon. I spent 23 hours getting there because of missed flights and bad weather. I did all this on a Friday night, to get there for a meeting Saturday morning. I stayed through the festivities Saturday, then went home Sunday. This had happened too many times, and it wasn't worth it any more. Heck, everybody knew me and they'd heard all my stories. I couldn't bring them anything new.

My wife Hannah and I on a couple of Trail Cats.

The end came one night in Peoria, Illinois. I leaned up against a wall and stared at all the handshaking and drinking and speech-giving. I said to myself, "Why am I here, why am I doing this?"

A friend of mine, Eric Menssen, was standing with me. I turned to him.

"Eric, this is the last meeting I'm going to. I'm not going to any more."

"Sure, Edgar, sure," he laughed.

But it was true. It had gotten to the point where I disliked it more than I liked it. I decided to leave Polaris, but they never forgot me. Even though I no longer work for them, Polaris to this day furnishes me with snowmobiles, garments, watercraft and ATVs, whatever the product line is. They've been great.

I left Polaris in the late '80s, but it was not for a life of idle retirement. Many things were on my plate. I'd started my own firm, the May Corporation, to build high-comfort wheelchairs; and I was in a business with long-time friend Gary Lemke, having started a small company called All Season Vehicles in 1983. Those enterprises would heal me and would bring the financial rewards the snowmobile industry never did.

Chapter 14

A TRIBUTE

As you sit across from Edgar Hetteen, in the office of his new home in Grand Rapids, Minnesota, you stare out across a wooded back yard, filled with six feet of snow and pine trees that struggle to hold their white burden. It is peaceful here, and it is where Hetteen belongs. Two snowmobiles sit purposefully and ready to go, a testimony to what Hetteen accomplished 40 years ago.

Indeed, by the mid-1980s, his legacy, his legend, was set in stone. Were he to do nothing else, he would go down as the grandfather of snowmobiling. So the question has to be asked: What made a man in his mid-60s, when most are enjoying the fruits of their labor, decide to launch another business? It is perplexing. Some would say he couldn't resist another good idea, but it goes much deeper than that. The May Corporation, which builds high-comfort wheelchairs for the disabled, was a brainchild of karma, named after Hetteen's ailing mother. Though Hetteen had brought pleasure to millions with his snowmobile, and indeed, helped thousands with numerous other inventions, he still felt pressure to give something back.

He leans back in his chair and, though Hetteen often laughs and jokes and teases, he doesn't now. He is deep in emotion, and explains himself.

"So you say, 'Edgar, you've written a lot of checks on the bank of life, but where have you made any deposits? We're talking of a more meaningful contribution than just the fun of snowmobiling. And so the wheelchair became this, that through this device we can make things easier. That will be my deposit in the bank of life."

❦ ❦ ❦

My mother lived alone and was sick. She suffered from the early stages of Parkinson's. The days of her working at Polaris and as a reporter for the Roseau newspaper were over. The ancient Smith-Corona typewriter on which she banged out stories was in a closet, gathering dust. When she died several months later, in 1986, I would claim the typewriter as one of my cherished possessions.

My mother's name was May. She had been healthy most of her life, but now the degenerative brain disorder was stealing her. The onset was slow, marked by trembling. It progressed to the point where she had trouble remembering to take her medication or to turn off the stove. After she lost her driver's license, she began to fade for good. It was horrible. She knew what was happening to her, and that there was nothing anyone could do.

I was the only living child, so her care fell to me. I had to convince her to enter a nursing home. It wasn't something I wanted to do, but she was struggling hard.

"Mom, I think it's time that we had someone care for you in a home."

"No," she said in a frustrated voice. "I can't do that."

"I think it would be much easier on you."

"No," she said firmly. "I can't do that. If I go, they'll tie me up. I know they will."

As I left, I was struck with a sad thought: "My gosh, her mind is going, too. She thinks they'll tie her up." Finally, by necessity, she entered a nursing home in Warroad. It was a nice place, and I thought she'd be fine. And yet, soon after, when I visited her, my jaw fell to the floor. She was tied to a wheelchair.

A more painful sight I'd never seen. They used what appeared to be a bed sheet, slung between her legs and then around the back of the chair. The indignity. I was distraught, though I didn't blame the nursing home. They couldn't have patients falling onto the floor, which is what had happened to my mother.

The wheelchair was stealing her pride and reducing her humanity.

Originally, the collapsible wheelchair was designed to transport people. It wasn't equipped with support for a person's head, neck or shoulders. But over the years, as I knew too well, it had become the parking place for the disabled. As a result, elderly occupants often slumped forward, either resting their heads between their knees or slumping over the side. They developed painful pressure points and sometimes sustained nerve damage. The wheelchair should never have been used as an all-day chair, and yet, the practice was common.

As much as I searched, I could find nothing on the market that would replace the wheelchair and help my mother. I simply could not stand to think of her ending her days like that – trapped. Thankfully, I had some mechanical skills. It was time to take matters into my own hands.

Out of an old car I grabbed a small bucket seat, which I mounted on wheels. Mom used that for a while, but it was only a partial answer. The next step was to remodel a standard wheelchair with an adjustable seat instead of the standard sling. That gave her more comfort because I could adjust the angle of the seat and keep her from sliding out.

But as the days and weeks wore on, her condition deteriorated. She now slumped forward. I stood five feet from my mother, towering above this poor woman, this one-time thriving human being, the one who filled our farm home with love and wondrous smells from the kitchen. She slumped in the chair I'd built. Her head lolled between her legs and she stared at the floor. Spittle, drool, ran out of her mouth and descended in a line to the floor, where it formed a tiny pool. She'd been parked in front of the television, but she couldn't watch.

I removed the canvas backrest and replaced it with a cushion that could be angled backwards to keep her from falling forward. It was another big gain, but she soon developed a side slump, and her body was squeezed against the armrest. It had caused a severe pinch-point and, I'm sure, stinging discomfort. The solution was to make a pair of adjustable shoulder bolsters, which kept her from slumping sideways. Then came a headrest, tray and other accessories. My mother's posture was now good. Her lungs were stretched and her body unrolled. Her dignity had returned, and with it a sense of well-being. Several months later, May Hetteen passed away, but I was pleased that I had made her final days comfortable and dignified.

That experience, however, enlightened me to the horrors of wheel-chairs. I knew people were worse off than my mother. Perhaps they, too, could use a specially designed chair. Perhaps I could make life easier for them. In that moment, my obsession began.

At Arctic, in the '70s, one of my jobs was to find new products to manufacture. Long before my mother had problems, I discovered a device to help the disabled. It was a gas-powered three-wheeler into which a person would push their wheelchair. Then, by starting the little motor, he could drive around and be quite mobile.

In the research of that product, I spent time in Washington, D. C., at a series of workshops for long-term care patients sponsored by the Veteran's Administration, the Department of Transportation and the Rehab Service Administration. It was a great lesson and helped me understand those with disabilities.

Eventually, I came up with a system of mobility that extended not only to the little gas-powered job, but to cars and buses and trains and airplanes. However, my visions were never built because of Arctic's demise. They were put on the back burner, quite forgotten until my mother became ill.

With that however, I began to visit the disabled, researching exactly what they needed and wanted. The people were beautiful and intelli-gent, having all the hopes and fears and loves and joys I had, but trapped in a body that wouldn't respond. I realized just how fortunate I was. I could run and jump and talk; I wasn't confined. Therefore, I wanted to give them whatever creature comforts I could.

In 1986, we started developing a line of chairs. I hired Mike McKeever, a former employee of Arctic, and at my hobby farm 25 miles outside of Roseau, we set up shop. Though I still worked part-time for Polaris and with ASV, wheelchairs would now take up most of my time.

Our first project was to develop a home chair. It had to be narrow, so it could move through old homes. It had to look like a piece of furniture. It had to be comfortable and offer dignity. I worked day and night, as hard as I'd ever worked at Polaris and Arctic.

Most of my time was spent in the barn and in my aircraft hangar, crafting this new device. It no longer was a seat ripped from the hull of a junked car. It had become a recliner on wheels.

Respect came hard at first, however. Whenever one of my few employees answered the phone and the customer asked for Edgar, they would say, "Hold on a second."

Then they would add, "I think he's in the barn."

This did not help us, and we had to teach them to say I was on the factory floor, or some euphemism like that. Not, "He's out in the barn." They might just as well have said that I was feeding the hogs.

Nevertheless, we made progress. The chairs began to take form, and we were ready to sell. We advertised, and newspaper articles were written. We mailed out hundreds of brochures. We demonstrated, but like Polaris and Arctic before, sales were slow to start. Still, I didn't worry; it was early in the company. Money was not my motivation; in fact, Hannah and I took no salary. We were about more than dollars. That much was demonstrated when I received a call from a woman in Neche, North Dakota.

"I understand you build special wheelchairs," she said.

"Yes, I do."

"Well, I'm having a problem with my husband, and I'm wondering if you could help."

She sounded nice, and a little desperate.

"Tell me about your husband."

"I'm taking care of him at home, but it's so uncomfortable for him to sit in that wheelchair."

The moment she said she was taking care of him at home, I thought there's carpet, it'll be difficult to push, especially if there's a big person in the chair. In a house, there are bound to be narrow doors and narrow halls. These thoughts zipped through my head automatically, computing, as it were.

"Is your husband a big man?"

"He's six-foot-two, and I have to transfer him out of his wheelchair and into bed. He has a dialysis machine, and I have to move him when he takes treatment. It's tough. He has only one leg; the other was amputated."

Uh-oh. A big man with only one leg probably would cause balance problems in a chair. This wouldn't be easy.

"He can't talk, Mr. Hetteen. He can't do anything."

Had this been a typical business, I might have decided that her problems were not worth my efforts. She was a good 200 miles away, and I didn't even know if I could help her husband. But this was no ordinary business. Of course I would try. I had done as much for snowmobile customers, and to me, this was more important.

We were building two different chair models. Not knowing which the man would need, I loaded both into a van. One chair was better balanced and better suited for a person with one leg. It had smaller wheels and would be harder to push on the carpet. The other chair had bigger wheels and would push more easily, but it didn't have the flexibility in adjustments the man might need.

Neche, a town of a few hundred people, is well inside North Dakota and bumped against Canada. My trip took about three hours, and once in Neche, it was easy to find the house. I knocked at the door. An older woman, Beatrice, opened it. She was slight of frame, with gray hair in curls.

"I have a chair for you," I said with a grin.

I took one into the house, and left one in the van. Taking in both could have been overwhelming. I didn't take in all my accessories either, because that might have scared them, too.

She introduced me to her husband, whose name was Jim. He sat sadly in a wheelchair, slumped over and speechless. We began to transfer him into my chair.

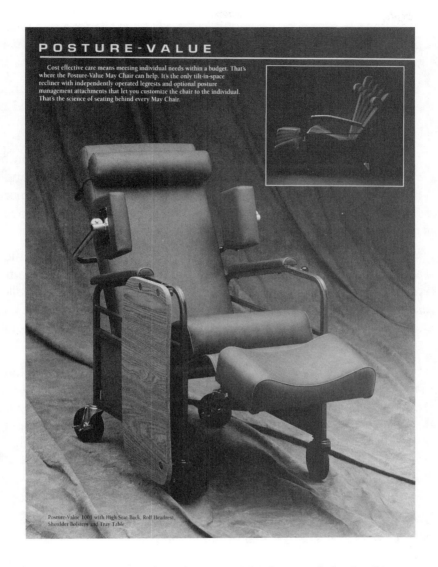

POSTURE-VALUE

Cost effective care means meeting individual needs within a budget. That's where the Posture-Value May Chair can help. It's the only tilt-in-space recliner with independently operated legrests and optional posture management attachments that let you customize the chair to the individual. That's the science of seating behind every May Chair.

Posture-Value 1001 with High Seat Back, Roll Headrest, Shoulder Bolsters and Tray Table.

This picture is from a brochure in which we advertised our wheeled recliner.

People like Jim generally sit on a sling of webbing. Each end is attached to a ring, so when you hook a lifting device to the rings, it hauls the person up. Jim was sitting on such a sling as I brought in the chair. Beatrice attached her hoist and pumped the handle. He was lifted while I moved my chair under him. Gradually, we dropped Jim down.

I felt under his leg, because for him to be comfortable, he needed support under the knee. With only one leg, it made my job difficult.

"Beatrice," I said, "we have to pick him up again. I have to reposition the seat."

She pumped the handle and hauled him up. I moved the seat just so, and we put him back down. He looked comfortable, despite the fact that he stared blankly ahead. But all too soon, Jim slumped forward.

"Beatrice, we have got to straighten him out," I said. "I'll reposition the chair so he won't do that anymore."

I did, and Jim again sat fine. But then, he fell over to the left. He was a toy doll, and I had to make adjustments so he would sit right.

"Beatrice, I have something in the van I think will help."

I got a shoulder bolster that plugged into the chair and supported his shoulders. He now was sitting real nice, so Beatrice and I turned to talk. All of a sudden, Jim let out a huge growl. As we turned, we saw his head was hanging backwards, and with an open mouth and a gurgle, he let out a noise that scared me as I'd never been scared before. I thought Jim had died on us, that perhaps I'd done something to kill him.

Fortunately, it wasn't that serious, and I wiped my brow with relief. I went out to the van and, this time, got a headrest. I brought it back and plugged it in. I adjusted it so his head was nice and stable. Now, he had good posture, but was sitting with his hands in his lap, rather effeminate.

Beatrice shook her head.

"I don't like the way his hands are sitting."

I again went out to the van and got a tray. I plugged it into the chair and placed his hands on it. Beatrice nodded. Thank goodness. I had nothing left in my bag of tricks.

It was late in the evening, perhaps 10 p.m., and I still had 200 miles to drive. As we sat at her kitchen table and watched Jim sitting comfortably, I felt guilty. I was having a hard time, a personal struggle of my own, a problem I never had selling snowmobiles. She was such a nice person, I didn't want to ask her to buy the chair. I mean, we had done something good for a human being, and now I was going to reduce it to an earthly thing like money? It shouldn't have been difficult for me, but it was.

I followed a suggestion once made by my friend Gary Lemke on selling with subtlety. I started to pack up my belongings, waiting for her to make the first move. I'd decided I wouldn't leave the chair unless she paid for it then and there. Despite my emotions, I just couldn't wait a few weeks for the money.

But when she looked at me with a warm smile and tilted her head, I knew I was finished. Though some may doubt it, deep down, I'm an old softy.

"Are you going to take the chair home with you?" she asked. "I don't know if I can pay you now. I could pay you in about a week."

"Well, I don't know, Beatrice," I said.

She paused and stared at me.

"Could you please leave it?"

"Yeah," I said, nodding gently. "I'll leave it."

I drove home, and as happened so often, arrived long after Hannah was asleep. The next day, I mailed Beatrice an invoice. Four or five days later, I got a check from her. With it was a handwritten letter, composed on wrapping paper you'd get at a butcher shop. She praised what the chair was doing for Jim, and I was glad I had given her a few extra days to pay for it.

I received many letters. Though I may not have made much money, they filled my heart.

One of my favorites came from a man in Grand Forks, North Dakota. We'd helped his father, the minister who had officiated at my wedding.

"It was so nice today to see my dad, Maurice, sitting straight up," he wrote. "He looked like a human being instead of a poor old soul all drooped over and hanging from a strap."

The first few chairs I sold convinced me that what we were doing was good, and that our chair could have an impact on life, like snowmobiles never could. I named my company the May Corporation, after my mother. The business was personal, more a relationship than a financial venture.

I had a shirttail relative by the name of Naomi. She was only 50, about to enjoy some of the best years of her life, when she was stricken with an aneurysm and became paralyzed. She was a beautiful person, a beautiful-looking woman. But now, she couldn't talk, couldn't eat by herself, couldn't do anything but lie all day long and stare at the ceiling.

I couldn't bear to see her that way, and I got her into one of my chairs. Instead of staring straight up from her bed, she then looked horizontally at life. She was back in a world that permitted her to leave the confines of the nursing home. She could get into the van, and her family could take her out for rides, could take her past the old house, could take her to public doings. It didn't change her illness, but it brought some dignity.

One day, in Naomi's nursing home, a nurse pulled me aside.

"It would be nice if she had better foot boards so she wouldn't get foot droop while she's sitting there," the woman said.

I pulled a chair next to Naomi. She stared straight ahead, unable to look my way. I smiled and touched her hand.

"Naomi," I said, "They tell me your legs aren't long enough, that you can't reach the foot boards."

Beneath her expressionless exterior, I could just tell she understood every word.

"Now don't worry, Naomi, because I've invented a leg stretcher, and I'm going to stretch your legs so you can reach the foot board. OK?"

I could tell she wanted to laugh.

Then I said, "Oh, Naomi, maybe we shouldn't do that. We'll put shoes on you with higher heels, so we won't have to stretch your legs."

She understood, I know.

"Naomi, I've started to build these chairs. The one you're in is a result of those efforts. I've named the company after my mother, who you knew so well."

I could see that she wanted to cry, because there was just a little quiver in her lips, and moisture gathered in her eye. She wanted to cry, but she couldn't do even that.

Being with Naomi and the disabled gave me insight into their world. It's why my wife and I spent so many years unpaid. What I saw drove me. At those nursing homes, they have a TV, and the residents are pushed in front of it. They drool on the floor, needing eyes on the top of their heads to see the television. To keep them from falling out of the chair, they might be tied or given drugs. Just like my mother.

According to a story in the *New York Times*, in the mid-'80s, more than 500,000 older Americans, many of them frail and demented, were tied to beds or wheelchairs. New federal regulations were in the works discouraging the use of physical or chemical restraints and indeed, many professionals were encouraging the use of recliners instead of wheelchairs.

Therefore, I fully expected our reclining chairs, which we named Wheelloungers, to take off rapidly. In an interview I gave the *Grand Forks Herald*, I predicted, "The Wheellounger will be accepted much faster than the snowmobile."

Unfortunately, I hadn't realized how entrenched the wheelchair was. The health industry seemed unwilling to let it go. It was a sacred device that was about as authentic as when I built an inch-and-a-quarter slide rail for the snowmobile.

I really wanted to get into nursing homes. I'd read there were more than 20,000 of them, and that didn't include Canada and the rest of the world. What potential! During the course of five years, I walked into so many. It was never easy.

I'd go up to the administrator. He would look me over as if I were some huckster selling snake oil off the back of a wagon. Sometimes he would be polite, but it was rare that he bought. Financially, it was not a good time for nursing homes.

I would explain what I had, a chair that would eliminate the problem of patients falling out of their wheelchairs. Here was a device that would keep their lung and chest cavities in position and eliminate the painful bedsores caused by sling-type seats.

The man usually asked one question.

"What does it cost?"

I would say anywhere from $1,500 to $3,000. The response would come all too quickly.

"Sorry, we don't have budgets for that."

After being asked to leave a dozen times, I learned not to ask for the administrator. Instead, I would ask for the head of nursing, who usually was a woman. I got more compassion from her. She might ask, 'What's your price?' but I'd quickly say, "I'll tell you, but first you have to listen to my story, and see what I have. Then we'll talk price."

I would tell my story and show her what the chair could do. When I finished, the head of nursing usually was on my side. We then could tackle the administrator together. Sometimes the ploy worked and sometimes it didn't; but having the director of nursing as my friend was always good. Whenever a patient came in who really needed a Wheellounger, the nurse would often talk to their husband or wife or children and say, "Hey, we can't buy this chair, but you can."

Eventually, to make it easier on nursing homes, we built a model at a much lower price. For the home-bound, our chairs were built to look like furniture, which was less threatening to a patient. But for the institutional market, we went with a utility-looking chair. I threw away all the wood and made one of metal, which was lighter and cheaper. Still, we kept it soft and cheerful, with bright, colorful upholstery. It was absolutely functional and helped us into the nursing homes.

Those first years were a whirlwind of activity for the May Corporation. A great many newspapers and trade publications wrote us up. Hundreds of calls and letters came our way. By 1987, we were attending conventions across the country, the biggest in Texas, where 700 Durable Medical Equipment (DME) dealers showed up and where 35 showed interest. In 1988, we had a deal with the Red Line Company of Minneapolis to take on our line. They were the largest DME dealer in the world with 120 sales representatives across the country.

In May of 1988, we moved the company from my barn to a plant in Grygla, Minnesota, about 45 miles south of Roseau. We had 11 employees, including me and Hannah. We were selling about 100 chairs a year.

Some of our patients had spastic episodes, so I made a model with heavy protective padding. Word got out, and unbeknown to me, one of them was sold to the Middlesex County Hospital in Boston. Soon after, I got a call from a woman named May Long, who identified herself as head of the Massachusetts chapter for people suffering from Huntington's chorea. Huntington's is a hereditary disease of the central nervous system, usually beginning in middle age and characterized by jerky movements, personality changes, and mental deterioration.

"We bought one of your chairs," this May Long said. "It's a good chair, but you're not quite there yet. Our patients are still having some trouble with it."

Though May Long and I became friends, I was put off by that comment. We hadn't built the chairs specifically for Huntington's, and I said so.

"I still would like to talk to you about possibly making some changes in your chair for Huntington's chorea," she said. "Will you come here if we pay your way?"

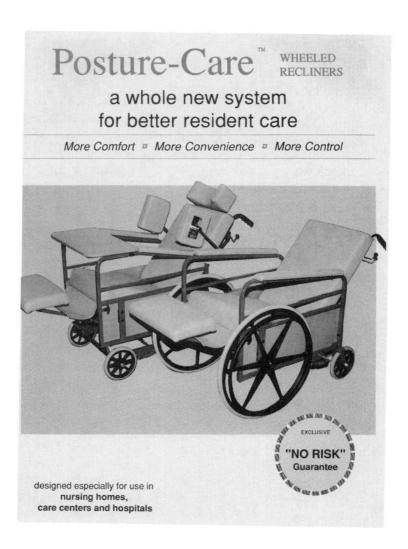

Posture-Care™ WHEELED RECLINERS

a whole new system
for better resident care

More Comfort ▫ More Convenience ▫ More Control

EXCLUSIVE
"NO RISK"
Guarantee

designed especially for use in
nursing homes,
care centers and hospitals

These were chairs that I specially designed for use in nursing homes and hospitals. They were pared down from the "fancy" home models.

Never one to turn down a possible sale, especially since it seemed tailor-made, I said sure. She sent me a ticket and I flew to Boston. May Long picked me up at the airport, and we drove to Middlesex County Hospital.

Awaiting me was an unwanted surprise. I was expected to give a lecture on what the chair could do for victims of Huntington's chorea. May Long led me into a large conference room, and I came face to face with people who weren't my peers by any stretch. They were rehab engineers, physical therapists, occupational therapists and nurses. They waited for me to enlighten them.

What the heck was I supposed to say? I was an eighth-grade graduate out of country school. It was every bit as bad as when I had to face the head engineer at International Harvester, or when I had to face implement distributors at a huge hotel in Chicago. But if you know your product and know what you're doing, you can speak with authority. It was just another example of taking a challenge and making it an opportunity.

The hospital people were very nice, and I made a special chair for sufferers of Huntington's chorea. I sent it to the hospital, and it worked well. So much so, that they would buy several more chairs.

I did my best for those with Huntington's. I went to many state meetings; one was in San Francisco, just before the big earthquake in the fall of 1989. I was standing with my chairs when up wandered a petite woman. She had along her mother, who suffered from Huntington's.

The lady asked if her mom could be put in the chair. I looked at this jerky, almost drunk-looking woman, and I said sure, hoping the Wheellounger would help. It didn't. Not one bit. The lady was so stricken, the chair failed to contain her. Back and forth she banged. As I watched her pain, I grew despondent. The chair was good for most victims of Huntington's, but she was one I couldn't help. Or so it seemed.

The woman and her mother left disappointed, and the episode bothered me the rest of the day. I couldn't get the image of that poor lady out of my head. Overnight, I came up with a plan, and the next day, I found them again.

"Look," I said, weary from mulling it over all night, "I will build a special chair, an absolutely special chair that I believe will take care of your mother. When it's finished, I'll send it to you. The price of the chair will be $1,500. You give me $750 now, and if it works, you can send me the remainder. If it doesn't work, don't send me any more."

Back home, I slaved over the new chair. I put in different adjustments, different angles, and built a petite chair that would fit such a lady. Finally, I sent it to her. It must have worked real well, because after a short time, we got the other $750 in the mail.

It can be easy to give up when you have a device that does 80 percent of the things it should, and then you find something it doesn't. But often, by not giving up and by studying and researching, you can make it do almost anything. Too often, people lose heart the first time their gadget doesn't work.

In the end, I regret we couldn't have helped more people. But while I was with the May Corporation, I sure did try. We worked with victims of Lou Gehrig's disease, of which my friend, Burt Johnson, recently died. And I went to as many hospitals as I could. Sometimes I was welcomed, but sometimes, like once in New Jersey, I was thrown out because they didn't want to hear what I was saying. They didn't want to be told the wheelchair didn't work, and was actually causing additional pain and discomfort.

I worked with Alzheimer's patients, who were difficult because their disease was a progressive one. They slumped in wheelchairs, and I gazed into their eyes, perhaps to catch a glimmer of humanity. It was like staring into a black hole.

We worked with people who had multiple sclerosis, and we worked with the obese. We built a chair for a lady in Florida who weighed 640 pounds. She couldn't get out of bed, but once she got the chair, suddenly she was able to get up and around. The chair sold for $3,000, a small price to pay for mobility.

By 1990, we'd made reasonable penetration into the health care market. The market was becoming aware of the May Corporation, and we should have been on the verge of rapid growth. Many physical therapists in the Twin Cities were behind us, as were others, such as the home health care industry. The future looked relatively bright.

By then, however, I was 70, an age when I no longer wanted to work seven days a week. I suppose I was slowing down, just a little bit. Moreover, my goal has never been to run a company forever. I'd never done that, not even at Polaris or Arctic.

It was time to move on, and I considered selling the May Corporation. Ultimately, I hammered out a deal with a man I knew from my days at Arctic. I sold him the majority of my stock in the May Corporation, and he became its CEO and president. I agreed to leave the board of directors and to no longer have a say in how things were done. In return, the new president was obligated to pay me a royalty on sales for the next five years. I looked on it all as partial payment for the four-and-a-half years my wife and I had toiled.

I remain a fairly large stockholder in the company, and I hope, in the balance of my life, that I would receive something from the stock. If not, however, I will have felt good because even though all the innovations I developed are not being worked on, I know thousands of people enjoy life a bit more than they would have without the May Corporation.

I do, however, experience mixed emotions about leaving. You see, I wanted a chair that could be built to design, that could be customized for the individual. No matter what symptom a person had, we would have been able to assemble a chair just for them. I wanted other devices and aids that could help the disabled, perhaps even motorized vehicles such as I'd hoped for at Arctic.

I thought my vision would continue, and it really should have. We certainly had the talent and the know-how to make it work. But the new owner has gone his own way. He wanted to build an inexpensive, standardized chair to sell to the masses. I wanted that too, but it had become his main goal, and it seemed to me the company was forgetting all the special people of the world.

Though he had a right to abandon my plans, it was tough on me. I'd worked so hard to build the May Corporation, and I'd invested so much emotion. It had been a challenge of a much different kind than the snowmobile. I'd wanted to show people that wheelchairs were not sacred, to prove that we could do better out on the farm. I'm comforted that we changed lives, and I'm comforted that the company still builds standardized chairs, but we really could have done so much more.

However as I left, I did not look back and ponder what might have been. Too much was going on to waste time like that. Remember, I'd co-founded a company called All Season Vehicles in 1983. Most of my time had been spent with the May Corporation, but ASV now would be put on the front burner.

Chapter 15

FINDING GOLD – AGAIN

It would have been so easy to give up. Even the May Corporation, which he'd put his heart and soul into, didn't work out the way he'd planned. It was a small success but certainly didn't give Edgar Hetteen financial freedom. But as the wheelchair saga was unfolding, in the background was a small struggling company in Marcell, Minnesota, called ASV. Hetteen had helped its president, Gary Lemke, found the company back in 1983. Almost daily, the two spoke on the phone. A few times a month, Edgar would venture down to Marcell and offer advice.

ASV now is experiencing rapid growth. Its stock has exploded, vaulting from $6 in spring of 1996 to a value of $36 before splitting three-for-two on Jan. 21, 1997. As of this writing in the winter of 1997-98, it's hovering around $27 a share. The company itself is worth millions.

Amazing. Hetteen has now been responsible or partly responsible for three multi-million dollar companies and for perhaps hundreds of people becoming millionaires. Finally, on paper, so did Hetteen.

I am now 78, and I am having a wonderful time. Aside from not being able to fly any longer, which is a disappointment, I live nicely. My wife and I have built a wonderful new home in rural Grand Rapids, Minnesota. It is set down a pleasant country road and is surrounded by great pines, which in the winter droop heavily with snow. My shop is full of interesting projects on which to tinker, and one of my rooms in the new house is full of video and special effects equipment, my latest hobby.

It is a good life. I owe much of it to the success of a firm called All Season Vehicles based in Grand Rapids. It is a company of which I've been a part for well over a decade. Just like Arctic Cat and Polaris, it has grown far beyond its early years. Company revenues reached more than $12 million in 1996, and have doubled for 1997.

Back in 1983, all of this was only a smattering of possibilities and ideas, with little money behind us. But in starting this new company with my friend Gary Lemke, I had the same excitement and anticipation I had in 1944 with Polaris and in 1961 with Arctic Cat. My heart beat fast just thinking about it.

You might say that ASV began, really, in the mid-'70s. Arctic Enterprises was rolling. We couldn't build snowmobiles fast enough. Money poured in. They were the glory days, and to celebrate our successes, we honored the dealers who helped us most. And each year, we singled out the very best. If a dealer met certain quotas, he got a trip to the Caribbean or Hawaii or to Mexico. On every trip, there was a guy called Gary Lemke and his wife JoAnn. I wanted to know who this guy was, this fellow who sold so many snowmobiles. It turned out that Gary had the Cat Shack in Grand Rapids, and the more I got to know him, the more I understood that he was a talented dealer, in a class by himself.

Over the years, we grew to be good friends. When he made trips to Thief River Falls, we typically met and discussed business. But a few years later, when Arctic went bankrupt, Gary lost his dealership and I lost my job. I opened my car lot, and it wasn't much later that Gary and I started talking. He had an idea for a tracked vehicle the size of a small truck with rubber tracks in back and wheels in front. It would compete against the bigger snow-grooming machines. Gary believed there to be a niche in the market for that size, that type and that price range, and for a machine that could also be used in the summer.

Our talk amazed me. Way back in the '50s, I'd had similar ideas. I'd always been fascinated by such things and built a whole slew of all-terrain equipment. One in particular was a four-wheeler. It was a nifty machine, but in 1958 I nearly scrapped it for material. However, the local game warden stopped by and caught a glimpse of it behind the shop.

"Gee, I would like to have that, except I don't have any money in the budget" he said. "But, Edgar, there's a 26-foot cabin cruiser lying up at Isle, Minnesota, on the shore of Mille Lacs. The state can't use it anymore. I have permission to trade that boat even up for your swamp buggy."

Since I was going to scrap it anyway, I agreed. I hauled that 26-foot cabin cruiser to Lake of the Woods, and it became "The Polaris." We used it to entertain customers. It had an enclosed cabin with a galley, a head, and slept four.

A few years ago, that same four-wheeler came up for sale at an auction, somewhere near Lake Mille Lacs. I said to myself, "Gee, I would like to have that for a keepsake." I sent word to the auctioneer that I would pay $600 for it. It sold for $1,800, and I didn't get it.

So you see, my background wasn't only snowmobiles and straw choppers. It also was lying in the mud and the swamps, or playing with tracked vehicles and wheeled vehicles for off-highway use. We had a four-wheeler called the model 1000 at Arctic that was an extremely capable little machine and was in the lineup of equipment when I sold my holdings to Lowell Swenson. We built mechanical-drive, half-tracked vehicles that, when I see the old pictures, still look pretty good today. They even work well, as evidenced by that auction in Mille Lacs.

Gary had similar thoughts and similar sketches. Neither of us had much money, but we sat down and plotted anyway.

In the meantime, I went back to selling those darn cars, and Gary went back to a business he'd begun called Marcell Manufacturing, which built snow-grooming equipment and imported a Swedish tracked vehicle.

Then it just happened one day in 1983. I got a call from Gary Lemke. Gary had been working hard in Marcell, a small town north of Grand Rapids, and he had lined up a group of potential investors, retirees who lived in the beautiful countryside of that small town.

"I'm going to have a meeting down here in Marcell with this group," Gary said. "I'd like you to come down for it."

"What sort of meeting?"

"I think I have them pretty much convinced to invest, but I want them to hear about your background. I'd like you to take them through the years of starting Polaris and Arctic, and explain what those companies are doing now."

Both Arctic and Polaris were bouncing back nicely.

"I'll be there, Gary."

I drove the five hours to Marcell's sparse downtown, consisting of a lumber mill, a bait shop, a church and Marcell Manufacturing. I walked into the plant, and found the makeshift office. It was there the men and women had gathered and where the future would be forged.

The charter investors listened as Gary spoke, and then I made a speech. We talked of Arctic and Polaris and the experiences there. We talked of Gary's accomplishments and how we knew exactly what we were doing, how we were certain of success. We might even have shown films of the early snowmobile days.

We talked about the machine, though it only existed in our imagination and on paper. It was vapor, just a dream.

"How much would that take?" someone asked.

The answer was about $70,000. It actually was a small amount to begin a manufacturing company, and the investors didn't take long to decide. A gentleman named Spike Graham stood up. He was of medium height, build, and had a sparkle in his eyes. He was 80, but could have been 50.

"Well, what do you think?" Spike asked. "Are we going to go? Are we going to go with these fellows?"

It took the seven families about four seconds to raise their hands and vote yes. They were retired folks, who'd saved their money and lived on what they'd earned over a lifetime. They didn't need us as an investment. Moreover, they had no guarantee they would ever get their money back. The difference, I believe, is that they trusted Gary Lemke to the ends of the earth, as did everyone in Marcell. They would learn to trust me as well.

This large ATV was a prototype I built in the mid-'50s at Polaris. It was never put into production, though it worked. Here we plow through snow. It was a forerunner to the ideas and inventions that came at All Season Vehicles.

The money went into ASV's bank account, and we had the green light. Gary and I put no money into the company, so the obligation and pressure to spend the $70,000 wisely and to succeed for those people was tremendous. We desperately wanted to prove their faith in us, but I never questioned our ability. It never crossed my mind we might lose the money. I was more confident in this venture than any before.

We would initially take no money for ourselves. I'd just sold the car lot and had built up some reserves, so I could afford it. But I don't know how Gary did it. He had a wife and two children at home, and he was risking a lot. He'd shut down his manufacturing business and was putting it all on the line.

And yet few who knew Gary Lemke thought he would fail. In the '70s, he turned his Arctic dealership into a little money mill. It was one of the best Arctic ever had, and we owed Gary a lot. On Saturdays, as winter approached, a line of cars could be seen stretching down the road on their way to his Cat Shack. If not for Arctic's bankruptcy, Gary probably could have retired off his dealership.

Now, he was starting anew. But you just knew he would succeed because Gary had unique talents. His numerous abilities usually are not rolled up in one person, but in him was the chutzpah of an entrepreneur and the cunning of a shrewd businessman. His tenacity and drive started ASV and kept it going through ups and downs. His salesmanship sold it to investors when perhaps no one else could have done so. His mechanical inventiveness led to the introduction of the tracked machine, and he earned a hard-to-get patent for its steering mechanism. In my life, I have worked with many talented people, but Gary Lemke is one of the few giants of the business world, and I enjoy calling him my friend.

With everything set, Gary began work on his concept, the tracked vehicle, which would move in snow and in mud and in swamps and everything in-between. We spoke on the phone almost every day; and two or three times a month, I drove to Marcell to offer any advice I could. Gary always ran his ideas by me, not necessarily for approval or a turndown, but I'd say I liked it or I didn't like it, and he would act accordingly.

Driving into Marcell was a peaceful experience. It's a small town, and ASV was built beside the only road, a narrow avenue to drive carefully when you meet another car. The brown metal building was set on a large patch of sand and gravel. When it rained, the parking lot became a muddy stew; when it snowed, it turned to ice. The building was relatively small for manufacturing, but it was large enough to start. The offices were moved from the plant to an old antique shop 20 yards away. It was losing its bricked face and had been a shambly disaster on the inside before Gary tossed out the junk.

The prototype began slowly. I wasn't there much, but I know Gary practically lived on that factory floor. He would drag himself home long after midnight, only to rise a few hours later to do it all again. He lived on adrenaline. He saw the machine in his mind, saw how the hydrostatic drive would work, how when you turned the steering wheel to the right, the left track would speed up and vice versa when you turned the wheel left. His vision, he knew, would revolutionize snow-grooming. Gary was not a trained engineer, but he knew instinctively how machines worked; and the prototype took shape.

About this time, I took Gary aside and made a few things clear. This would not be a rerun of Polaris and Arctic, where I played every position.

"Gary," I said, "the company that has two heads is a freak. When an animal is born with two heads, it's exhibited at the county fair, and I don't think we want to be exhibited at the county fair. Therefore, I'll be perfectly comfortable if this company has one head – yours."

We had that understanding real quickly, and I've never regretted it. Over the years, there has been a lot of common ground between Gary and myself, which isn't to say we agreed on everything. If we agreed on everything, one of us wouldn't be needed, and the guy not needed might have been me. It was good to have disagreements, but Gary always made the final decisions.

With the prototype progressing, it was time to hire an engineer. We needed someone who could draft and do blueprints. While at Arctic, I worked with a fellow named Stuart Boelter. We became good friends and for several years, Stu and I often arrived home late from work. We spent a lot of time at Plant No. 5, which also was known as the Legion Club. With Arctic rebuilding, Stuart was on the job market and living in Brainerd. I suggested we hire him, and Gary did. Stu brought to the table a wealth of engineering experience, technology and know-how that was very helpful in the design of our new machine.

In the winter of 1983, the prototype was born. It didn't look much different than the Track Truck looks today. It had 18-inch-wide tracks driven by hydrostatic drive and a 60 horsepower Ford engine. In the front were mounted skis or rubber tires. Though it was similar in many ways to the old machines built at Polaris, it was different, too; my vehicles had used mechanical drives. Our prototype worked so well. Clearly there was a bright future.

Did I know how great a future? Yes, I sure did. I knew we'd be hugely successful, and it was no surprise when it happened. That feeling had been different at Arctic and Polaris. I knew that they, too, would be successful, but not to the extent they were. At ASV, I knew it all along.

How did I know? It's pretty simple. I sat down and I made a list of our assets, as you should do when starting a business. The assets were the people, their technical abilities, their experiences, and their know-how. When I added it up – Gary, Stuart, myself and a talented young employee named Cary Safe – we had a darn good list. We had a few liabilities, too – such as the lack of money – but the assets proved to me ASV would have success.

Over the next several months, more employees were hired. They, too, were good people and added to our assets. Gary was laying a good, strong foundation on which greatness could be built. With that base, we could take on the much older, wealthier snow-grooming companies.

ASV, I came to notice, had the same common denominator as did Arctic and Polaris. My snowmobile companies began small, with a few dedicated people, who never used a watch, rarely used a calendar, and who were absolutely dedicated to what they were doing. They ate, slept, did everything for the good of the company. They lay all night under wet old snowmobiles, working and sweating over the task at hand, and I know their wives grew sick of coming in second-best. This they did at Arctic and Polaris. This they do at ASV.

ASV people don't mind working long hours and don't mind getting dirty. Could it all have failed? Yes, I suppose so, but with all those things going for us, the possibility seemed unlikely.

It took several months, but finally the day arrived when we brought the Track Truck to market.

We started by showing it at trade shows and demonstrating it to snowmobile clubs. It was deja vu for me. I'd done that all before, and I knew the struggles to come. I recalled my days of trying to sell the snowmobile when nobody had seen a snowmobile, of people thinking it went on water.

With ASV, little had changed. We were presenting a new concept, a better way. The marketing process would be an educational one. We had to teach people why they should buy. As with snowmobiles, it would be a constant struggle to compose ourselves as we were bombarded by questions.

One of the early trade shows was in southern Minnesota. Gary and I worked the booth all day long and were beginning to droop. It had been a day of answering questions, and it still wasn't finished. Around 4 p.m., this old-timer walked up. He stepped with slow deliberation, his feet moving tiredly up and down until he reached me and the Track Truck.

He looked it over.

"What's this hook for on the back of this thing?" the old man asked, squishing up his face.

"It's so you can pull something," I said with as much patience as I could muster.

"Why would you want to do that?" he asked.

The old man walked away slowly, and I shook my head as he disappeared into the crowd, perhaps to bug another entrepreneur.

Another guy walked up and looked at the back of the Track Truck. It had a box similar to any truck.

"What's this box on here for?" he asked.

The Track Truck by ASV is at home in the snow.

"You'd use it just like you would on your pickup," I said.

"I don't have a pickup," he responded, like something out of an Abbott and Costello routine.

One guy took a look, and said, "Is that front-wheel drive?"

"No," I said. "It's not front-wheel drive." I wanted to ask, "Do you think those little bitty rubber tires in front pull that huge track mechanism behind?"

Another guy turned up when Gary was alone in the booth.

"Boy," he said, "I sure like your vehicle. It's just exactly what I want. If you could take the tracks off it and put on wheels, I'd probably buy one."

The tracks were its main feature.

We criss-crossed the country, trailering that Track Truck behind as we moved from town to town, listening to exasperating questions, and getting frustrated that they weren't selling faster. It is difficult to trust in yourself when things go slowly, but you have to. If you want to succeed, you keep plowing ahead, and listen to the questions. Occasionally, on these slow days, we had to make our own fun just to keep up a smile.

At a show in Tulare, California, Gary went to get a cup of coffee while I held down the fort. There had been exasperating questions all day long, and I was getting a little punchy. A few minutes after Gary left, a guy walked up and said he had a few questions. Some of them I couldn't answer.

"Well, gee, I can't help you with everything, but the president of the company is here and he can help you," I said. "He'll be back pretty soon. What's your name?"

"Bill."

Bill walked around our vehicle, looking at it like guys do, almost like staring at a pinup.

"Hey," I said to him. "Let's have some fun with Gary when he comes back."

The guy turned my way.

"When he comes back, he'll be wearing a red cap. You walk up to him and say, 'Hi Gary. How are you? Don't you remember me?'"

The fellow smiled and chuckled. He agreed to the farce.

"Now," I said, "you walk away and come back in a few minutes, so it looks like you're arriving for the first time."

A few minutes later, Gary emerged from the crowd. He walked into the booth. I grabbed him by the shoulder, a sly smile on my face.

"Gary, there's going to be a guy you don't know who's going to walk up here any second. He's going to say, "Gary, how are you? Don't you remember me?" You turn to him and say, "Yeah, you're Bill, aren't you? How the heck are you?"

Five minutes passed and finally the fellow sauntered up to the booth. He spotted Gary in his red hat.

"Gary," he said loudly and happily. "How are you? Don't you remember me?"

"Yeah," Gary said, slapping him on the back. "You're Bill, aren't you? How the heck are you?"

The guy's chin fell to his chest.

"Son of a gun," he said, glancing my way, where I couldn't contain a smirk. He looked back at Gary. "He got me, didn't he?"

It was a terrible thing to do to a prospective customer, but it was just one of those things that spontaneously happened. When you're on the road, you make entertainment any way you can.

❦ ❦ ❦

One thing was for certain. With little room for error, the Track Truck had to take off quickly. Despite the initial investors, money was tight. Gary pinched and squeezed and we worked hard. Sure enough, with a lot of calls and a lot of pushing, sales picked up. ASV did $700,000 in sales the first year, and we were able to stay in business. Numbers for the Track Truck continued to climb the following year, but a funny thing was happening with the machine and our customers. They were not

The Posi-Track's low ground pressure and rubber tracks allow it to be used in just about any kind of terrain.

satisfied with it, entirely, and began to bolt on attachments. They were using it for brush-cutting, mowing and snow clearing. They used it for things it was never designed to do.

On a hunch, one weekend in 1988, Lemke and Cary Safe ripped a Track Truck in two and wound up with a tracks-only vehicle. It was a twin-tracked machine that was extremely versatile, could go nearly anywhere, and performed well in any weather. It was a substantial breakthrough, and we immediately saw the promise. With this new vehicle, we could work in the areas that have no roads. It was exciting. We went to equipment shows to determine if people really needed it, and the answer came back a resounding, "Yes." We then said to ourselves, "With the Track Truck, we are a one-product company. We should have some insurance; we should have something that sells year-round. We need to put capital into this new machine."

We did. While Track Trucks supported the company, we worked on the new vehicle. We called it the Ag-Track and then, later, the Posi-Track. The Posi-Track differed from other small tractors and bulldozers because of the rubber tracks it rode on. The machine weighed 5,800 pounds, much less than small dozers, and its 18-inch-wide tracks displaced the weight so its ground pressure was 1.5 pounds per square inch, about the same as a house cat. That allowed the vehicle to drive over nearly any terrain – sand, swamp, mud – without bogging down, while surfaces were left without ruts.

In those years, I split my time between Polaris, the May Corporation and ASV, working long, long hours. In my mid-'60s, I was going quite strong. The May Corporation took up most of my time. Polaris was mostly a weekend thing, and Gary never was demanding at ASV. More demanding than anything was my own conscience. Where should I spend my time?

And as I grew older, the long hours did get the better of me. I reached a point where I said, "Holy gosh, I just can't sit on three stools." With that realization, I left Polaris and eventually sold some of my stock in the May Corporation. ASV was my future.

The Posi-Track moves in just about any terrain and does just about any job.

But as with any company, there were ups and downs. As we devoted more and more time to the Posi-Track, Track Truck sales dropped and continued to drop through 1991. We had to raise more money, we had to raise a lot. Gary and I did just that, taking in another $400,000 from investors. By 1992, we'd been working on the Posi-Track for four years, but we needed some sales. It was much like Arctic and Polaris had been, when any day might break the company. Often, Gary saved us by selling a Track Truck or a Posi-Track a day before an important bill was due.

With Gary practically standing on his head to make sure the company survived, the Posi-Tracks began to sell, though slowly at first. It wasn't easy because they were new. People didn't understand them. It was the same stuff all over again.

We displayed it at a farm show in California. The other equipment there was much larger and seemed so massive that we felt a little puny. Gary, always imaginative, had a pile of wood shavings brought in. He then drove the Posi-Track up the pile and perched it on top. It could be viewed more easily.

A little guy came up and walked around it.

"Where do the shavings come out?" he asked.

We shook our heads. The shavings, we told him, did not come out of the Posi-Track. The Posi-Track did not run on wood-shavings and did not create the huge pile. But the question was indicative of the fact that everything we had was so different and so strange that it prompted those kinds of remarks.

Finally, however, in 1992, ASV showed its first profit since 1987. We took in $2.9 million and earned $225,000. The following years were even better, and we've continued to grow. We now have four products on the market – the basic Posi-Track and a high-performance model, plus the old Track Truck and a much larger snow groomer. I believe ASV will continue to grow, and perhaps outdistance even my wildest imagination.

ASV's Posi-Track and Track Truck sit side-by-side after a hard day's work near the North Pole.

The Posi-Track has gained a loyal following. We count among customers Gallo, which operates several in its vineyards; Gazprom, Russia's largest oil company; and Pierre duPont's Longwood Gardens in Pennsylvania. They use them at Squaw Valley, where they argue over who drives it next. Mary Hart, a reporter on Entertainment Tonight, and her husband, Burt Sugarman, have one on their farm in Montana. Even driving one is a recently retired board member of Ingersoll Rand, which ironically owns the Melroe Company that builds BobCat skid-steers, the machines against which Posi-Tracks most directly compete.

ASV has signed up high-profile machinery dealerships. Among its 65 dealers is RingLift in Jacksonville, Florida, one of the largest Caterpillar dealers in the country, and Hyster Sales Company on the West Coast, one of the biggest BobCat sellers. Others include Thompson Machinery, with five locations in the Midwest, and RDO Equipment, which recently came on board with John Deere dealerships in Minnesota, North Dakota and South Dakota. We also have many influential investors, too numerous to list, but so important in our growth.

The Posi-Track DX, another new vehicle from ASV, demonstrates the company's ingenuity and forward thinking.

ASV has moved from its cramped surroundings in Marcell to a new, 102,000 square-foot plant in Grand Rapids. I have a nice office and I show up most every day, though my hours aren't long. While I realize Gary Lemke has been the real force behind the company, I'd like to take some pride in what has happened. I now own quite a bit of ASV stock and once again, on paper, I'm worth more than a million dollars. I don't say this to brag but to demonstrate it is never too late for anyone willing to pursue their dreams.

I've no doubt ASV will continue to thrive. With its high-class dealers and prominent investors, we have a solid foundation. And with our people, so talented and so dedicated, never wearing a watch – just like those I had at Arctic and Polaris – there seems to be only one way to go. Straight up.

Chapter 16

NEVER GIVE UP

Everybody wants to succeed. It's human nature. So why are so many people stuck in jobs they don't like, wishing and hoping they could earn more money? Why are so many people scared to pull the trigger and shoot for their dream? Likely because it is tough and it is risky. You might lose, you might fail. But for Edgar Hetteen, that was never a concern.

Way back in the 1800s, Charles Duell, commissioner of the U.S. Patent Office, urged President William McKinley to abolish the office.

"Everything that can be invented has been invented," Duell argued.

Of course, it wasn't true. But there is a sense among people, during whatever age they live, that everything has been done, that nothing is left to do. Hogwash. Today, there are more opportunities than ever. All you have to do is find them, and then work.

Do not listen to those who say you are wrong. Trust yourself and your own ability. I mean, just look at the history of the entrepreneur, and how mistaken so-called experts have been. Look at some expert opinions down through history:

Tom Warner, president of Warner Brothers Pictures, 1927: "Who the hell wants to hear actors talk?"

Thomas Watson, IBM Chairman, 1943: "I think there is a world market for about five computers."

Thomas Alva Edison, 1880: "The phonograph is not of any commercial value."

Albert Einstein: "There is not the slightest indication that nuclear energy will ever be obtainable."

Darryl F. Zanuck, head of 20th Century Fox, 1946: "Video won't be able to hold onto any market it captures after the first six months. People will soon get tired of staring at a plywood box every night."

Dr. Dionysus Larder (1793-1854), Professor of Natural Philosophy and Astronomy at University College, London: "Rail travel at high speeds is not possible because passengers, unable to breath, would die of asphyxia."

Wilbur Wright to his brother, Orville, 1901: "Man will not fly for fifty years."

Marechal Ferdinand Foch, professor of strategy and commandant at the Ecole Superieure de Guerre, France, 1911: "[Airplanes] are interesting toys but have no military value."

Dr. Richard van der Riet Wooley, British Astronomer Royle of Britain in 1956: "Space travel is utter bilge."

President Rutherford B. Hayes, 1876, concerning the telephone: "That's an amazing invention, but who would ever want to use one of them."

Even the experts can be wrong, and often are. People should trust in themselves, should take risks. We've talked about a wide range of businesses that I've been involved in. We've talked about farm implements, Bug-O-Vacs, pool tables, combo desks, entertainment centers, grain elevators, straw choppers, wheelchairs, snowmobiles, ATVs and countless other things. Perhaps I took too many risks. Today, however, it seems people are scared to try anything new, or a little risky. I was never scared to try. It was the fascination of living life to the fullest, of not getting stuck in a humdrum existence, that was my concern.

I fear society is teaching us to conform. We hate to be conspicuous, we hate to be different, we hate to stick out like a sore thumb. Yet how will our world develop, how will we progress without the Edisons, the

Fords and the Westinghouses, the unique people of the earth? I grow worried, because I think we're getting away from a time when there was an incentive for people to be different.

I've had a long-standing belief that if you want to do something, you just do it. You don't worry whether it's going to flop, because that's the surest way it will. You don't worry about whether it's going to fail, because you have calculated the risks to the best of your ability. I calculated the risks when I began Polaris and Arctic and the May Corporation, and when I got involved with ASV. I believed the risks were worth it, and they certainly were.

There is an old saying that your reward is directly proportionate to the risk you take. I believe that. If you want to build another pair of shoes, another TV set, another me-too item, your chances of failing diminish; however, your reward is also smaller, because you have competition and fixed perimeters on what you can charge. But if you have a product that is different, there is greater risk, and much greater reward.

People have made much of the fact that I have been involved in four successful companies over my life, three of them very successful. I do not take complete credit for them, especially ASV, which you have to put in a different context. But I think there are similarities between all of my companies.

I think something special happened at those places. We energized people, helped them become even greater than what they were. We did it at Polaris, at Arctic, at the May Corporation, and it has also happened at ASV. The legacy of hard work has been passed down from employee to employee. Our drive for perfection has become tradition. It's the only thing I can say on a personal level. The heritage has continued, and it is why these companies are still successful.

So many of those people in Roseau and Thief River had their very first job at either Polaris or Arctic. Some of them never had another, and many of them became very, very successful. Consequently, what we taught them, either by demonstration or by word of mouth, sank in, and they have passed it on.

Did we know what we were doing? Unconsciously, maybe. In the beginning, David, Allan and I knew we had a job, we knew we had deadlines, and we knew we needed money or we couldn't continue. There was an inborn pressure, an inborn tempo that was set. So maybe by accident we instilled something in these people that has lasted.

Moreover, we succeeded by surrounding ourselves with such good people, by not being scared to hire someone smarter than us. On occasion, people ask for my autograph. I give it to them, but I feel silly. I mean, why should I give somebody an autograph because of ideas I had? The ideas didn't necessarily succeed because of what I did, but because of the people around me, and because of those to follow, who not only used my ideas but added their own.

I remember the first time one of our employees left Polaris. We were pretty small, and he was our shop foreman. When he left, we thought we would fall apart. But you know what happened? We got someone else to be our shop foreman, and it went even better. The old foreman had taught us everything he knew, and the new man taught us what he knew.

It seems I've been able to attract good people. I don't know if I was attracted to them or vice versa. I often wondered, how did the snowmobile create the wonderful people who bought them? But the snowmobile didn't create them. The machine was the catalyst that brought people of the same caliber together. So probably, if I've performed any function at all, it was as a catalyst. The people were already doers, already great, long before I came along. We simply formed an alliance. I like to think we helped each other get a little better. We developed a work ethic and a tenacity to stick with it and to solve problems.

There is no reason in the world why anyone can't achieve their goals, as we did. There is no reason to think you can't do better than an eighth-grade graduate from the farm. You might think the opportunities are all gone, but they're not. I believe if I were starting out now, I could be even more successful. With enough hard work, enough dedication and by surrounding yourself with good people, anyone can succeed.

❧ ❧ ❧

I'm glad I did all the things I did. I have no regrets, because if I changed any of them, the fabric of my life would unravel. At this point, I would have no desire to go back to either Polaris or Arctic and become a part of their corporate bureaucracy. And as for going back to the wonderful, romantic, frantic things that Allen Eide and I did, I don't want to do that either, yet I wouldn't sell the experiences for anything.

It's not in my character to go back. Snowmobilers have one thing in common and it is this: When they go riding, they rarely turn around and come back on the same trail they've just traveled. They've already been there and don't want to go back and see all the same things. They want to make a circle and come around from another direction. That's the way I've lived my life, and I think the success I've had comes from such an attitude.

I've now read through my book, and I've asked myself, what's the message here? What am I trying to say?

I've come to a couple conclusions:

Success comes from many different places. It comes from that tenacity, it comes from perseverance, and believing in yourself. Those ingredients are shown in every person that has achieved his dreams. Even though I once took an aptitude test that told me I wasn't good at anything, I didn't believe it. I knew I was capable and didn't listen to anyone telling me different.

This makes me think there must be something in us, an inner drive that makes us try these things, that made me fly an airplane to Alaska for the first time, that made me go from the Bering Sea Coast to Fairbanks on those old snowmobiles. It's to conquer, maybe just yourself and your own feelings.

The May Corporation, as an example, was another challenge – tackling the health-care world, a world I knew so little about, and yet dealing with people who were much more knowledgeable than I. It was a sacred world, it was a closed world, it was a little, select world, and being able to get in there, talk to them, get recognition, and accomplish things was a reward. The farm equipment meeting in Chicago, which I remember so vaguely, was another accomplishment.

I look at the things I've done and I say, "Why have I done them?" It didn't seem very smart for a person like myself to try such things. I have to believe there was an inner drive that compelled me. Maybe it's an inner drive that nags us and becomes an obsession. I don't know. Fortunately, people throughout the ages must have had that urge.

Society judges a man's accomplishments by the amount of dollars he has. That shouldn't be. As I look back, I can say I'm absolutely successful in life, with or without money. I've satisfied every need. I satisfied that inner drive, and in the end, the financial rewards did come.

I thank that inner drive for my happiness and hope more people find it within themselves.

POSTSCRIPT

Upon finishing Edgar Hetteen's autobiography, you may think his commitment to the sport of snowmobiling has waned. You may think at age 78, gone from the business for more than 15 years, that he doesn't worry about the path his sport is taking.

Not true. It keeps him up nights.

By the end of 1972, 36 people had died from snowmobiling accidents in Minnesota alone. The machines were public enemy No. 1. Edgar Hetteen spent most of the next few years working out ways to make snowmobiles safer. From his work, we got things such as brake lights, crash-resistant gas tanks and anti-theft devices. We got a better trail system and safety training.

In 1972, he was there to save an industry. In 1997, when history again called, he naturally threw himself into the fray.

The winter of 1996-97 was a hard one for the responsible snowmobiler, and especially a hard one for Hetteen. Twenty-six people had died in Minnesota as a result of snowmobile accidents through the end of January, and the state lawmakers were busy throwing bills at each other as they scurried to meet public outrage. At the same time, the Minnesota Snowmobile Advisory Committee called a meeting to get a handle on the outcry. The pressure was intense, most of it negative. Television stations were having a field day with the deaths, and newspapers openly asked the question: Are snowmobiles safe?

The MSAC convened in White Bear Lake, and the members chatted briefly before settling down to the task at hand. Into the room stepped Hetteen, and though he may not like being called a legend, he is. He walked softly, smiling and bantering with those he knew. To those he didn't know, he was an icon and a hero.

Dan Collins, an employee of the Minnesota DNR and at least in his 40s, stepped tentatively to Hetteen. It was as if he were nine years old and asking for an autograph from Mickey Mantle.

"Mr. Hetteen," he said, "I met you once 20 years ago. I was in awe. When you entered the room, people cleared a path. You had such a persona about you."

"That is very kind," Hetteen said.

Collins was flattered. He blushed slightly.

Hetteen no longer is a paid lobbyist for the snowmobile companies. Aside from gifts showered on him by Polaris, he is an average citizen, with no commitments to Arctic or Polaris. And yet, he was there when it mattered.

Hetteen drove the three hours to White Bear Lake that day out of a sense of purpose. So many people were dead from snowmobile accidents. They'd been drinking, speeding recklessly, or both, and the industry was getting a black eye. Those few lost souls were, in a sense, besmirching Hetteen himself.

"This is about an industry I love," Hetteen said as the meeting began. He scratched his beard and paused for a moment. He likes to scratch that white beard.

Hetteen spoke to absolute silence. He had earned it. To snowmobile people, to those who love the outdoors, he is a part of history. They do not interrupt or fidget when he speaks.

"Snowmobile people are the finest in the world," Hetteen said. "It irks me that a few people trying to prove that they're the Marlboro Man and drinking and driving are hurting the industry. It's giving me a bad name."

It certainly had not been a good year. The first death of the season occurred on November 17 in Lake of the Woods County, not far from the very woods where Edgar, David Johnson and Allan Hetteen tested that first snowmobiles more than 40 years earlier. A 30-year-old man had paused for just a moment, perhaps to gaze at the scenery, or simply to stretch. It was late, about 10:30 p.m. He'd been riding with a group, but they were somewhere behind. In an instant, another snowmobile flew in fast from the dark. It struck and killed him.

According to the Lake of the Woods County Sheriff's Department, the driver of the snowmobile had been drinking. Of the batch of deaths in the winter of 1996-97, alcohol was usually the culprit. And with that came speed.

But as far as much of the media was concerned, the alcohol and the speed were symptoms of the main problem: Snowmobiles were dangerous. Sure, the Minnesota Legislature had offered several bills that would reduce the legal limit of alcohol, but as the Minnesota Snowmobile Advisory Committee began its meeting, it appeared alcohol was not the main concern.

"I am bothered by calling it 'the sport of snowmobiling'," Collins said. "Sport, to me, is competitive. I race to be first, I race to win. It conjures up images of racing to the finish line. What I'm trying to encourage is to get beyond snowmobiling as a sport to the idea of it as transportation."

He went on.

"The farthest thing from our minds would be a 500-mile snowmobile race across the state. It should seem as weird as thinking of a car race on I-35E from St. Paul to Duluth."

Hetteen pleasantly disagreed with the notion that he and the industry have pushed a "sport" onto the public, a sport that now causes deaths. Indeed, that couldn't be farther from the truth. Those first snowmobiles were intended as utility machines, not speed sleds. But a funny thing happened on the way to selling those things. The customers decided they were fun. And though Dan Collins of the DNR might have had a point, it likely would be easier to devolve man than take the sport out of the heart of the snowmobiler.

"We had no plan to turn snowmobiling into a recreational society," Hetteen explained. "Actually, we were just building it because we were too lazy to use snow shoes. But in the process of doing that, we found that it was fun. We said, 'Hey, this is a great thing.'"

So instead of a campaign to take the sport away, Hetteen would just as soon see the snowmobile industry hit the drunks.

"When I look at Arctic Cat and Polaris and the talent they have at their advertising agencies, there are subtle ways to do this, and if they don't work, something drastic is called for," he said. "Tobacco gets to our kids in subtle, clever ways. I would like to think that we could come up with something that would make me feel like an outcast if I pull up at the tavern and I'm one of the few to walk up to the bar. If we can make them feel like stupid jerks, we'll be halfway to our goal."

To Hetteen, stopping the deaths is urgent.

"We're looking at a lot of embarrassing questions, and we're looking at a heck of a big industry to protect," he said.

As in 1972, change is at hand. In addition to tackling drinking and driving, snowmobiling faces another challenge. The trail systems throughout the country simply aren't large enough to accommodate the millions of sleds in use.

"It's a trail system built in the '70s trying to accommodate the needs and technology of the '90s," said Leo Hassman of the DNR about Minnesota's trails.

Moreover, snowmobile usage has tripled since 1988. Riders have been forced to highway shoulders on their way to the trails, resulting in more accidents. To ease some of the congestion, it seems, the trail system will have to be expanded. Also, Hetteen said, a safety campaign is needed, one that will teach how to ride responsibly.

As in 1972, the sport of snowmobiling has hit a turning point. As in 1972, Hetteen is getting the word out to save the industry he loves.